The Political Economy of Reform
in Post-Communist Poland

ECONOMIES AND SOCIETIES IN TRANSITION

General Editor: Ronald J. Hill
*Professor of Comparative Government
and Fellow of Trinity College
Dublin, Ireland*

Economies and Societies in Transition is an important series which
applies academic analysis and clarity of thought to the recent traumatic
events in Eastern and Central Europe. As many of the preconceptions of
the past half century are cast aside, newly independent and autonomous
sovereign states are being forced to address long-term, organic problems
which had been suppressed by, or appeased within, the Communist
system of rule.

The series is edited under the sponsorship of Lorton House, an
independent charitable association which exists to promote the academic
study of communism and related concepts.

The Political Economy of Reform in Post-Communist Poland

Janice Bell

Office of Research,
United States Department of State, USA

ECONOMIES AND SOCIETIES IN TRANSITION

Edward Elgar
Cheltenham, UK • Northampton, MA, USA

Published by
Edward Elgar Publishing Limited
Glensanda House
Montpellier Parade
Cheltenham
Glos GL50 1UA
UK

Edward Elgar Publishing, Inc.
136 West Street
Suite 202
Northampton
Massachusetts 01060
USA

A catalogue record for this book
is available from the British Library

Library of Congress Cataloguing in Publication Data

Bell, Janice, 1968–
        The political economy of reform in post-communist Poland / Janice
Bell.
        p. cm.— (Economies and societies in transition)
    Includes index.
    1. Poland—Economic conditions—1990—Public opinion. 2. Poland—
Economic policy—1990—Public opinion. 3. Poland—Politics and
government—1989—Public opinion. 4. Public opinion—Poland. I. Title.
II. Series.

HC340.3 .B45 2001
338.9438—dc21

                                                                  2001023164

Electronic typesetting by Lorton Hall
ISBN 1 84064 123 1

Printed and bound in Great Britain by MPG Books Ltd, Bodmin, Cornwall

Contents

Figures

Tables

Acknowledgements

This book is based on the PhD dissertation, *The Effects of Economic Transition on Voting Patterns in Poland, 1990–1997*, written while at the School of Slavonic and East European Studies, University of London. The author would like to express gratitude to Tomasz Mickiewicz of SSEES for his extensive advice and comments on the draft chapters of this book over the past several years. Sincere thanks are extended to Alan Smith, who acted as dissertation adviser, and to Jacek Rostowski and Martin McCauley at SSEES, to my PhD examiners, Judith Shapiro and Karen Henderson, and to Helen Wallace and David Dyker at the University of Sussex. Lukasz Konopielko also provided comments and suggestions throughout. Many thanks to Stephen Shaffer and Dina Smeltz of the Office of Research, US Department of State, for approving the use of survey data in this book, and for their encouragement and support during the completion of this manuscript. Many thanks also to the series editor and to Christine Gowen of Edward Elgar Publishing for their painstaking work in editing this volume.

The author benefited from the comments of participants at various conferences where sections of this text have been presented. This includes the session 'Public Opinion after the Fall of Communism', at the World Association for Public Opinion Research conference, 17–21 May 2000, in Portland, Oregon; the conference *Democracy in Central Europe*, held on 3–4 September 1999, at the Jagellonian University, Cracow; and the annual conference of the Irish Association of Russian and East European Studies, 15–17 May 1988, at Queen's University, Belfast.

Financial support for the dissertation was provided in part by the Overseas Research Scheme (UK) and a grant from the American Association of Women in Science. Financial support also came from an Individual Research Opportunity Grant from the International Research and Exchanges Board (IREX), with funds provided by the National Endowment for the Humanities and the United States Department of

State under the Title VIII programme. None of the organizations listed above is responsible for the views expressed in the book.

All the findings, interpretations and conclusions presented in the book are the author's own, and should not be attributed either to the United States Department of State or to the US government.

Introduction: Assessing Poland's Political and Economic Transition

Ten years after the collapse of communism in Poland, there is still an active debate over the impact of the transition to a market economy on Polish society. Since few think the socialist system could have been preserved, the debate mostly focuses on who has gained and who has lost during the transition, and whether things could have turned out differently – which usually means whether the process could have been *less* costly or *less* traumatic than it has actually been.

The relation of what are often called the 'social costs' of transition and voting behaviour in Poland's new democracy is also a matter for debate. In response to the strong showing of communist successor parties in Central European elections during the mid-1990s, Elster *et al.* (1998, p. 293) wrote that '[t]he revival of pro-communist feeling in several post-communist societies is more readily understandable when it is recognised that economic reforms have led to declining living standards for the majority of the population, at least "in the short run".' Others have argued how shock therapy reforms have 'come at a high social cost and opponents of shock therapy approaches to reform have made compelling arguments about the political fall-out which would result from the high social costs of shock therapy' (Rose 1999, p. 196). Deriving lessons from Latin America's experience in the 1980s, Przeworski (1991) was one of the first to focus on the consequences of market reform, and specifically the rising rate of unemployment, on political support for the post-communist reform process, a theme later taken up by economists including Rodrik (1995).

This concern re-emerged with surprising vigour in late 1999, ten years after the fall of the Berlin Wall. A May 1999 survey of the Polish public found that half (53%) thought the situation in Poland was 'going in a bad direction' (including 76% of farmers).[1] In September 1999, the leader of Poland's largest opposition party warned of a 'social explosion',[2] as farmers and workers marched in protest against the policies of a government rooted in the Solidarity opposition. Although arguably less affected than other transition countries by the Russian and emerging markets crises of 1997–1998, Polish unemployment began to rise again after more than four years of decline (from 9.5% in August 1998 to 11.9% in August 1999). GDP growth rates slowed, from 6.8% per annum in 1997 to 4.8% in 1998 and 4.1% in 1999,[3] although this was still one of the highest growth rates in Europe.

The shock to public confidence was compounded by confusion surrounding the governing centre-right coalition's 1999 introduction of no fewer than four controversial reform programmes (of the pension system, the health care system, local administration, and education). Unlike the reforms of 1990, these new policies were met with scepticism. Several months into the reform, an OBOP poll found that half (49%) the public thought people had neither lost nor gained from these reforms and a similar proportion (45%) saw them as a failure (only a reported 4% saw these reforms as a success).[4]

These recent twists in the transition path seem to have unnerved a public which had become accustomed to high growth rates and the prospect of rapid economic convergence with the European Union. Indeed, the EU's tough stance in the ongoing accession negotiations may have made the Polish public more anxious about their country's relatively rapid progression towards closer integration with west European institutions, and its unknown impact on living standards and welfare.

By the time of the events of 1998–1999, many Poles had already formed fairly clear perceptions of the positive and negative aspects of transition. Full shelves in shops and personal freedom are widely seen as successes of the past decade, while unemployment, the difficult situation in the agricultural sector, the lack of housing, fears for personal safety and security, and the increase of disparities in wealth in society are seen as failures.[5] Poles also appear to have developed a general agreement on the winners and losers of the transformation. As of late 1999, about four in five Poles considered business owners to be among those who have most profited from the transformation, and two-thirds think that workers in the central state administration, activists in the Solidarity trade union and directors of state enterprises have benefited. Among the losers, farmers and unskilled workers are most frequently mentioned.[6] But do these various

attitudes towards the economy translate into political preferences, and if
so, how?

This book combines basic methods of applied political analysis of
voting behaviour with an overview of the economic changes which the
political theory says underlie voters' support for or rejection of systemic reform. After the overview of the main theoretical approaches to
transition in Chapter 1, public opinion data provides further insight into
the assumptions and attitudes which underpin political choice (Chapters
1 and 2). Subsequent chapters address two standard methods of
analysing the impact of the economy on voting behaviour. Chapter 3
considers whether voting in Poland falls closer to the 'sociotropic' or
'pocketbook' model, with trends in income and unemployment
examined in detail. Then, regression analysis of the socioeconomic
voting model (which given the absence of an adequate time series
employs regional data) presents its own interesting conclusions
(Chapters 4 and 5). In particular, these initial findings indicate the
primary role of unemployment in explaining variations in support for
the main political parties. Furthermore, patterns of coefficients for
regional income, unemployment, and party support allow some first
intuitive readings of the constituencies of the most central parties in
Poland. Chapter 5 also tests the interpretations of Chapters 4 and 5
through examining data on households and individuals. It finds that the
public holds reasonably accurate assumptions about the winners and
losers of transition, and there is a discernible link between worsening
living standards and support for leftist parties. Chapter 6 summarizes,
and makes some proposals about the individual process of choosing a
party or candidate.

This book can be considered complementary to other works on the
politics and economics of transition, in that it seeks to incorporate
political and economic analysis into a unified work. Among previous
studies, Slay (1994) and Johnson and Kowalska (1994) provide
overviews of not only the first years of Poland's economic transition,
but also the policies and politics surrounding this process. Milanovic
(1998) presents a comprehensive survey of income, inequality, poverty,
and social policies in eighteen transition countries. This book connects
the empirical analysis of the social costs of reform with public choice
type voting models (for example, Fidrmuc 1997, Pacek 1994) to test
the implications of redistributions of income and consumption for
political support for reforms.

4   *The Political Economy of Reform in Poland*

NOTES

1. CBOS data from an April 1999 survey cited in *Dziennik Internetowy Polskiej Agencji Prasowej*, e-mail edition, 25 May 1999.
2. 'Zrezygnujcie z władzy już dziś', *Rzeczpospolita*, internet edition, 21 September 1999.
3. Główny Urząd Statystyczny (GUS), *Biuletyn Statystyczny*, 1999, No. 6, p. 20.
4. Polish Press Agency, *Dziennik Internetowy*, e-mail edition, 29 September 1999.
5. OBOP data from a survey of 1,062 Poles age 15 and over, conducted 15–17 May 1999, cited in Polska Agencja Prasowa, *Dziennik Internetowy*, internet edition, <<http://dziennik.pap.com/Pol/pol.html, 7 June 1999>>.
6. CBOS data from an April 1999 survey cited in Polish Press Agency, *Dziennik Internetowy*, e-mail edition, 25 May 1999.

1. Winners, Losers, and Why it Matters for Politics

1.1 THE POLITICAL ECONOMY OF POLAND'S 1993 PARLIAMENTARY ELECTION

The victory of post-communist parties in the 1993 Sejm election spurred a number of explanations of how economic factors contributed to the electoral victory of post-communist forces. Chan (1995) attributed Poland's 1993 election result to three factors: social hardships caused by transition, widespread disillusionment with post-Solidarity parties' domination over the political arena, and the revised electoral system,[1] the latter of which was an important factor behind the ability of the Democratic Left Alliance (SLD) and Polish Peasant Party (PSL) to gain 67.9% of seats with only 35.8% of the popular vote.

Gibson and Cielecka (1995) conclude that the SLD attracted votes from groups which 'lost out' from economic reform, including state sector and budget sector workers, pensioners, and employees of state farms. The SLD's winning platform, in this interpretation, centred on greater social spending and a more evenly distributed 'sacrifice', as demonstrated by a close correlation between higher unemployment and SLD support. In contrast, Zubek (1995) emphasizes the role of the SLD's successful transformation to a social democratic party in their electoral success. Through the use of 'independent' allies, including future prime minister Cimoszewicz, and the mobilization of the OPZZ trade union, the SLD cultivated an image as a professional, experienced and pragmatic party which was able to campaign credibly on labour and living standard issues. In the 1993 campaign, the SLD blamed the 'severe economic hardships and rapidly growing unemployment' (Zubek 1995, p. 293) on the Democratic Union (UD) and the Suchocka government, centring their criticism on the excessive speed of transition and proposing remedies based on the preservation of the state sector, agricultural protection, increasing pensions, and rejecting the 'doctrinaire' monetary policies of the UD government.

While statistical and opinion data can be used to measure changes in economic performance, it is a different matter to measure people's perceptions of change and their attitudes towards reform, whether positive or negative. Overall, there seemed to have been a general shift from popular support for reform in 1989–1990, followed by a degree of disillusionment as expectations of material enrichment failed to materialize as soon as expected.

Unlike earlier situations where radical reforms were enacted in Poland in face of strong public opposition, the threat of economic collapse in 1989 and the ruling Polish United Workers' Party's (PZPR) lack of legitimacy created a level of public support for the radical policies of the Balcerowicz Plan among politicians and the public alike.[2] In contrast to classic models where individuals oppose reform because they are uncertain about how the economic reform plan will affect them personally (that is, the identity of winners and losers) (Fernandez and Rodrik 1991), the Polish electorate appeared to be biased in favour of reform because of the tremendous costs and instability of the crumbling socialist system (Chapter 6). But, as with most new governments' honeymoon periods, this one could not last. Rather than having to overcome initial public resistance to reform, the post-communist reformers' initial command of enormous public support was soon depleted as the full impact of transition made itself felt. Balcerowicz (1995) himself characterized this honeymoon period as a phase of 'extraordinary politics'.

One cause of the disillusionment was arguably that, because no one could have accurately predicted the scale of the transitional recession, many forecasts were overly optimistic. During the first months of reform, the successes were obvious: the inflation rate was still high but stable, liberalization policies put an end to shortages and brought full shelves and inflows of previously scarce consumer goods. But although people were prepared to experience some hardships on the road to a market economy, the scale of the drop in real wages constituted a real shock. When the transformation entered its second and then third year, enterprises started actively shedding more labour, more firms were threatened with bankruptcy, budget austerity began to bite into education and health spending, and wages were stagnant, with all these factors contributing to a pessimistic social mood and a growing sense of opposition to reform, especially among those less able to take advantage of the new economic and social environment.

Those least best able to cope with reform were, as Kitschelt (1992) phrased it, people with 'market-variant skills': people who were in demand and treated well under socialism, but ended up at the bottom of the ladder under the market. The level of economic uncertainty (as measured by, for instance, income and unemployment levels) is higher for these groups. An increase in the number of the 'losers' of reform (including the unemployed, those working in less competitive sectors, living in depressed regions, and so on) could potentially shift political preferences away from pro-reform parties towards those backing more redistributive policies.

1.2 SOME PERSPECTIVES ON THE POLITICAL ECONOMY OF REFORM

Studies of the interaction of politics and economic reform in Poland have been developed not only in political science and economics, but also in sociology (including works by Wnuk-Lipiński, Rychard and Staniszkis among many others), anthropology (for example, Wedel 1992), and geography (for example, Parysek *et al.* 1991; Weclawowicz 1994). For the purposes of this book, it is useful to compare the main political economy approaches, which Haggard and Webb (1993) classify into three categories: (1) the effect of political institutions on adjustment, (2) how the design of the economic reform programme influences the pattern of political support or opposition, and (3) the relation between economic conditions and the politics of reform.

Political Institutions and Adjustment

Institutional constraints can arise from the political or electoral system, and typically include incentives for politicians (to gain and retain office), distributive conflicts (for example, between different social or sectoral interests), and ideology. Alesina (1994) notes that models which take such constraints into account are useful in explaining why countries with very similar resource constraints and economic problems can have very different economic performance. Studies of the political business cycles (Nordhaus 1975) and the impact of partisan preferences (Hibbs 1977, 1987; Alesina 1988) examine electoral and party systems and macroeconomic performance in established democracies. Themes include the effects of coalition and single party governments on inflation and unemployment, the incentives whereby fragmented party systems can lead to potentially destabilizing economic policies, and also how parties target different segments of the population or interest groups. One influential application of this approach (Haggard and Kaufman 1989) studied stabilization programmes pursued under autocratic versus fledgling and established democracies, and concluded that authoritarian systems are not better than established democracies in stabilizing; consolidating democracies appear marginally better although not as good as stable democracies. Although originally developed in reference to Latin America and East Asia, these ideas have subsequently been applied to the new democracies in Central and Eastern Europe. Like numerous Latin American countries in the 1980s, post-communist states such as Poland and Russia inherited a disastrous macroeconomic situation, the legacy of the expansionary policies pursued by failing authoritarian regimes and a subsequent stabilization and liberalization under crisis conditions.

Design of the Programme

This type of approach asks whether reform programmes can be designed to optimize the building of political constituencies in favour of reform. Compensation for losing groups may be justified not only in terms of social justice, but it may be expedient to sustain political support, or at least to minimize political opposition to reform. However, compensation can be counterproductive if it undermines the reform programme, for example when it takes the form of protectionism or transfers from the state budget to specific groups which seriously damage efficiency. Another concern is whether reforms can be sequenced, either to institute complementary reforms (for example trade liberalization to deflect the impact on enterprises of lower domestic demand, the provision of health and education services to the disadvantaged) or to build constituencies in favour of reform.

Economic Conditions

This type of political economy model, and the one used in the following chapters of this book, analyses the impact of economic performance on political outcomes. Haggard and Webb emphasize three special qualifications to public support for economic reform: (1) The longer the crisis, the more tolerant and accepting the public will be of radical reform; as the crisis becomes less critical, reform becomes less urgent and distributive pressures and resistance to reform increases. (2) Similar to the credibility argument from rational expectations, present reform programmes are influenced by the outcomes of previous reforms, and the perceived chance of successful reform after a string of failures may depend upon its receiving support from former opponents of reform (Lopez Murphy and Sturzenegger 1994). (3) The distribution of income pre- and post-reform can affect the level of consensus for reform. Alesina and Tabellini (1987) conclude that greater inequality leads to greater polarization of parties, greater areas of policy blocking by the opposition, and therefore less efficient politics. Furthermore, it is expected that there may be a lag in the public's perceptions of changes in the economy, particularly improvements, as there is some discounting of initial signals of change in order to take account of normal fluctuations in economic indicators.

1.3 THE COSTS AND BENEFITS OF REFORM

The nature of economic reform means that some sections of the population will inevitably lose, at least in the short run. If this proportion if large enough, their protests may endanger the continued political viability of the reform. In the longer term, the political consequences of the social costs of reform depend largely upon whether the negative economic effects constitute a *permanent* state of affairs, or whether by being an offshoot of transition they are *temporary*. As time passes, the question becomes how widely the benefits of post-recession growth will be distributed and what this will mean for political behaviour.

Assuming the proper mode of analysis is a political economy model which focuses on economic conditions, the next step is to make a distinction between the aggregate and distributional effects of economic reform, as well as between short-term and more permanent changes (Przeworski 1991). For instance, Poland's 'big bang' resulted in transitory shocks, including a temporary inflationary surge and a reduction in output. But the overarching purpose of transition is to increase aggregate welfare, and over the longer run there has been a net improvement in output and consumption once the 'transformational recession' had passed.

Although the socialist system was notoriously inefficient, its dismantling fundamentally changed how people lived and coped to meet everyday needs. Under 'real socialism' in Poland, the allocation of resources was determined by political criteria (Kornai 1992). With transition, distribution is much more comprehensively determined by market relations, and greater disparities have emerged in income and wealth. A social safety net was set in place at the start of transition, but its coverage was limited and payment levels relatively low. While people with 'transferable skills' including foreign languages, a high level of education, or specific and marketable skills had reason to expect they would survive or even succeed in the market economy, very low-skilled and poorly educated workers and people without a reliable income source who could rely on the socialist welfare system experienced a great deal of uncertainty about their welfare under the new system.

While macroeconomic data indicate that the Polish economy is restructuring and becoming more diversified, a new type of economic uncertainty has fallen upon households. Labour market status is still the most important factor in living standards and poverty, but its security and remuneration are now open to market forces. Living standards in households where the main income earner is unemployed, dependent upon social benefits, or both, are falling behind those of the average household. Households with private sector incomes, including both employees and entrepreneurs, are experiencing wage growth above the norm. All in all, such a wide and apparent gap between the rich and poor is still a relatively new state of affairs in Central Europe.

The following chapters present findings which indicate that the economy affects political choice in Poland in ways similar to those identified in interest-based voting models used for advanced market economies. Furthermore, distributional effects are among the most significant economic factors affecting election outcomes in Poland. Economic voting in Poland is dynamic and reflects the changing distribution of winners and losers. Public opinions also demonstrate fluidity – notably an overall increase over the first years of transition of a rising threat from unemployment – as well as a relatively constant influence of occupational and skill levels on voting preferences. At both the regional and individual level, those who have borne greater costs of transition have tended to use their vote to oppose candidates identified with radical, market-oriented reform, and to support candidates running on a more redistributive or populist platform. Survey data have repeatedly found that supporters of the liberal-leaning *Unia Wolności* are the most positive about future consumption, followed by centre-right voters who support *Akcja Wyborcza Solidarność*. Those favouring the post-communist *Sojusz Lewicy Demokratycznej* and the agrarian *Polskie Stronnictwo Ludowe* are the most negative.[3] Overall, political preferences have been surprisingly stable and radical politicians mostly marginalized. In Poland's transition, groups of winners and losers emerged quite quickly, with a gradual but perceptible improvement over the 1990s. Moreover, the public appears to gauge the balance of costs and benefits of reform against economic performance, notably the aggregate growth rate. For instance, when the growth rate slowed in 1998–1999, the public became less likely to evaluate the current economy as better than that during the socialist period.[4] There may also be a perception lag if short-term fluctuations in economic indicators cause genuine improvements (such as reduction in unemployment) to be noticed only after a delay.

The struggle over distribution and the role of the state in the economy is not something new or unique to post-communist countries. As Fernandez and Rodrik (1991) stress, the proportion – and composition – of the population relatively better or worse off will change during reforms, and this can shift the level of political support for the government and its policies. However, there are rising signs of a swing between the two main political blocs from election to election, and as the political situation has stabilized, we may be seeing a paradoxical repolarization of party identification along ideological or historical divisions.

It is reasonable that under the chaotic conditions of reform, it would take time for social and occupational groups to develop informed preferences about their economic interests. Publics in transition countries have indeed become able to define and articulate their interests at different speeds and levels of coherence. Those who had both a coherent identity and economic interest before transition and who stood to lose once government support was withdrawn – notably Polish farmers and low-skilled industrial labourers – *entered* the reform period with something to defend and strong grassroots organisations through which to pursue these goals (for example Solidarity and the Polish Peasant Party or PSL). In contrast, new groups such as business owners and service sector employees who largely stood to gain from the market economy have actually faced legal impediments to the organization of their interest representation (Mickiewicz and Bell 2000, Chapter 5). While socioeconomic groups and sectors need time not just to organize formally but to ascertain which policies will best further their interests, there are indications that perceived links between economic status and voting emerged fairly early in Poland's consolidating democracy.

Another factor in the politics of economic reform is timing, and in particular of the balance between the honeymoon period of 'extraordinary politics' and the perhaps unavoidable disillusionment or political fallout resulting from the 'social costs' of reform. During the period of extraordinary politics, there is high public support for reform and confidence in reformers (Balcerowicz 1994, 1995). The government should take advantage of this window of opportunity to push through necessary but temporarily painful policies. Perhaps the most important constraint on economic policy comes when the political capital of the 'extraordinary politics' phase is depleted.[5] By this time, the government is held more accountable for policy outcomes, but a quick and coherent reform programme would have put into place the foundation to enable the economy to begin to recover. Growth then creates new supporters of reform among those for whom circumstances and opportunities have improved.

However, critics of rapid reform assert that because transition has had an unequal and painful impact on people's welfare, this is harmful not just for reasons of social stability and social justice, but also because of the potentially destabilizing effect for Poland's fledgling democracy (for example, Kabaj and Kowalik 1995). Furthermore, because of the trade-off between the speed and social impact of reform, it is argued that it is better to reform gradually to mitigate social costs and preserve public support for change. However, this argument has not been proven, and in fact Central and East European countries which have made more gradual reforms, such as Russia, Ukraine, Bulgaria or Romania have experienced greater declines in welfare. Yet, as Rychard (1996, p. 468) notes, both sides of the debate over winners and losers 'even if they are based on some empirical data, are strongly ideologically biased'.

Four other factors which probably influenced the public's attitudes towards material living standards during transition can be mentioned here. First, living standards were highly politicized long before the start of transition. From the time of Gierek in the 1970s, the communist party's rule was primarily legitimized through promises of continuous improvement in consumption and material living standards. Although Poles eventually rejected one-party authoritarian rule in favour of democracy, political legitimation through delivery of improved living conditions has remained a constant.

Second, a certain amount of disillusionment with reform could have been affected by overly optimistic expectations about how quickly the economy would rebound. There were widely varying forecasts among economists. It was generally acknowledged that open unemployment would emerge during transition,[6] but few predicted how high the rate might go. Kołodko was among the most pessimistic: since stabilization programmes had led to unemployment rates of 10% to 20% in Bolivia[7] and 21% in Chile,[8] jobless rates were likely to climb at least as high in Poland. Rostowski (1989) predicted peak unemployment rates of 25-40%. Most other prognoses from late 1989 concentrated on inflation stabilization and on production and consumption. The Central Planning Office (CUP) made three estimates of the outcomes of the 'big bang', even the most conservative of which turned out to be wildly optimistic.[9] Their *worst case* estimated that GDP would fall 5% in 1990, consumption would be down 6%, and accumulation (investment) by 3.3%, and this in an environment where firms reacted slowly to the market. CUP's moderate prospect put 1990 GDP at the same level as 1989, and the most optimistic scenario saw GDP *growth* of 3.8%, consumption rising 3.4% and investment up 1.8%, with firms adapting easily to the market. As Table 1.1 shows, these outlooks under-estimated the scale of contraction.

However, the public did perceive a threat to their welfare, most especially from unemployment. As the jobless rate rose, people felt a greater threat of joblessness. In November 1990 (the date of the first

Table 1.1 GDP, inflation and unemployment in Poland 1989–1999

	1989	1990	1991	1992	1993	1994	1995	1996	1997	1998	1999
GDP	0.2	–11.6	–7.0	2.6	3.8	5.2	7.0	6.0	6.8	4.8	4.1
CPI	585.8		12.2	14.3	16.4	32.2	27.8	19.9	14.9	11.8	7.3
Unemployment	–	6.5	12.2	14.3	16.4	16.0	14.9	13.2	10.3	10.4	13.0
Real wages (net)	9.0	–24.4	–0.3	–3.7	–2.9	0.5	3.0	5.7	–	–	–
Real wages (gross)	–	–	–	–	–	1.7	2.8	5.5	5.9	3.3	3.1

Notes: GDP: annual growth rates, constant prices; CPI: average annual Consumer Price Index; Unemployment: year-end registered unemployment rate; annual change in average net and gross monthly wages in the national economy, constant prices.

Source: GUS.

presidential election), 48% of respondents thought there was a distinct possibility of losing their job, whereas in October 1991 (the first freely contested parliamentary election), this figure was 55% (more in Chapters 2 and 6).[10] More vulnerable groups also began to feel more at risk. For example, sizeable majorities of those in occupational groups with above-average unemployment rates – unskilled workers (78%) and agriculture and forestry employees (98%) – thought it likely that they would become unemployed in the near future. Similar patterns emerged among people with vocational education, a group which also had above-average unemployment rates. But this symmetry between actual and perceived threats has not been reflected across regions (Chapter 4). Fear of becoming unemployed has been greater in urban regions such as Warsaw and Cracow, which have the lowest regional unemployment rates, and lower in high unemployment areas like the north-east.

Finally, while the Polish public have varying opinions about the best speed and extent of market reforms, there is a high level of agreement that the state should continue to have a role in providing social benefits. After nine years of transition, across most social groups and political allegiances Central European publics strongly support state participation in the provision of social services including child care for pre-schoolers, pensions, and universal health care (Table 1.2). Those who consistently favour private provision compose a small but coherent group within each society.

The case of Poland is different from the established and (more or less) stable US economy, on which these models are often based. Poland's economy was still not in equilibrium during the time period being studied here. Because of the transition from a planned economy, the dual programme of liberalization and stabilization, not to mention the emergence of open unemployment, complicates any attempt to apply traditional concepts such as a trade-off between inflation and unemployment. While concerns about the impact of inflation on living standards dominated the early, stabilization phase of transition, unemployment soon came to dominate public concerns about the economy and personal well-being in transition economies.

Moreover, it should be asked whether voters attribute the distributional consequences of transition to the incumbent. The transformation of the economic system and the resulting (re)distribution of national wealth and income was intentionally undertaken by acts of

Table 1.2   Support for state provision of selected social benefits (%)

	Bulgaria	Czech Republic	Hungary	Poland	Romania	Slovakia
Free health care						
All	68	92	69	65	63	95
Only the poorest	29	6	27	24	34	4
None, all private	3	1	4	9	4	–
Pensions						
State	86	73	89	88	74	74
Own savings	11	23	10	9	21	23
Child care						
State-funded	72	80	61	56	78	84
Parents pay	23	17	34	38	17	14

Source: Office of Research 1999.

government, which opened determination of wages and prices to market forces. As shown in Chapter 2, the public evaluation of transition was rather negative. However, the tone of the public debate in the 1993 and 1997 campaigns suggests that most people attribute current economic benefits to the incumbent, while lasting adverse effects appear to have been blamed on the transformational reform programme.

The rise of unemployment in Poland has been linked to a sharp split in the electorate between more market-oriented and more interventionist or redistributionist parties. The main political beneficiary from high unemployment has not been radical or populist parties, but rather the post-communist Alliance of the Democratic Left (SLD). The ability of the SLD to attract disaffected voters may have defused (and diffused) the potentially destabilizing demands of economically disadvantaged groups. Although the prospect of EU membership and ideological debate between political parties has so far blunted some groups' demands for redistribution, to paraphrase Wnuk-Lipiński, egalitarianism is the philosophy of the less able and the poor while meritocracy, which requires knowledge and ability, is the philosophy of the energetic, enterprising, educated, able, and motivated.[11]

Furthermore, when it comes to articulation of interests and their expression through voting, politics in Poland is 'still "traditional" in Rokkan's sense: it was driven mostly by the economic grievances and distributional issues of well-defined social groups' which have been fairly constant and do not display significant fluctuations in allegiance (Ekiert and Kubik 1998, p. 102).

Any observer of Polish politics will be aware that party allegiance and voting behaviour are far from fully determined by economic factors. Indeed, the aim of this book is not to say that Polish voting behaviour is completely determined by socioeconomic status, but rather to investigate the extent to which it is. History also plays a large role in Polish politics, and echoing Lipset and Rokkan's (1967) classic paper, a significant cleavage between post-communist (SLD and PSL) and anti-communist (AWS, UW, ROP, UP, UPR) parties continues to delineate party contests and the lines of acceptable coalition building in Poland today. Another, secondary cleavage lies between secular and Catholic-traditionalist tendencies. Among the post-communist parties, SLD could be placed in the former but PSL in the latter category. As regards to the anti-communist parties, UW is more closely identified with secular values of civil liberty and tolerance. Post-Solidarity centre-right parties such as those in AWS and right-wing groups like ROP both emphasize Catholic and traditional values, but AWS is generally more pro-reform (balancing a classically liberal constituency and a substantial trade union membership) while ROP uses more protectionist slogans. Smaller parties, such as the economically protectionist but secular KPN and the libertarian UPR have become only marginal presences on the political scene. Of these two cleavages, however, experience shows it is easier to bridge the secular–traditionalist divide than the post-communist and post-Solidarity split.

NOTES

1. From a proportional list system to majority constituency seats, introduction of thresholds: Gebethner (1997, p. 11).
2. See Małkiewicz (1994) and Chmaj (1996) for details on the 1989 election and the 'contract Sejm' which operated until the 1991 elections.
3. Demoskop data from a survey of 998 Poles age 15 and over, conducted 7–10 May 1999, quoted in Paweł Grelak, 'Gorzej, ale nadal nieźle', *Rzeczpospolita*, internet edition, 18 May 1999. For an earlier but more detailed analysis, see Halina

Frańczak, 'Konsumencki profil elektoratów', *Rzeczpospolita*, internet edition, 22 July 1997.
4. This book's approach is closer to the public choice than the rational expectations school of thought in that people act rationally, but may have imperfect information and may be wrong in their understanding of economic mechanisms.
5. *How* this capital is depleted is probably attributable not only to tangible consequences such as losing one's job or sustaining a cut in real pay, but also to 'expired' expectations. That is, many people expected any transformational recession to be relatively shortlived. As these psychological deadlines passed, willingness to tolerate continued hardships probably also declined.
6. S. Chelkowski, 'Co z tym bezrobociem?', *Życie Gospodarcze*, 12 November 1989, p. 2.
7. *Życie Gospodarcze*, 24–31 December 1989, p. 3.
8. *Życie Gospodarcze*, 3 December 1989, p. 1.
9. *Życie Gospodarcze*, 10 December 1989, p. 4.
10. CBOS (1991), 'Opinia społeczna o planie Balcerowicza i kierunku prywatyzowania gospodarki', Report No. 816/91, November, p. 12.
11. 'W peletonie', *Rzeczpospolita*, internet edition, 18 June 1999.

2. Public Views on the Costs and Benefits of Transition

Retrospectives on the ten-year anniversary of the fall of the Berlin Wall reappraised the developments of the past decade. The impact of transition on living standards and the public's disappointment with the realities of life after communism were often cited as failures. But others saw the reforms as having been a success. A *Business Week* article placed the most advanced post-communist countries – the Czech Republic, Hungary, Poland and Slovenia – ahead of most west European countries in the *Zeitgeist* of labour market flexibility and European integration. Moreover, 'by almost every measure' (GDP per capita, inflation, unemployment, cars per 1,000 people and male life expectancy) 'life ... has improved'.[1] A more realistic appraisal noted that '[w]ith the influx of complexity into everyday life, Poles have to make more and more decisions. The majority of the population is not educated and sophisticated enough to make those decisions and that can make people unhappy, even though things are improving year on year.'[2]

Before analysing transition's 'social costs' and their relation to voting patterns, this chapter reviews public opinion on the consequences of political and economic transition for society and the individual, focusing on the periods surrounding each of Poland's five national elections in the 1990s.[3] The time span under consideration here can be roughly divided into four phases: pre-reform crisis (late 1980s), the period of extraordinary politics (1990), the transformational recession (1991 to 1994), and the current – but not trouble-free – recovery (1995 to 1999).

Analyses of the collapse of the socialist system and the implementation of Poland's 'big bang' reform programme often rely on assumptions about the nature of the deterioration of public confidence in the communist government after its repeated tries at reform. This failure of public confidence fed into the reflexive growth in popular support for the political and systemic alternative offered by the Solidarity-led opposition (Staniszkis 1991; Kamiński 1991). Balcerowicz (1994) called this surge in public acceptance of market and democratic reform and the resulting window of opportunity for policy initiatives the period of 'extraordinary politics'.

Another interesting relationship is between public attitudes towards the state of the economy, politics, their own economic well-being, their expectations for economic improvement, and how these have evolved over the 1990s. Over a relatively short period, unemployment and living standards replaced inflation and broader reform issues as the most important problems facing the country, according to public opinion surveys. Moreover, survey data show that across time and across social groups, there is a fair amount of consistency in identifying the most likely winners and losers from transition (Chapter 5). Survey data also indicate a significant level of interrelation between attitudes toward political and economic reform, both in the abstract and in their evaluations of outcomes so far (Chapter 6). Public attitudes to political and economic reform are adaptive, but are based on strong pre-conceptions formed early in the process.

Other factors, particularly the contrast between the unified post-communist parties and the fractious post-Solidarity groups, have also affected political choice. Early in the transition, public support for post-Solidarity parties was adversely affected by the public in-fighting between political leaders, especially the 'war at the top' manifested between Wałęsa and Mazowiecki in the 1990 presidential race. In contrast, the post-communist Democratic Left Alliance (SLD) gained legitimacy and retained popular support in part through its remarkable discipline and outward unity (Zubek 1995). In fact, the SLD's 1997 campaign literature emphasized exactly this point, stating: 'We do not want another "war at the top", for which everyone pays.'[4]

2.1   PUBLIC OPINION DURING THE CRISIS AND COLLAPSE OF REAL SOCIALISM

Pre-1990 survey data from Poland's state public opinion research organizations[5] illustrate the poor state of public morale in the months leading to political and then economic transition. Figure 2.1 plots political attitudes in the two turbulent years prior to the breakthrough of 1989. At the start of the timeline, November 1987, Gorbachev had been in office for two and a half years, and *perestroika* was creating a powerful legitimizing force for reforming socialist systems. The lower line in Figure 2.1 indicates a worsening in the public's evaluation of the current political situation from late 1987, with a rise in the summer of 1988 after a rash of wildcat strikes, but then a sharp decline in August and September (coinciding with the Magdalenka talks which set the conditions for the Round Table negotiations). From September 1988 to the spring of the following year, views stabilized and even improved, but more as a response to the growing coherence of the opposition than any ability of the PZPR to regroup. The Messner government resigned in August 1988, and it took until October to form the Rakowski government. In October, the public was divided over whether Rakowski was a good premier (37% yes, 31% no, 32% don't know).[6] Public debate over Poland's crisis intensified, fuelled by the November 1988 televised debate between Lech Wałęsa, then leader of the

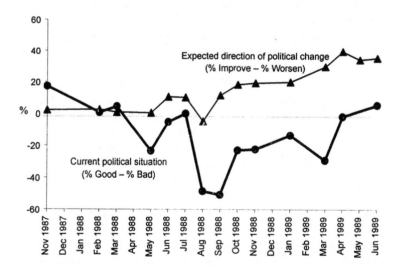

Source: CBOS 1989.

Figure 2.1 Public opinion on the political situation

Solidarity trade union, and the OPZZ leader Alfred Miodowicz, which quickly moved from a discussion of the future of trade unions in Poland to a full-scale debate over the situation in the country and its future.

Although public optimism grew as the possibility of some political concessions became more possible, survey data indicate that a minority consistently maintained at least some degree of confidence in the PZPR (Polish United Workers' Party) regime, thought that the economy and political situation were really not too bad, and apparently failed to anticipate the rapid dissolution of socialism (as did many outside observers).

In the late summer of 1988, a majority (62%) believed that the forthcoming round-table talks between the government and the opposition would lead to an agreement,[7] and they were not disappointed. The Round Table talks got under way in February 1989, and on 5 April 1989, representatives of the ruling coalition and Solidarity signed an agreement which provided for the re-legalization of Solidarity, faster marketization of the economy, and semi-free elections within the context of constitutional reform. In addition to being able to contest 35% of seats in the Sejm, all 100 seats in the reinstituted Senate were to be openly contested on a free ballot.[8] The Round Table Agreement went further than what Solidarity leaders had hoped to achieve, but soon events outpaced even this deal. Although it was planned – and expected – that the democratic transition would take four years, Solidarity's clean sweep of nearly all the contested seats and the failure of most of the Communist and allied lists to garner enough votes in the first round provoked a more rapid collapse of the political order.

Survey data indicate, however, that there was still some persistent uncertainty. Almost half (45%) of respondents foresaw an improvement in the political situation by April 1989, but a third (32%) expected no change (6% saw it as worsening).

While optimism about the political system grew after autumn 1988, expectations of future economic performance moved along a different dynamic, remaining persistently and deeply negative over this same period (Figure 2.2). By June 1989, 84% described the economic situation as bad (3% good, 12% neither good nor bad).

In October 1987, the government used a vaguely worded referendum to try to gain a popular mandate for a planned austerity programme (the 'Second Stage' reforms, meant to follow through on

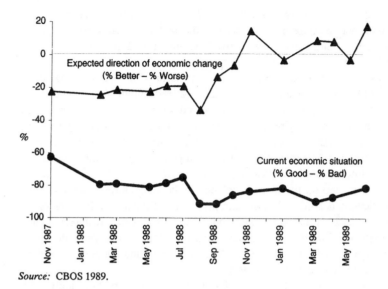

Source: CBOS 1989.

Figure 2.2 Public opinion on the economic situation

the 1981 'WOG' reforms; see Slay 1994, pp. 38–40). However, the referendum failed,[9] mainly because the public had the (mostly correct) suspicion that this reform would primarily mean more price rises. Still, the Party leadership pressed ahead with a moderated version of the reform programme (for example, projected price rises for 1988 were reduced from 57% to 40%). Even before the plan was implemented, there was a sharp public outcry and the government backed away from implementing the reforms with any real vigour. For example, partially compensatory wage rises were granted. It is no wonder that the government was cautious, as consumer price rises had triggered large-scale social unrest four times previously in the years since the Second World War. The first palpable effect of the Second Stage was a large increase in prices for most consumer goods and services, including a 60% increase in the CPI, a 49% rise in food prices, and services up 63.5% for the year as a whole.[10] The second effect was a wave of labour unrest in April and May 1988.

While never as optimistic towards the economy as the political situation, from the autumn of 1988 a rising share of the public perceived that there was a chance for Poland to improve its economic prospects. In part, this may be because the economy was sliding toward crisis and perhaps people thought the situation could not get much worse. A September 1988 OBOP survey found that 45% of those surveyed believed material living standards would not improve under Rakowski (22% thought they would); also 45% believed that there would be no radical economic reform (23% thought there would be).[11] By June 1989, about as many expected worsening (29%) as expected an improvement (26%) in 'material conditions' – meaning material living standards. A separate poll in November 1989 found that three-quarters (75%) agreed that 'what is happening today in the country is a step towards shaking Poland free from its troubles' (5% said that it was the first step on the road to Poland's collapse). These broadly defined indicators accord with most interpretations of the social dynamic of the time: that events over the course of 1989–1989 fostered greater optimism towards the prospect of political change, but also a deepened recognition of the critical state of the economy and the need for radical reform to halt the deterioration.

In the run-up to the June 1989 elections, Solidarity's economic platform was broad, with general commitments to the free market, entrepreneurialism and decentralization. By this point, the PZPR advocated similar policies and had articulated specific reform proposals to be implemented within the socialist framework. Solidarity tended to confine its economic policy discussion to criticisms of the existing system and the impossibility of reforming it. One important aspect of the build-up to the political and economic breakthrough was that the Solidarity opposition avoided directly debating economic policy with the PZPR, preferring to have its leading economists issue critiques of the Party's programme and its (often contradictory) policy pronouncements. As in 1980–1981, during the Round Table talks Solidarity negotiators concentrated their efforts on promoting social protection issues, such as wage indexation. At this point, the opposition was wary of being lured into accepting even partial responsibility for an economic policy that was probably doomed to failure without making any appreciable political gains in return. The Party was directly and absolutely blamed for all of the post-war economic miseries, from falling standards of living to the depreciating capital base.

Hope for a brighter and more prosperous future, coupled with a rejection of the existing system which failed in its promise to provide this future, led to growing popular support for the institution of a market economy. One of the more sceptical observers of public opinion (Kolarska-Bobińska 1989) termed this the 'myth of the market': wherever real socialism failed to provide improved living standards, the market would correct these failures and deliver prosperity and efficiency. Such optimism, however, seems to lead inevitably to disappointment and disillusionment. Since most Poles had little direct experience of a market economy, Kolarska-Bobińska equates this trust in the market with a kind of faith. Yet whether support for economic reform was realistic or idealistic, the public's rejection of the existing system undeniably increased the political pressure on the PZPR to relinquish power.

2.2 EVENTS AND OPINIONS DURING POLAND'S ELECTIONS: 1990–1997

1990: Changing Views of and Expectations for Transition

Compared with the lack of confidence in the chances for successful reform under the PZPR, the public believed that the first non-communist government under Mazowiecki would be able to garner confidence from society (80%), radically reform the economy (61%), and bring about improvements in living standards (55%).[12] Over the course of just one month (September 1989), the share who thought Tadeusz Mazowiecki would be a good prime minister rose from 76% to 81%.[13]

In response to the January 1990 'big bang', Poles felt that society as a whole reacted negatively but that they themselves were ready to accept its hardships. In January 1990, at the very moment of transition, a CBOS survey found that nearly half (48%) thought that society reacted to the recent price increases with 'indignation' rather than 'resignation' (33%), 'understanding' (15%), or 'indifference' (2%).[14] Slightly more described their *own* reaction as 'understanding' (26%) or 'resignation' (28%); two out of five (38%) said they reacted with 'indignation' (5% with 'indifference'). Furthermore, most thought that the government enacted its radical price liberalization programme either to end queues and empty shelves (39%) or to let prices adapt to the reality of production costs (37%).

Over the first half of 1990, CBOS data shows falling support (42% in January, 26% in July) and rising opposition (from 9% to 24%) for the government's stabilization programme.[15] One month later (February 1990), 65% thought that the reforms would improve the economic situation; 15% disagreed. However, most expected that economic improvement would follow relatively quickly – six out of ten thought that improvement would come in two years or less[16] – indicating one potential source of disillusionment with reform which could emerge over time. These optimistic expectations were rarely contradicted in the media; few economists or politicians voiced the possibility that reform would be a costly and protracted affair. As time passed, those who expected a relatively quick recovery were increasingly disappointed as the recession persisted, potentially diminishing public willingness to accept further hardships.

In January and in September 1990, OBOP found that nine out of ten Poles considered the economic situation to be poor.[17] Over the first nine months of 1990, Poles began to realize that economic recovery would be a long process. Whereas in January Poles tended to think the economy would pick up within a year (25%) or two (16%), by September they were more likely to think that economic recovery was three to four (21%) or more than five years (21%) away (ibid.). People were even less certain about when their own situation would improve. By the time of the November 1990 presidential election, the first fully free election after communism's collapse, Poland was experiencing a severe transformational recession. GDP declined by approximately 12% in 1990, a sizeable drop even considering the potential bias from statistical distortions. Nearly 6% of the labour force was unemployed in November, up from 0.3% in January and 2.4% in May 1990. Industrial production was down 15.3% for the year, with important industries such as metallurgy and textiles particularly hard hit. Overall, inflation was gradually easing. The monthly CPI in November was 4.9%, which was a definite improvement from 79.6% in January but an increase over the low rate in August (1.8%) (GUS figures). Both imports and exports were rising, but unemployment and the delayed threat of further labour shedding increased the level of personal economic insecurity (Bell and Mickiewicz 1997).

Poles' confidence in their democratic institutions was also shaken. Over the course of 1990, from January to September, fewer expressed confidence in the government (a decline from 82% to 61%), the Senate

(75%–60%), and the Sejm (78%–59%) (ibid., p. 3). Despite this, in October more than half (57%) of the Polish public had a positive opinion of the activities of the Mazowiecki government.[18]

Table 2.1 contrasts the actual polling results from the first round of elections with pre-election preferences as surveyed by CBOS and the Office of Research. Overall, the survey results are rather accurate, although the Office of Research survey overestimates support for Wałęsa and underestimates Tymiński's support.[19]

Table 2.1   Vote in first round of presidential election, 27 November 1990 (%)

	Official data	CBOS poll	Office of Research
Wałęsa	39.96	36	50
Tymiński	23.10	26	17
Mazowiecki	18.08	22	20
Cimoszewicz	9.21	6	6
Bartoszcze	7.15	8	5
Moczulski	2.50	1	2

Source: Rzeczpospolita, 1–2 December 1990; CBOS, 1990, 'Elektorat na tydzień przed wyborami', Report No. 683/90, November, p. 15 (N = 1017); *Polish General Social Survey*, 1992, (N = 1647); Office of Research, 1990.

In the actual election, held on 25 November, no single candidate won an absolute majority in the first round, requiring a second round which was held on 9 December. The first round of the presidential election was closer than perhaps expected, with a surprisingly strong finish by Stanisław Tymiński, a shadowy émigré who ran on an explicitly populist platform. Tymiński surprised observers by capturing nearly a quarter of the vote. Tymiński attracted the protest vote from those who felt they were the losers of reform and who were sceptical and fearful of the changes under way. But Tymiński's more libertarian statements appear to have attracted support from some wealthier individuals more opposed to state control and supervision of the economy. But the fact that neither Tymiński nor his Party 'X' ever again finished anywhere near as well as in 1990 might be evidence that the Polish electorate was also surprised by the first round results, thus making them more conservative in how they express discontent.

With hindsight, Mazowiecki's third-place showing might be understandable given the recession taking hold of the economy at that time. Yet Mazowiecki and his supporters were taken by surprise, as just a few months before he had drawn wide-ranging popular support (see Balcerowicz 1995, p. 298). But Wałęsa's result was also a surprise: not only did he not win outright in the first round, but he was given a run for his money by a complete political outsider with no track record or grassroots support. Although Wałęsa benefited from his long political record, he was undoubtedly hurt among floating voters by the 'war at the top' between the more socially and economically liberal camp of Mazowiecki supporters and the Christian Democratic camp which rallied behind Wałęsa (although one of Wałęsa's main criticisms of Mazowiecki was that his government had not pushed ahead quickly enough with economic reform and decommunization).

The candidate backed by the ex-communist Social Democracy of the Polish Republic (SdRP), Włodzimierz Cimoszewicz, finished relatively poorly, mostly because of the SdRP's still-fresh association with socialism. Yet a hard-core of about 10% continued to vote for the former communists. The candidate of the post-communist Polish Peasant Party (PSL, successor to the socialist-era ZSL), Roman Bartoszcze, came in fifth, but in the next parliamentary elections the PSL's grassroots support and extensive organization enabled it to fight off challengers for the peasant vote, including Rural Solidarity and its successor party, PL – *Porozumienie Ludowe*.

1991: Party Fragmentation and Public Uncertainty

After Mazowiecki's defeat in the 1990 presidential election, he resigned as prime minister and was replaced by the leader of KLD, Jan Krzysztof Bielecki, who served in that post until the October 1991 parliamentary election. In late 1991, Poland's transitional recession had fully taken hold; output and real wages were still falling and unemployment was growing apace. Much of the state enterprise sector was in danger of financial collapse because of high taxes and declining profitability. The worsening budget deficit made it impossible to grant further subsidies to industry. The education and health sectors were squeezed, and farmers were demanding protection from cheap

imported food. Farmers, state sector employees, health sector workers
and of course pensioners were all voicing increasingly strident opposition to the burdens of fiscal austerity and adjustment.

By the time of the 1991 election, the public mood towards reform
had decidedly soured. More than half (57%) of Polish adults thought
that the country was going in the wrong direction (31% thought it was
moving in the right way), and seven out of ten were 'not very' (50%) or
'not at all' (19%) satisfied with the course of economic reform (Office
of Research, 1991b). At the same time, there was some optimism: more
than half (58%) agreed that 'in the long run, everyone is better off'
under the market.

At about the same time, CBOS found falling support for the
Balcerowicz Plan (Figure 2.3), a growing sense that the Balcerowicz
Plan should be modified or replaced by a 'completely new economic
programme'.[20] There was a moderate rise in the proportion who said

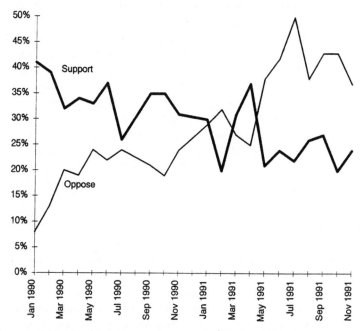

Source: CBOS, 1991, 'Opinia społeczna o planie Balcerowicza i kierunku
prywatyzowania gospodarki', Report 816/91, November.

Figure 2.3 Attitudes towards the Balcerowicz Plan, 1990–1991

that privatization was going 'too quickly' (13% in June 1990 and 34% in October 1991),[21] and a slight increase (from a third in October 1990 to half in October 1991) who thought the Balcerowicz Plan should be amended or scrapped (ibid., p. 12). Between February and August 1991, the proportion who thought that the Bielecki government's economic policy did not have a chance of leading the country out of crisis doubled (from 23% to 50%) – not because fewer thought that government policy did have a chance of succeeding (stable at 45% to 47%), but because those who were previously unsure (32% in February, 3% in August) became more negative.[22]

Uncertainty about the scale of the resulting transitional recession led to an intentional if unofficial policy of publicizing optimistic forecasts about the likely scale of the contraction and the speed of the recovery. Balcerowicz (1995, p. 309) cites not only his psychological and intellectual difficulty in making predictions, but also his resistance to the 'constant demand to commit "the fallacy of misplaced concreteness": to say when exactly when things would get better.' Anecdotal evidence suggests that these were not all sins of omission. In August 1989, *Tygodnik Solidarności* allegedly suppressed Jacek Rostowski's forecast that unemployment rates could soon reach 40%.[23] This approach to public relations can be contrasted with Klaus's approach in Czechoslovakia, where a full year was spent preparing the public for the potential hardships as well as opportunities of reform. Part of the information problem may have come from honest underestimations by official bodies of the difficulties in adjustment which would affect production and consumption. Managers of state enterprises and government economists seemed to be stuck in the mind-set of the planned economy. Articles of the day indicate that managers sincerely thought that, once liberalization made material and labour inputs more available, production would soar.

The extraordinarily high expectation that the 'big bang' would be successful partly rested upon political factors stemming from the recent capitulation by the communist party and the correlated, tremendous legitimacy of the Solidarity government. However, the radicalness of the Balcerowicz Plan, with its rejection of reform of the socialist economy and embrace of the market, reinforced its economic credibility. One advantage was its formulation within a coherent framework of liberal market economics. The embrace of market economics not only reflected the general rejection of the failed systems of socialist and market socialist economics, but it also embodied the liberal orthodoxy among academic and professional economists. The public's rejection of the socialist system and acceptance of its opposite was reinforced by the domestic and international policy-making elite's emphasis on liberal theories.

Not only were Poles becoming less sure about the economy's future course as the election neared, but there was considerable uncertainty about the election outcome. An important reason was that Poland's first open parliamentary election, held in October 1991, used an almost pure system of proportional representation to allocate seats in the lower house of parliament (the Sejm). No minimum national threshold was required. More than one hundred individual parties were officially registered, causing confusion among the electorate in their attempts to distinguish between these parties, many of which had ill-defined platforms, were centred on individuals, and often had similar names. The result was that a number of marginal parties gained parliamentary seats despite having attracted a very small share of the total vote (Table 2.2).

Table 2.2   Shares of votes in 1991 parliamentary election

	No. of votes (thousands)	% votes	No. of seats	% seats
Unia Demokratyczna	1382.1	12.3	62	13.5
Sojusz Lewicy Demokratycznej	1344.8	12.0	60	13.0
Wyborcza Akcja Katolicka	980.3	8.7	49	10.7
Porozumienie Obywatelskie Centrum	977.3	8.7	44	9.6
Polskie Stronnictwo Ludowe 'SP'	973.0	8.7	48	10.4
Konfederacja Polski Niepodległości	841.7	7.5	46	10.0
Kongres Liberalno-Demokratyczny	840.0	7.5	37	8.0
Ruch Ludowy 'PL'	613.6	5.5	28	6.1
NSZZ 'Solidarność'	566.6	5.1	27	5.9
Polska Partia Przyjaciół Piwa	367.1	3.3	16	3.5
Chrzescijanska Demokracja	265.2	2.4	5	1.1
Unia Polityki Realnej	253.0	2.3	3	0.7
Solidarność 'Pracy'	231.0	2.1	4	0.9
German minority	132.1	1.2	7	1.5
Others	630.8	12.7	24	5.1

Source: Rocznik Statystyczny (1993, p. 73).

The functioning of the 1991–1993 Sejm was greatly hampered by this division into numerous small, ill-defined, and constantly shifting parties and clubs.

The largest pro-reform party running in the 1991 elections, *Unia Demokratyczna* (UD, successor to Mazowiecki's ROAD organization) won 12% of the vote, just 0.3% more than the SLD coalition. Although UD included some of the more popular politicians in Poland – including Tadeusz Mazowiecki (59% favourable) and Jacek Kuroń (75%) – the dominance of Leszek Balcerowicz (46% favourable, 44% unfavourable) and the Balcerowicz Plan in public debate may have caused some Poles to perceive the UD as being too rigorously ideological and not sufficiently pragmatic in their pursuit of liberal economic reform.[24] The Polish public has consistently favoured a more gradual approach to policy making over a more radical one (in September 1991, 75% favoured gradual reform, 12% radical, 5% none),[25] and may have begun to punish politicians too closely identified with radical reform.

If this idea is at all true, the KLD is more likely to have been affected than UD. In the 1989–1991 governments, the KLD exercised an influence over policy disproportionate to its limited membership and electoral support. Although, in the weeks before the election, opinions towards Prime Minister Jan Bielecki were highly favourable (66%), the minority government was under attack from the opposition for its decision to stick to its policy of fiscal austerity, for the worsening macroeconomic situation, and for the government's handling of controversial issues such as privatization and pension reform – all factors which were not helped by the government's rather limited attempt at public information.[26]

In a sign of things to come, the SLD coalition drew almost level with the UD in the percentage of votes gained in the 1991 election. Although individual politicians aligned with SLD were themselves either unpopular or unknown,[27] the post-communist left began to make inroads in gaining support as a legitimate social democratic party.

However, the event which defined the 1991–1993 parliament was not just the less than resounding support for pro-reform parties but the abundance of tiny parties that won representation in the Sejm (Table 2.2). The proportional representation system impeded the functioning of the parliament and the nascent party system: not only was the Sejm highly fragmented, but once installed nearly a quarter of deputies changed political alliance or party at least once during the parliament's tenure. Many political representatives lacked a clear party identity and the national list system left few with any sense of a definable constituency to represent. Coalition building was difficult and governments unstable: the Suchocka government included seven partners prior to the no-confidence vote in July 1993.

The Solidarity coalition gave rise to a multitude of small groups and parties which ran in the 1991 election under a number of banners. One electoral coalition organized around *Zjednoczenie Chrzescijańsko-Narodowe* (National Christian Union – ZChN) ran on a traditionalist and pro-Catholic platform; *Wyborcza Akcja Katolicka* (WAK, or Catholic Electoral Action) and *Porozumienie Obywatelskie Centrum* (Centre Alliance, POC, later PC) tied for third place with the PSL, with 8.7% of the vote each. Overall, one vote in ten went to either the Solidarity trade union (*NSZZ 'Solidarność'* – 5%) or the pro-Solidarity peasants' union (*Porozumienie Ludowe* – 5.5%), both of which ran their own candidates. In all, the parties somehow aligned to the post-Solidarity centre-right gained 30% of the total vote and a third of the Sejm seats.

Other parties that gained seats in the 1991 Sejm include the PSL (8.7%) and the KPN (7.5%), headed by Leszek Moczulski. Over time, the PSL would see its fortunes rise and then fall, while the KPN and other radical and populist parties such as Korwin-Mikke's UPR and Tymiński's Party 'X' eventually lost any real significance.

1993 Parliamentary Election: Political Rebirth of the Left

As the parliamentary election approached, the centre-right was impeded by their negative evaluation among the public. By May 1993, four out of ten Poles (42%) were ready to accept a government headed by the SdRP (leading party in the SLD coalition).[28] In the end, the seven-party Suchocka government was brought down by abstentions of Solidarity deputies in a no-confidence vote. New elections were called, but one of the last acts passed by the parliament before it was dissolved was an amendment of the electoral law.

The messy collapse of the Suchocka government produced a deep cynicism before the election and a strong 'honeymoon' period of positive attitudes afterwards. Thus, OBOP surveys found that, before the 1993 election, a majority of Poles said the country was headed in a bad direction (66% bad, 19% good in June; 51% bad, 21% good in

September).[29] Similar shares also said the economy was in weak or bad shape, while attitudes were slightly more positive towards the political situation (36% neither good nor bad, 41% bad in September).

From a nearly pure PR system, under the new electoral system 391 seats in the Sejm were to be elected by a smaller number of multi-member territorial constituencies (with three to seventeen seats, depending on population) and a smaller share of seats (69) became distributed through a national list system. Thresholds of 5% for political parties and 8% for coalitions were also set.[30] As intended, these changes caused a sharp decrease in the number of parties represented in the 1993–1997 Sejm, and this has indeed stabilized the political system. While the media again focused on the confusing array of parties in the 1993 campaign, the situation had improved from 1991. About 65 parties registered as nation-wide candidates, compared with more than 100 that registered in 1991. Whereas 29 parties and coalitions attained Sejm seats in 1991, only 6 groups made it into the 1993 parliament (Table 2.3).

Table 2.3   Share of votes in the September 1993 Sejm election

	No. of votes (thousands)	% of votes	No. of seats	% of seats
SLD	2815.2	20.4	171	37.2
PSL	2124.4	15.4	132	28.7
UD	1461.0	10.6	74	16.1
Unia Pracy	1005.0	7.3	41	8.9
Katolicki Komitet Wyborczy 'Ojczyzna'	878.4	6.4	–	–
KPN	795.5	5.8	22	4.8
Bezpartyjny Blok Wspierania Reform	746.7	5.4	16	3.5
NSZZ 'Solidarność'	676.3	4.9	–	–
Porozumienie Centrum	610.0	4.4	–	–
KLD	550.6	4.0	–	–
UPR	438.6	3.2	–	–
Samoobrona	384.0	2.8	–	–
Partia 'X'	377.5	2.7	–	–
German minority	84.2	0.6	3	0.6
Others	848.8	6.1	1	0.2

Source: Rocznik Statystyczny (1994, p. 77).

Some of the more interesting opinion polls were conducted after the election. OBOP data show that, after the election, views were slightly more balanced. Although nine out of ten still thought the economy was in poor shape, and three out of four (76%) described the social mood as negative, there was a slight improvement in the share who said they were dissatisfied with the way democracy was developing in Poland (60% in October, compared with 77% in June and 75% in August).[31] In addition, there was a moderate decrease in the number who thought that material living standards would worsen in the future (37% in June, 22% in October), and a rise in expectations that it would be the same (34% to 40%) or better (19% to 27%). Another OBOP survey taken after the election found that a majority thought the election result would have a positive impact on problems in agriculture (62%), and pluralities expected improvement in unemployment (46%) and living standards (43%; about a quarter expected no change in any surveyed area).[32] But despite the negative environment surrounding the election, a majority of Poles believed that the 1993 results were a confirmation that Poles were capable of participating in democracy (ibid., p. 6).

The drafters of the new electoral law could not foresee that the changed electoral law would lead to the overrepresentation of the two post-communist parties in the Sejm. The SLD and PSL together won 35% of votes, but gained two-thirds of its seats. Although there were many prognoses of the devastating effects of the new system on small parties, during the few months spanning the no-confidence vote, the enactment of the new electoral law and the election campaign of 1993, the fragmented centre-right in particular was unable to overcome rivalries and personal conflicts to form larger groups and coalitions. The right lost so resoundingly to the left because it did not form coalitions to mobilize the electorate under one election committee. Even President Wałęsa, who was so strongly opposed to the post-communists, was unable to resist this result, and soon thereafter a coalition government was formed between the SLD and PSL, with PSL leader Pawlak as prime minister.

In general, SLD supporters tended to take an 'anti-clerical, post-communist' orientation, favouring abortion rights, support for state industries, and opposition to Christian values and economic liberalism. PSL voters, perhaps the most clearly defined electorate, were predominantly rural, opposed to market liberalism, and against integration into Europe. By contrast, supporters of UD are clearly identified with pro-market and pro-European sympathies and are against subsidization of agriculture, but like SLD voters are opposed to a prominent role for Christian values in election campaigns.[33] UD's vote share fell in the 1993 election, but its greatest loss was that it was largely without potential allies in the parliament.

This was because while the small, post-Solidarity parties of the right[34] attracted about 20% of the total vote, they won only 3.5% of the seats in the Sejm. The centre-right paid for their reluctance to trade off individual party identity and independence for a greater probability of gaining seats as part of an electoral coalition.[35] The only other parties represented in parliament where the pro-Wałęsa BBWR (whose supporters were pro-market with a Christian outlook), the social democratic Unia Pracy, and KPN (whose supporters tended towards statism and conservative social values) – too diverse a selection to form an influential opposition.

Not surprisingly, this Sejm lasted its full term. However, it was not without its tensions and scandals. Waldemar Pawlak's tenure as prime minister ended in May 1995 over allegations that he was more con-cerned with increasing the PSL's assets and power rather than with improving the situation in Poland outside of agriculture. He was fol-lowed by Józef Oleksy, whose term as prime minister was cut short in December 1995 by allegations of connections with Soviet and Russian spies. Finally, Włodzimierz Cimoszewicz took office in 1995, and governed over a relatively balanced government policy until elections in 1997; the calm of this period was assisted by the victory of the SLD candidate and former communist-era junior minister Aleksander Kwaśniewski over Lech Wałęsa in the 1995 presidential election.

1995 Presidential Election: Post-Communist Consolidation

After taking office, the SLD–PSL government somewhat slowed the pace of reform, but this did not put a brake on the economy's growth. In 1995, GDP expanded at the fastest rate in any year since 1990. Unemployment (14.7% in November) and inflation (21% for the year) were high but coming down. Real wages were rising (up 4.5%) and there was a greater sense of social peace (the number of strikes fell from 429 in 1994 to 42 in 1995).[36] Still, two million fewer people were working than in 1989. The SLD–PSL government had enacted some agricultural policies such as minimum guaranteed prices and import price equalization payments, but not at the level demanded by farmers. Pensions had been keeping pace with consumer prices, if not average wages.

Despite the favourable economic indicators, public opinion through the first half of 1995 shows that Poles remained likely to say that things in Poland were going in a bad (54%) rather than good (26%) direction, that the economy (48% bad, 36% neither good nor bad) and the political situation (47% bad, 34% neither good nor bad) were both in a poor state. Moreover, the tendency was to think that little would change over the next year or so on any dimension.[37] Although at this point reforms were starting to turn into real, measurable gains, this sense apparently had not fed fully through into public perceptions.

The political situation was rockier than that in the economic and social spheres. There were constant tensions between the interventionist tendencies of the PSL and the macroeconomic conservatives in the SLD, and the coalition was continuously at odds with President Wałęsa. Wałęsa's key tool was his control over the three 'presidential ministries': foreign affairs, defence and the interior ministry, although by the time of the election both defence minister Kołodziejczyk and foreign minister Olechowski had been forced to resign (the former by Wałęsa; the latter following government revelations of links to business). Wałęsa was also seen to be destabilizing the system, such as through his veto of the 1996 budget and then his threat to dissolve parliament for failing to pass a budget, and the fight over political appointees to the state broadcasting board.

What credit there was to gain from the economy went to the SLD, which had controlled the key economic ministries and the post of prime minister for the preceding year. Thus, in promoting Kwaśniewski, the SLD was able to combat Balcerowicz's argument that the high growth was made possible by the tough policies of 1990–1991, and instead for the SLD to take credit for Poland's improving situation. Moreover, the SLD's track record in office dispelled the right's claim that electing candidates linked to the former regime would lead to a return to communism.

The first round of the 1995 presidential election was extremely close, with Kwaśniewski winning just 2% more of the vote than the incumbent, Lech Wałęsa (Table 2.4). The OBOP exit polls are very close to the official results, signalling little impact of the residual hesitancy to admit publicly that one voted for the post-communists or

Table 2.4   Vote shares in the first round of the 1995 presidential election (%)

	Official results	OBOP exit poll
Kwaśniewski	35.1	34
Wałęsa	33.1	33
Kuroń	9.22	10
Olszewski	6.9	7
Pawlak	4.3	4
Zieliński	3.5	4
Gronkiewicz-Waltz	2.8	3
Korwin-Mikke	2.4	3

Sources: Official election results: *Mały Rocznik Statystyczny,* 1996, pp. 73-74; OBOP data: *Gazeta Wyborcza,* 6 November 1995, (N = 1145), p. 1.

for the controversial former premier Pawlak, an act which Marody (1995a, p. 268) suggests was sometimes seen as 'morally improper behavior'.

The personal characteristics of the candidates appear to have been more influential in the 1995 election than in the 1990 contest. A post-election OBOP survey for *Gazeta Wyborcza* found that half (54%) of Kwaśniewski's first round supporters chose this candidate because he had 'a responsible character [and] individuality', whereas 46% of Wałęsa's supporters were motivated 'because it was impossible to support any other candidate'.[38] Kuroń and Olszewski came in substantially behind the leading candidates. Despite his personal popularity, Kuroń may have been hindered not only by concerns about his health but also because of anti-Semitic feelings. Likewise, the National Bank of Poland president, Hanna Gronkiewicz-Waltz, is also popular, but fared poorly in this contest. Although she may have attracted some votes away from Wałęsa in the first round, the second round results suggest this did not make much of an impact in the final result. In the second round, Kwaśniewski won over Wałęsa by a very narrow 52% to 48%, a difference of about 650,000 votes.[39] Unlike Wałęsa, Kwaśniewski has maintained a remarkable level of public support since assuming office, with seven out of ten Poles consistently favourable towards Kwaśniewski.[40]

1997 Parliamentary Election: Systemic Consolidation

The 1997 parliamentary election was consequential for several reasons. First, the 1993-1997 parliament was the first in the post-communist era to run the full length of its legal mandate, indicating a stability that was absent before. Second, the centre-right formed a political alliance which finally bridged the divisions that had plagued them for most of the 1990s, contributing to a reduction in the number of candidates and parties. Gebethner (1997) indicates this also to be a sign of consolidation and stabilization of democracy in Poland. Whereas, in 1993, the amended electoral system resulted in a parliament which did not represent a third or more of the voting public, the further concentration of the party system in Poland increased the proportionality of seat distribution. The number of parties and election committees registered for inclusion on the national list declined from 29 in 1991 to 19 in 1995 and just 10 in 1997; the number of groups which ran in one or more electoral districts also fell. The other key political event of 1995 occurred on 25 May, when the constitutional referendum passed, with 6.3 million votes in favour and 5.6 million against, but on a turnout of only 43% (Gebethner 1997, pp. 11, 15).

In late 1997, macroeconomic conditions were even better than during the 1995 presidential race. GDP expanded by 6.8% in 1997, one of the fastest rates in all of Europe. Annual consumption growth was also strong at 6.9%. Registered unemployment (10.3% for 1997) was headed downwards, having fallen 3% during the first eleven months of 1995 and 6% since the previous general election. Over the same period, both real wages (7%) and pensions (6%) also grew. The pace of privatization and other reforms slowed under the SLD–PSL government, but fiscal policy was more cautious than some expected. Social spending increased: transfer payments as a share of total state expenditures rose (from 32.6% in 1993 to 36.4% in 1994), as did total government debt (from 12% of GDP in 1991 to 24% in 1994) (Blazyca and Rapacki 1996). As a result, inflation fell more slowly than expected, although the gradual deceleration of inflation and the creeping exchange rate peg made these rates rather stable and predictable.

However, the economy played a lesser role in this election than in previous ones. To a greater or lesser extent, the main parties agreed on the general dimensions of economic policy, with debate tending to focus on details such as the rate of personal taxation and budgetary spending on social policies. There was a surprising degree of consensus on eventual European Union membership, including implementation of the *acquis communautaire*. The most divisive issues during the campaign harked back to the ideological split between the PZPR and Solidarity, including decommunization and 'lustration' (*lustracja*). Jasiewicz (1998) argues that the similarity in socioeconomic attributes and policy-related attitudes makes economics a poor predictor of voting behaviour in 1997, thus bringing the ideological cleavage between the two main political camps back to the fore (see Chapter 6).

In Spring 1997, a CBOS poll found the Polish public divided over whether the 1990–1993 'post-Solidarity' governments (28%) or the 19931997 SLD–PSL government (22%) did more for reform in Poland (27% said they were the same). While evaluations of the incumbent government may not have been overwhelmingly positive, in July 1997 half (50%) said that the coalition government had behaved more or less as expected.[41] In general, consumer confidence in 1997 did not show the dynamic rise seen over the course of the 1995 campaign. Consumer confidence and public attitudes on the economy's prospects were dampened by the devastating floods which hit Poland in the month before the election. This led to a rather subdued tone for the campaign; mudslinging was largely absent until about the last week before the poll. In the weeks prior to the campaign, AWS and SLD were running neck and neck, separated by no more than five points.[42]

In the 1997 race, Poland's party structure was in practical terms whittled down to four effective parties or coalitions: AWS and SLD at the centre-right and centre-left, and UW and PSL flanking these two parties (Table 2.5). Because the race appeared so close, closer than the final results suggest, the volatility in pre-election opinion polls seems to have led to some degree of strategic voting, to the benefit of the two largest blocs and to the detriment of smaller and more interest-specific groups such as PSL and UW, as well as more ideologically-driven parties such as the ROP and UP.

The SLD actually increased its total support from 1993, but the poor showing of its coalition partner PSL, along with worsening relations between the two, meant that the post-communists went into opposition. Under the slogan 'good today, better tomorrow', the SLD focused during the campaign on an appeal to those who profited less and bore a disproportionate share of the costs of transformation, mostly through a pledge to increase wages, pensions and social assistance.

Table 2.5 Vote shares in the 1997 Sejm election

	No. of votes (thousands)	% votes	No. of seats	% seats
Akcja Wyborcza Solidarność	4427.4	33.83	201	43.70
Sojusz Lewicy Demokratycznej	3551.2	27.13	164	35.65
Unia Wolności	1749.5	13.37	60	13.04
Polskie Stronnictwo Ludowe	956.2	7.31	27	5.87
Ruch Odbudowy Polski	727.1	5.56	6	1.30
Unia Pracy	620.6	4.74	–	–
Krajowa Partia Emerytów i Rencistów	284.8	2.18	–	–
Unia Prawicy Rzeczpospolitej	266.3	2.03	–	–
Krajowe Porozumienie Emerytów i Rencistów	212.8	1.63	–	–
Blok dla Polski	178.4	1.36	–	–
German minority	51.0	0.39	2	0.44
Others	62.9	0.47	–	–

Source: GUS, *Mały Rocznik Statystyczny 1998.*

As noted, the most significant development of the 1997 parliamentary election was the formation of a centre-right political bloc. After failed attempts to create wider coalitions for the 1993 and 1995 campaigns, the *NSZZ Solidarność* leader, Marian Krzaklewski, took the initiative in forming a federation of 40-plus disparate groupings which shared a general anti-communist ideology and a conservative social outlook.[43] Despite some polls which indicated that votes could be lost by such a coalition,[44] Solidarity Electoral Action (*Akcja Wyborcza Solidarność*) attracted most of the votes given to the fragmented parties of the right in 1993, and came first in the 1997 election (Table 2.5). AWS gained the highest share of the vote and the greatest number of seats in the Sejm, and won 51 of 100 seats in the Senate. The fact that this centre-right coalition gained the largest share of seats indicates that its relative lack of parliamentary representation in the 1993–1997 Sejm was more a reflection of its failure to form an electoral coalition than of any insuperable shortcomings in the institutional development of a representative democracy.

Among the smaller parties, Unia Wolności (the party formed by the merger of UD and KLD in April 1994) fared better than predicted, with a last-minute surge in support. For most of 1995, UW received about

7–8% support in the polls, jumping to 10% in August and 15% in the last pre-election poll in September.[45] Although Balcerowicz placed the party as one of the 'centre-left', there is a continuing split between those on the left such as Jacek Kuroń and those more on the right, including Hanna Suchocka and Donald Tusk (Rothert 1997). The PSL's decline continued in the 1997 election, with its 7% support marginally lower than that in 1993. Only one other party, Jan Olszewski's Movement for the Reconstruction of Poland (ROP), managed to enter parliament. It has already split, and is unlikely to make it into the next parliament as things stand. The Union of Labour (*Unia Pracy*, UP) just failed to cross the 5% threshold.

Overall, the 1997 election was even more a contest between two large political machines than the 1995 presidential vote was. Together, AWS and SLD won 79% of the seats in the Sejm; only three other parties plus the German minority gained representation. ROP came in just over the 5% threshold and gained six seats, while Unia Pracy came in just under the threshold and won no seats. The most critical factor in deciding the outcome of this election was not the SLD's pragmatism, or the PSL's poor image, or any sudden conversion of the Polish public to UW's liberalism. Rather, the election results strongly indicate the importance of voter turnout (see Chapter 5).

2.3   WINNERS AND LOSERS IN PUBLIC OPINION

Through each of Poland's democratic elections, a number of key themes have emerged and re-emerged to define public debate over Poland's future. In some cases, general principles, such as concern over material living standards, can find their expression through changing along with the economic circumstances (such as a falling concern about inflation and a rising awareness of unemployment). This section also considers the Polish public's evaluations of the present system compared with that under communism, and their perceptions of the distribution of winners and losers in society. Finally, there is evidence of a general consistency in the public's attitudes towards economic and political reform over the 1990s. In other words, people tend to hold consistent attitudes either for or against economic reform. And while a positive view of economic reform tends to be linked to favourable general attitudes towards Poland's transformation, for a minority the material losses experienced under the post-communist transition are outweighed by the gains in political and personal freedom.

Unemployment and Opportunity Seen as Most Important Consequences of Transition

Perceptions of the most important problems facing the country appear to have evolved with actual circumstances. In late 1990, most Poles named society-wide issues such as economic reform (41%), the environment (17%), democratic reform (10%) and the cost of living (8%) as the 'most urgent issues' facing Poland (Office of Research 1990). By spring 1999, Poles were focused on issues related to economic well-being: unemployment (29%) and living standards (16%), followed by economic issues in general (10%) and economic reform (9%).[46]

Unemployment also tops the list (59%) in a 1999 poll of the most important negative changes which have occurred since 1989.[47] In the same survey, when asked to name the most important *positive* changes of the past decade, four out of ten (42%) named 'full shelves', along with freedom of speech (21%), political freedom and a multi-party system (17%) and the free market and private enterprise (15%). Both positive effects of transition – such as increased choice and quality of goods and better opportunities in education and employment – and its negative effects – such as unemployment, increased crime and rural poverty – weigh in individuals' calculations of the costs and benefits of transition. Each of these factors also features in people's conceptions of the 'social costs' of transition, as shown in the following chapters of this book.

Consequences of Transition for Living Standards

In addition to asking individuals to evaluate their current living standards, the question of gains and losses during transition can also be approached through questions which compare present circumstances with those under the socialist system, such as the standards of law and order, the political situation, or even 'life in general'. These questions are interesting not only because they indicate the range of views held by different social and economic groups, but also because they can also give a perspective on whether and how perceptions of the present and past are developing over time.

A spring 1999 survey (Office of Research 1999) found that attitudes towards whether the present situation is better or worse than ten years ago depend on how the question is asked (Figure 2.4). Poles are most positive about the current political system, with six out of ten saying that the situation today is better; about half say that the economic situation is better now. But views are evenly divided over whether 'life in general' is better or worse than before 1989 (45% versus 47%), although more are positive now than in 1992 (when 34% said life was better, 52% worse) or 1993 (37% better, 54% worse) (Office of Research data).

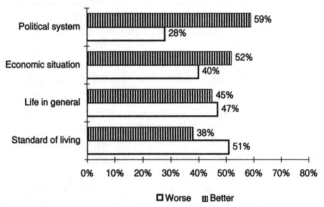

Source: Office of Research 1999.

Figure 2.4 Situation today compared with under communism, Poland, Spring 1999

Central Europeans' opinions of whether they are worse or better off than under communism vary not only from country to country, but also across social groups within each country. Compared with countries such as Bulgaria or Russia, where the structural dislocation has been worse and political support for economic reforms weaker, Poland as a whole is clearly better off than a decade ago. But also unlike countries which have enacted reforms more slowly, where standard indicators show that a decisive majority is worse off now, Polish society is about evenly divided into those who perceive themselves to be either winners or losers.

That said, Poles are considerably more optimistic about the impact of transition than publics in other Central European countries, and they are the only public from the six countries surveyed which has become substantially *more* positive over time (Figure 2.5). Only Czechs have nearly the same level of optimism, but this has declined in recent years. Just one in four in Bulgaria, Hungary and Slovakia, and one in three in Romania, view life now as being better than before 1989.

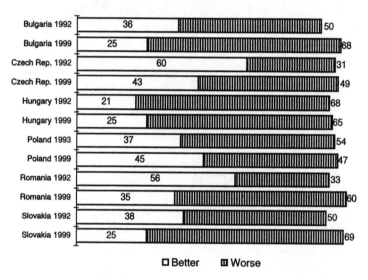

Source: Office of Research 1992–1999.

Figure 2.5 'Is life in general better or worse now than under communism?'

In 1999, half (51%) of the Polish public said that the past ten years had had a *bad* effect on living standards in the country, although evaluations were now more positive than in 1992 (82% bad). In the same survey, almost half (45%) described the financial situation of their own household as 'fairly good' (2% 'very good', 38% 'fairly bad' and 14% 'very bad'). Like the results in Figure 2.4, this suggests that the Polish public is almost evenly divided into those who feel they have benefited

from the reforms, whether materially or otherwise, and those who feel
they have not. These views have been remarkably stable over the past
few years (Figure 2.6). There has been more fluctuation in the proportion saying the economy's performance was 'good'; this view generally
rose between 1990 and 1997, but then entered two years of decline, in
part mirroring the slowed GDP growth rate.

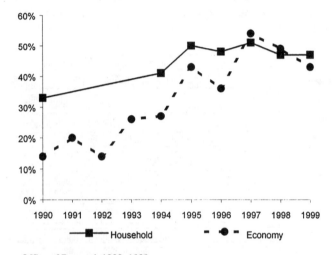

Source: Office of Research 1990–1999.

*Figure 2.6   Current situation of economy and household finances (%
              saying each is 'good')*

The events of 1997–1999 are politically important because of the
reversal of a long-standing trend where people tended to estimate
their own household's financial situation as better than that of the
wider economy. In 1997 these estimates converged and subsequently
remained parallel, although they are not very strongly correlated
(0.353).

Further dynamics in people's perceptions are apparent in responses
to whether the political and economic systems were better or worse
than under communism. Data from annual surveys (Table 2.6) show
that while optimism about the relative status of the economy and
democratic system peaked in 1996–1997, a majority continues to say

that the present situation is better – although the margin is narrower regarding the economy than the political system.

Table 2.6   Economic and political system now versus under communism (%)

	1992	1993	1994	1995	1996	1997	1998	1999
Economy								
Better	19	31	38	53	62	62	56	52
Worse	67	59	53	37	25	25	30	40
Politics								
Better	60	61	52	60	61	61	53	59
Worse	23	23	36	28	26	28	33	28

Source: Office of Research 1992–1999.

Winners and Losers

Rychard (1996, p. 467) notes that the concept of winners and losers depends not only upon empirical data to identify the most vulnerable and most advantageously placed groups in society, but also upon wider conceptions of the costs of transition within social and political life: 'We can learn about power and localization of social conflict not only from the "objective" locations of the losing and winning groups, but also from how images and stereotypes on the subject held by, for example, political elites and different social groups emerge.' Public opinion data from before and after the 1990 launch of Poland's marketization programme illustrate people's preconceptions, expectations and understandings of market reform.

The concepts of 'winners' and 'losers' can prompt a lively and wide-ranging discussion. This section reviews a few key concepts and guidelines to shape the discussion.[48] A standard way of defining winners and losers is via social class. Poland's class structure was indelibly marked by the socialist system, but since the late 1980s one of the most interesting developments has been the emergence of social groups which were small or almost non-existent before. At the broadest level, the emergence of an entrepreneurial class as well as a large population of unemployed introduced new high and low bounds between the 'haves' and 'have nots' in Poland. In official statistics, new categories were created to include 'self-employed' and 'non-wage income' (that is, unemployed and benefit-dependent) household types into the household budget surveys, this being just one example of how working definitions in the statistical agency have changed to meet a transforming economy (Chapter 4). Another interesting development is the speed with which success in the post-communist economy has come to follow the patterns exhibited in advanced market economies: those with education, skills and personal contacts adapt more easily under either system. However, personal attributes undoubtedly also play a vital role in forming 'winners'.

Moreover, the 'gains' and 'losses' from systemic reform may not all be measurable in terms of income or wealth. Public opinion data indicate that a fraction of Poles feel that life is better, but primarily because of political freedom rather than economic gain. Even when the idea of 'better' or 'worse' is restricted to economic performance and well-being, it may not be possible to separate out the impact of transition on different aspects of economic life, much less measure the improvements in quality, choice and supply which are among the greatest utility-increasing effects of liberalization (Roberts 1993). Some losses affect individuals and specific groups, such as factories or regions, while most of the public is able to benefit from transition's positive effects such as the end of shortages.

Standard demographic or occupational categories are weaker than might be expected in explaining attitudes towards life in post-communist Poland. Recent survey data (Office of Research 1999) show that the clearest breakdown is by age: half (56%) of those under 30 say life is now better, whereas six in ten of those over the age of 60 say life now is worse. Those with lower educational attainment (primary or vocational) tend to be negative, whereas those with secondary and higher tend to be positive. Although individual occupational groups are quite small, white collar and skilled workers tend to say life is better, whereas the unemployed, pensioners and unskilled workers tend to say life is worse. However, there is little variation across other indicators of experience: those who had been unemployed and those who had changed jobs vary little in their attitudes from those who have not. State and private sector employees, as well as the self-employed, have similar outlooks, as do those who do and do not attend religious services regularly.

The apparent link between education, age, and attitudes toward transition can be explained to a large extent by individuals' relative positions in the labour market. The young and well-educated, especially those living in larger cities, are more optimistic about the benefits of the market, while those older, out of work, less-educated, and dependent on social benefits are understandably more sceptical. While these factors can explain a good deal of the variation in attitudes across the public, the indications are that people hold fairly consistent views towards transition – more coherent, perhaps, than the demographic data might suggest. Chapter 5, which looks more closely at socioeconomic status, shows interesting relationships between perceptions and empirical data on welfare.

Finally, in the midst of current concern about the costs of transition for society, it is easy to lose sight of the privations and difficulties of the socialist period. 'Real socialism' should not be idealized as an era of free health care, cheap food, full employment, and inexpensive utilities. In *Heart of Europe* (1984), Norman Davies summarized the reality of life in Poland in the mid-1980s:

> The social effects of the protracted crisis have best been described as 'pauperization'. A rich country has been beggared; and it is the ordinary people who suffer the consequences. The standard of living sinks, while prices rise together with all the other indices of social distress In 1985, an estimated one-third of the population lives below the subsistence level ... The waiting time for apartments varies between 15 years in Warsaw and 26 years in Wrocław ... One of the worst records of environmental pollution in Europe ... has produced an alarming rise in infant mortality, in environmental-related diseases, and in the overall deathrate. Life expectancy is falling. A Health Service stretched beyond endurance, which has survived for years on medical aid from the West ... has seen surgical wards closed down for want of elementary equipment. (pp. xiii–xiv)

Consistency in Attitudes Towards Political and Economic Reform

Although this chapter has used a number of different surveys, there is a surprising consistency and comprehensible evolution in the public's attitudes towards political and economic reform. Recent survey findings indicate that attitudes have become relatively more positive, but still only half of Poles say they have gained from the changes since 1989 (Office of Research 1999).

All four questions summarized in Figure 2.5 evoke highly correlated responses (Table 2.7),[49] with the relation especially strong between estimates of 'life in general' and 'standards of living' now, followed by views towards 'life in general' and the current 'political system'. Overall, nearly half the public is consistently negative or consistently positive across these four measures.

Table 2.7 Correlations between situation now versus under communism

	Standard of living	Political system	Economic situation
Political system	0.4749		
Economic situation	0.4548	0.4039	
Life in general	0.6056	0.5884	0.4439

Note: Spearman correlation coefficients; $\varrho = 0.000$ for all (two-tailed test).
Source: Office of Research 1999.

Simple observation indicates that at least some of those who say life is better than under communism also say that living standards and the economy are comparatively worse. About one-quarter of those who say life is better than before 1989 describe their own financial situation as bad and also say that transition has had a negative impact on living standards. However, this should not detract from the very high relation between satisfaction with economic and political reform and with life now, as Table 2.7 shows.

Moreover, there is a high level of consistency among these groups. In particular, those who feel that they have benefited from reform tend to give more support to specific market reforms while those who see their situation as worse under the present system are more in favour of interventionist policies.[50] When factor analysis is performed with a wide range of questions on political, economic, social and international affairs and attitudes, a strong factor emerges – one relevant for the subject of this book – namely, the heavy loading on variables for 'life in general', living standards and the Polish economy now in comparison with the position under communism, and also on the present state of Poland's economy and the political system now compared with before 1989.

Other factors which also influence perceptions of having gained or lost from transition include a pro-West orientation, a preference for a more limited role for the state in the economy (all positive), and political alienation (negative). Yet this does not detract from the strong relationship between individuals' evaluations of their own living standards, the state of the economy, and the performance of the political system now compared with under communism. Moreover, this connection persists across the tenures of successive governments. As subsequent chapters argue, there is a shared perspective concerning which social groups have benefited most from reform and which are more at risk, although in the case of pensioners this is not always accurate. Second, personal characteristics feed directly into support for political and economic reform. Third, these attitudes have significance for voting behaviour, as will be discussed in Chapter 6.

Understanding Acceptance and Disillusionment with Reform

Through the cycles of public acceptance and dissatisfaction with reform, social scientists have come up with several frameworks through which to examine and think about the assumptions upon which public attitudes are formed and the factors which cause people to amend their beliefs and preferences. This section reviews some of the key ideas that have been most influential in thinking about how people understand transition.

'Myth of the market'

As shown in the opinion data, Poles greeted the radical Balcerowicz Plan with a high degree of support and acceptance. In this view, acceptance of the market lay not so much in public acceptance of how market mechanisms work, but rather in the belief that the market economy was the opposite of 'real socialism'. Attitudes towards democracy and the market in the 1980s contribute to an understanding of popular support for radical reforms. Frentzel-Zagorska and Zagorski (1993) theorize that, whatever negative characteristics were attributed to socialism during the years of deepening public dissatisfaction, the market economy – as the opposite or antithetical system – was seen as possessing positive and almost miraculous qualities. The socialist order was fundamentally unjust, so democracy, the private sector and the market were preferable in that they were not unjust. However, they tended not to pay sufficient attention to capitalism's down sides.

Kolarska-Bobińska (1990) uses the concept of the 'myth of the market' to describe how competition and the market mechanism were set in opposition to the planned economy. As the centralized system became progressively less able to fulfil the material aspirations of the 1970s, so grew the belief that only the market could provide. Kolarska-Bobińska emphasizes that this support for the efficiency of the market did not rest on public approval of market determination of higher remuneration for more valuable skills, or from a deep understanding of production and consumption. Instead, the 'myth of the market' was rooted in observations of the superior consumption patterns in the West, without proper consideration of the meaner and harsher aspects of capitalism.

Such conclusions are not the sole domain of sociologists. For instance, the economist Stanisław Gomułka (1994) also emphasizes the importance of perceptions of what economic reform would deliver for its political acceptability. In the late 1980s, the severity of the economic crisis compounded disbelief in the administration's ability to reverse trends. As much of the economic misery was at times exaggerated in the public perception, so the scale of benefits to be had from a free market was potentially aggrandized in similar disproportion. At the moment of transition, acceptance of the market was high despite lack of familiarity with it. This was possible because of the rejection of socialism rather than acceptance of the market. The problem with this scenario is that support for market democracy could be eroded if the expected goods were not delivered on time. There is little scope for the value of democratic ideals in the face of sustained hardships, which links back into the interpretation of election results as the consequence of generalized discontentment with the course of economic reforms.

Legitimacy

Another way of conceptualizing the origins of the high levels of public support for the Mazowiecki government's economic policy is linked to the concept of legitimacy. Kaminski (1991) defines legitimacy for a socioeconomic regime as the public's willingness to 'acquiesce to the existing distribution of power and privileges', but not through fear of the regime's coercive use of force. Legitimacy may be established through the force of tradition, religion, law or a charismatic leader. However, in his interpretation of the Polish situation, Kaminski identifies the source of the legitimacy of the socialist state as having depended upon its ability to deliver rising economic performance, as measured through increased consumption and improved standards of living. As the regime's ability to deliver the goods deteriorated, continued passive acceptance of the regime was based not on its legitimacy but, as Kaminski argues, on negative legitimation. By negative legitimation, he means that beyond a dependence on the state to fulfil most basic needs (work, housing, education), other motives such as a sense of security in welfare terms, a sense of irreversibility of the political order, and fear of the unknown alternatives, can also promote people's accommodation of the regime. Fear of the alternative can create passive acceptance of the *status quo*.

But what triggers the public's rejection of the *status quo*? As in war of attrition models, there must be a threshold beyond which continuation of the *status quo* becomes costlier than the probable cost of reform. Under an authoritarian regime, willingness to mobilize in favour of reform must also be tempered by the likelihood that the regime will use coercion to defend its position. After the transition, the question arises of how long the legitimacy of the new regime will last. The general feeling seems to be that, as in the 'extraordinary politics' idea, the political capital from effecting political and economic transition is itself transitory. If governments under the new, democratic system do not pay attention to generating coalitions of support for reform, then public opposition to the distributive impact of transition will grow.

Making this sort of argument depends upon a different definition of legitimation. Legitimation, according to Rychard (1992), depends upon whether people 'accept and subordinate themselves to the existing institutional system'. It is widely agreed that, by the end of the 1980s, the communist regime suffered from a chronic and irrecoverable loss of legitimacy. Yet democratic governments also have to concern themselves with maintaining legitimacy, defined as an acceptance of the institutional system. Rychard expressed the fear that the post-communist, democratic governments would not place sufficient attention on creating a base of legitimation for the reform process. The system needs an addressee, and the 'legitimacy gap' of post-Solidarity politics originated in the lack of overt constituency building once the previous system had been rejected. Post-socialist legitimacy is strong in terms of ideology and everyday behaviour, but particularly weak in the area of institutions. This lack of legitimacy of political institutions led to low voter turnout and depressed confidence levels. Passivity towards reforms, Rychard asserts, may become resistance because Poland focused more on values than on interests, the expression of which is essential for the proper functioning of economic and political institutions. Furthermore, support based on emotion is more susceptible to manipulation than that based on reason. Rychard seems to imply that transition will mean a move from a generalized to an interest- and sector-specific calculation of whether to accept the institutional structure. While agreeing with the importance of growing differentiation of interests, the idea that the Mazowiecki government's neglect of developing value-led acceptance of reforms led to growing active opposition to the costs of reform should not be exaggerated.

The material interest of the individual is the primary influence on the personal acceptance of or opposition to transition. However, social status, conditions of work and level of personal consumption in the new system are not known in advance. In calculation of future economic and social status, individual characteristics such as age, education, capabilities, talents and preferences are also important, and one might also add further connections. Individual attitudes may be predicted by certain fundamental variables, including people's perceptions of their own capabilities and their present and future skill use in employment, their expected earning levels (and how quickly these are or are not reached), and expected changes in living standards and consumption levels, especially when privileges such as special access to goods and services in short supply become redundant. Expectations of future well-being are based on this imperfect knowledge as well as on ideas about the rules of the game under markets and democracy, in comparison with the known rules under the existing system. By contrast, the 'market myth' theories cited above proposed that these calculations are based on antitheses of the worst aspects of the socialist system.

One important factor to remember is that the political debate over economic reform in Poland was not primarily between proponents and opponents of the market economy. The goal that Poland should develop towards a market-oriented economy modelled on the advanced systems of the West has long been widely accepted. Rather, the core of the debate has been over the distribution of costs and gains from market reforms, and increasingly on the role of the state in the economy.[51]

The most volatile political issues have centred on demands for subsidization – and continue to do so. Take, for instance, the political importance of sectors such as agriculture and mining. About one-third of voters come from rural areas which are primarily dependent upon agriculture. In each parliamentary election, rural voters have not only made up an important element of the floating vote, but each time they voted against the incumbent. The agricultural sector has had a hard time adjusting to the market economy, and successive governments have done little to advance the adjustment of the rural economy. Yet, as in many other countries, the countryside is conservative and tends to be more interested in receiving subsidies to support the continuation of established activities than in undertaking reforms which may raise efficiency but which also threaten to change and displace traditional livelihoods. Balcerowicz (1995, p. 358) attributes farmers' opposition to reform primarily to the elimination of the windfall gains in 1989 (while there is no evidence to suggest that all farmers profited equally, or that most of the gain did not in fact go to the still largely state-run agricultural wholesalers). In the next paragraph, Balcerowicz argues for the need to shift excess labour from agriculture to 'more productive sectors'. It is not too difficult to see how farmers might find a policy aimed at putting a proportion of them out of business to be excessively ideological.

NOTES

1. 'Europe Ten Years Later', special report, *Business Week*, 8 November 1999, pp. 57–66.
2. George Kolankiewicz, quoted in 'Market realities hit Poland', 13 November 1999, <<http://news.bbc.co.uk/hi/english/special_report/499/09/99/iron_curtain/newsid_460000/460885.stm>>.
3. The public opinion data primarily come from three sources: published reports from CBOS (Centre for Public Opinion Research, Warsaw) and OBOP (Bureau of Public Opinion Research), and also a ten-year series of survey data from the Office of Research and Media Reaction of the United States Information Agency (since October 1999, the Office of Research of the United States Department of State),
4. SLD, 1997, *Dobrze Dziś – Lepsze Jutro, Program Wyborczy Sojuszu Lewicy Demokratycznej*, Warsaw, p. 5 (author's translation).
5. Osrodek Badanii Opinii Publicznej (OBOP), founded 1958, formerly part of the

56   *The Political Economy of Reform in Poland*

state broadcasters but now under the Taylor-Nelson Sofres group, and Centrum Badanii Opinii Społecznej (CBOS), founded in 1982 as a semi-state organization.

6. OBOP, 1988, 'Opinie Społeczne o powołaniu M. Rakowskiego na stanowisko premiera', Report No. 32/496, 19 October.
7. OBOP, 1988, 'Opinie Społeczne o rozmowach "Okręgłego Stołu"', Report No. 31/496, 29 September. In the same poll, 55% agreed that recent strike actions were right (28% not right).
8. The remaining 65% of seats in the Sejm were to be contested by party lists composed of candidates selected by the Party.
9. Despite receiving the majority of votes cast, because of voter absenteeism the required absolute majority of all eligible voters was not attained.
10. GUS, 1989, *Rocznik Statystyczny*, p. 122, Table 11 (202), p. 1220.
11. OBOP, 1988, 'Opinie Społeczne o powołaniu M. Rakowskiego na stanowisko premiera', Report No. 32/496, 19 October, p. 3.
12. OBOP, 1989, 'Opinie Społeczne o nowym rządzie', Report 25/527, 27 September, p. 3.
13. Ibid., p. 1.
14. CBOS, 1990, 'Społeczeństwo wobec nowej sytuacji rynkowej w styczniu '90', Report No. BS/11/3/90, January.
15. CBOS, 1990, 'Program Balcerowicza – jego zwollenicy i przeciwnicy', Report No. 651/90, August, pp. 9–10.
16. Five per cent said that the economy would improve in the next month, 13% within six months, 25% in one year, 16% in two years, 11% in two to three years, 16% in five or more years; 6% said it would not improve at all, and 15% did not know: OBOP, 1990, 'Opinia publiczna o programie Balcerowicza', Report No. 6/548, February.
17. OBOP, 1990, 'Nastroje społeczne we wrześniu 1990 r.', Report No. 33/575, September.
18. OBOP, 1990, '"Rok Mazowieckiego" w opinii publicznej', Report No. 43/585, October.
19. Polls taken close to the date of the election are obviously preferable to ones taken months or even years later. Comparisons of Polish survey data from a number of sources suggest that shifts in popular approval of politicians and parties may cause some voters to 'remember' their choices differently as time passes.
20. Between October 1990 and October 1991, fewer thought it best to continue with the Balcerowicz Plan in its current shape (from 8% to 5%) or to continue but make certain changes (from 39% to 27%). More preferred a new economic plan, either including the parts of the Balcerowicz Plan that worked (from 22% to 31%) or completely new (from 13% to 22%): CBOS, 1991, 'Opinia Społeczna o planie Balcerowicza i kierunku prywatyzowania gospodarki', Report 816/91, November, p. 12.
21. Too slowly: 47% in June 1990, 33% in October 1991; fast enough: 30% and 28%: ibid., p. 13.
22. CBOS, 1991, 'Społeczna ocena polityki gospodarczej rządu', Report 790/91, September, p. 5.
23. *Życie Gospodarcze*, 10 December 1989, p. 4.
24. It is possible to incorporate excessive ideological rigidity into a rational voting model: see Lopez Murphy and Sturzenegger (1994).
25. In November 1990, 32% said that reforms were 'too slow', 9% 'too fast', and 19% 'just right', similar to attitudes in May 1991 (36% 'too slow', 16% 'too fast', and 17% 'just right') (Office of Research 1990, 1991a). Eight years later, half (56%)

said they would have pursued 'more gradual' reforms if it all could have been done again (26% more radical, 6% no reforms) (Office of Research 1999).

26. One exception was Jacek Kuroń's television addresses while labour minister. Balcerowicz (1995, p. 309), in a section entitled 'Communicating with the Public', writes that he was basically too busy making policy to explain and publicize it, but praises a 'small group of very good economic journalists' writing for national papers. Certainly, more effort could have been put into the publicity machine. More significant, in Balcerowicz's view, were the negative 'by-products of the transition to democracy': the media's 'strong tendency to focus on the negative and the sensational' and the hostility of many leading Polish economists.

27. In September 1991, 20% were favourable towards Aleksander Kwaśniewski, 43% unfavourable, 39% don't know; and towards Włodzimierz Cimoszewicz: 27% – 44% – 29% (Office of Research 1991b).

28. CBOS, 1993, 'Lewica – Prawica – Rząd', Report 1003/93, May, pp. 20–21.

29. OBOP, 1993, 'Oceny wyborów do parlamentu i nastroje Społeczne w pazdzierniku', Report 39/93, October. See also CBOS, 'Nastroje Społeczne we wrześniu '93', Report No. BS/150/122/93, October.

30. *Ordinacja Wyborcza do Sejmu Rzeczpospolitej Polskiej*, 28 May 1993, at <<http://www.sejm.gov.pl/prawo/ordsejm/03_01.htm>>; see also Polish Press Agency, 'Sejm: Electoral Law' at <<http://www.pap.com.pl/ elections97/law/sejm/html>>.

31. Ibid.

32. OBOP, 1993, 'Opinie i ostatnich wyborach i nowo wybranym Sejmie', Report 41/93, October, p. 3.

33. CBOS, 1993, 'Przed wyborami – orientacje polityczne zwolenników' partii i ugrupowan wyborczych', Report 1047/93, August, pp. 7–9.

34. Ojczyzna, BBWR, NSZZ 'Solidarność' and PC. KPN also won 4.8% of seats with 5.8% of the popular vote; KLD (4.4% of the vote) and UPR (3%) won no seats.

35. For instance, controversy arose during the SLD–PSL government regarding alleged wrongdoings connected with the PSL's links with the Agricultural Economy Bank (BGZ), the PSL's anti-privatization stance, and its active lobbying for tax breaks and subsidies for farmers.

36. GUS, 1996, *Mały Rocznik Statystyczny 1995*, pp. 104, 118.

37. CBOS, 1995, 'Nastroje Społeczne w czerwcu '95', Report BS/130/110/95, June.

38. 'Jak Kwaśniewski głosy zebrał', *Gazeta Wyborcza*, 21 November 1995, p. 2.

39. GUS, 1996, *Mały Rocznik Statystyczny 1995*, p. 74.

40. For example, 73% expressed confidence in Kwaśniewski in a March 1999 CBOS poll (<<http://www.cbos.pl/SPISKOM.POL/1999/KOM045/KOM045.htm>>) and 79% were favourable towards Kwaśniewski in a May 1999 Office of Research poll. Moreover, Kwaśniewski won a second term in October 2000, in an election which saw Wałęsa's vote slump to a mere 1%.

41. The remaining 50% were split as follows: 9% better, 28% worse, 13% don't know: CBOS data quoted in R. Wróbel, 'Na współrządzeniu wiecej straciła partia chłopska'. *Rzeczpospolita*, 11 September 1997, p. 15.

42. 'Skok Unii'. *Gazeta Wyborcza*, 6–7 September 1997, p. 4.

43. A. Domosławski, 'Przeciw "Bolszewików"', *Rzeczpospolita*, 16 September 1997, pp. 18–20.

44. As discussed by Kamiński (1998, p. 11).

45. 'Ostatnia Prognoza', *Gazeta Wyborcza*, 19 September 1997, p. 1.

46. Office of Research (1999). Undoubtedly as a response to recent reforms, a few also cited pensions (4%) and health care (5%).

47. CBOS data cited in 'Ojczyzna malkontentów', *Wprost*, 19 September 1999, p. 27.

48. A debate summarized in Crow and Rees (1999).
49. Coefficients calculated via Kendall's Tau-b (a nonparametric measure of association for ordinal variables) provides the same results, except for 'economic and political system better now' (0.3862) and for 'economy and life in general now' (0.4250).
50. A comprehensive set of questions measuring attitudes toward transition, the political system, relations with the West, confidence in politicians, the state's role in the economy, nationalism and others was examined through exploratory factor analysis, using maximum likelihood and oblimin rotation. Trials using other factor analysis methods produced similar results, especially the strong first factor (see Chapter 5, Section 5.6).
51. This conflict between liberalization and redistribution may be illustrated by the conflict between external and internal pressures on economic policy. While the SLD–PSL government rapidly passed legislation to liberalize Poland's banking and tax regulations in preparation for joining the OECD (in August 1996) and, eventually, the European Union, they also made changes to the privatization law which generated serious concern about an increasingly interventionist role of the state in the economy.

3. Income, Unemployment and Voting in Poland

As discussed in the Introduction and Chapter 1, explanations of voting behaviour in Poland often look for connections to the level of, or changes in, the material welfare of the public, particularly how the distribution of income before and after reform can affect the level of consensus for reform. This chapter starts with a survey of income and unemployment in Poland during the 1990s, then it presents and tests a simple model of economic voting comparable to some which have been extensively used in advanced market democracies. The surprising conclusion is that, even despite uncertainty about the future and imperfect information on the economy, regional variations in income and unemployment are related to levels of support for the main political parties. These results are used to make prognoses about the socioeconomic profile of parties' electorates, which are tested in Chapter 5.

3.1 INCOME

Statistical Data During the Transition

When using economic data from the transition period, certain caveats need to be kept in mind. In the socialist economy, prices and quantities were predominately set by administrative measures rather than market forces. Administered prices reflected neither consumer demand nor even production costs. Controls on foreign currency, external trade and private sector activity constrained the supply on domestic markets. In these circumstances, money-based indicators use price indices to determine constant or real values (such as growth in GDP or monthly wages and salaries), which can be difficult to interpret in terms of actual consumption possibilities. Standard measures such as prices, wages and even quality become noisy indicators under conditions of supply problems and poor quality.

Transition introduces its own problems for creating stable indices. Moving from a system of multiple, overvalued and fixed exchange rates (which made imported goods very expensive compared with the wage in domestic currency) to a unified but undervalued exchange rate – whether fixed or free-floating – increased the purchasing power of hard-currency savings, but made imports more expensive (Milanovic 1993). Moreover, trade and price liberalization allowed most prices to be set according to demand, and also brought world prices to bear on the Polish market.

Measures of quantities, particularly production or output indicators, are subject to their own distortions. Every transition economy sustained sizeable falls in output, but the extent to which this represents a real welfare loss is disputed. Some of the statistically measured decline in output from the pre-transition to the transition period is considered not to have led to an equivalent fall in welfare. Under socialism, firms intentionally over-reported production to meet the imperatives of the plan, but with transition the incentive became to *under-report* production to evade turnover and income taxes. Also, some of the measured fall in output could be accounted for by the elimination of waste, whether in inefficient production practices or when firms stopped making unwanted goods (statues of Lenin are a commonly cited example). These effects would be recorded as a decline in output, but their impact on net production or general welfare would be neutral or even positive (Winiecki 1991). That said, a good proportion of the output fall was real and did result from shocks to demand (contractionary fiscal and monetary policies aimed at reducing aggregate demand) and supply (for example, price liberalization, shifting relative price structure and the slow response time of production in adjusting to the new demand patterns).[1]

Consumer Price Indices During Transition

A similar set of warnings can be made for the use of 'real' wages (where nominal values are deflated by a price index, usually either the consumer price index or purchasing power parity index) during the transition process. One reason is questions about the accuracy of the deflator. Even in advanced market economies, consumer price indices do not fully capture changes, not just in prices but also on balancing prices with other considerations such as changes in quality and innovation in the products which are available.

Set against the ways in which the consumer price index (CPI) is measured in market economies, the socialist-era retail or consumer price index is not strictly comparable because it often did not reflect the proper weights or prices of the average consumption basket of goods and services. Shapiro and Granville (1995) point out several specific distortions in the Soviet retail price index (RPI) which are also relevant to Poland, such as the omission of the prices for alcohol or 'luxuries' such as chocolate. Furthermore, prices at delivery and not at sale were used, which meant that, as shortages worsened, the RPI failed to reflect (illegal) price mark-ups, either those made by sales clerks in state retail outlets or those arising from the redirection of goods meant for sale at subsidized prices in state-controlled shops to sale through private transactions on the black (or grey) markets (Katsenelinboigen 1977). Black-market prices were not calculated into the cost of living, although prices in farmers' markets often were. Even using the parallel market, dollar exchange rates as an alternative deflator may not accurately reflect the relationship of international to domestic prices, as excess demand pushes up the parallel market exchange rate relative to the volume of the monetary overhang.

As of 1 January 1990, nearly all prices for consumer goods and services in Poland were freed, the currency was devalued to a fixed and unified 9,500 złoty to the dollar, and Poland's borders were opened to imports as well as exports. The response in the consumer market was immediate and dramatic (Sachs 1993b). The volume of available goods increased as imports flooded the market. Shortages disappeared almost overnight but many prices soared, with relative prices changing rapidly. As a result, households' consumption patterns changed quickly. This combination of factors undermined the ability of the consumer price index to measure the 'variations over time of the price of a fixed basket of goods and services representative of the consumption practices of all households' (Shapiro and Granville 1995, p. 12). Since the baseline basket of goods is usually updated once each year, the indices become less representative of households' actual behaviour until readjustment. Even then, the index may be perpetually catching up with a rapidly changing consumer market.

The changes in quantities and in relative prices bring us to another consideration, the influence of methodological changes on the accuracy of the price index. Socialist price indices normally used a Paasche index, which compares base period prices and current prices of the standard basket of goods, and so reflects only price changes. Most countries with market economies use the Laysperes CPI, invoving an index based on the base period consumption basket, but the Laysperes index has its own shortcomings. Because it uses fixed weights, it can neglect the 'second order effects due to substitution in response to relative weight changes' (Berg 1993, p. 46). The Paasche index reflects the new basket but may underestimate some of the changes in relative prices. The Laysperes index, on the other hand, may fail to capture actual purchases and overestimate price rises. Neither index can fully incorporate measures of the variety, quantity and quality of goods available on the market. Even in advanced market economies, consumer price indices may overestimate the actual rate of inflation by up to one point annually, thus underestimating changes in real incomes. Yet, despite the difficulties and inaccuracies of price indices spanning the pre- and post-liberalization economy, it is common practice to compare current real incomes with 1989 levels.[2] While the official consumer price index may not provide a completely accurate deflator for comparing living standards before and after the 1990 liberalization,[3] price indices are not irrelevant and they do tell an interesting story in themselves. One way in which this and following chapters will seek to minimize the distortions of price indices during transition is to use 1988 or an earlier year as the base year, or prices will be compared with other indicators such as consumption data.[4]

The role of relative prices[5]

Socialist-era prices often did not function to clear supply and demand markets, as they do in a market economy.[6] Although subsidies and price controls also exist in most market economies, the extent of subsidization was generally greater in socialist economies. The subsidization of basic consumption items was a political decision, meant to hold down the cost of living so even the lowest income households could maintain a basic living standard. Although cheap, the quality of goods and services was often poor, the choice limited and supplies unpredictable. But by and large most Poles felt themselves relatively insulated from destitution.

However, socialism's failure to produce (or import) sufficient durable goods to meet consumer demand meant that demand tended to 'spill over' from desired goods to available goods. Unable to buy what they wanted, the public tended to buy what they could get. This particularly increased the demand for food. During late socialism, the volume of food consumed by the average Pole was higher than in many west European countries.[7] The conventional wisdom was that in the socialist economy, food prices were held far below market-clearing levels. Podkaminer (1987) argued, on the contrary, that the observed excess demand for food was not caused by too low prices, but rather by the retention of controls on administered prices for and supplies of scarce durable goods and services. Furthermore, Podkaminer held that food prices were *not* abnormally low throughout the 1970s and 1980s, but that official food prices prior to 1989 were *higher* than their equilibrium levels. Therefore, the Party's decision to try to reduce excess demand by increasing administered food prices was wrong. What needed to be done was to increase the supplies and prices of durable goods and consumer services, thereby reducing the demand for food and clearing markets through higher non-food and services prices and (relatively) lower food prices. If Podkaminer was right, then price and trade liberalization in Poland should have caused a surge in the consumption of, as well as relative aggregate prices for, non-food goods and services.

One element of the Round Table agreement was that food price subsidization would be gradually reduced during 1990, allowing prices to rise gradually to market-clearing levels. Some price controls for agricultural inputs were to be kept, and a system of minimum price guarantees for farm produce was to be enacted. However, in August 1989 one of the last acts of the defeated communist government was to liberalize food prices completely, at a time when only 35% of the total volume of consumer good sales were sold at freely-set prices (Iwanek and Ordover, 1993, p. 158). The knock-on effects from consumer prices to indexed wages pushed Poland into a cost-push inflationary spiral. By December 1989, Poland was poised on the edge of hyperinflation. In response, a key step of the Balcerowicz Plan was to free nearly all prices, with the exception of essential goods such as energy and rents which were to rise gradually over time, while strictly limiting the money supply.

The impact of liberalization on cumulative price rises for food, non-food goods and services is shown in Figure 3.1. Overall, between 1990 and 1997 food prices rose *less* than non-food goods and services prices, suggesting there was some basis to Podkaminer's argument that food was not under-priced before 1990. However, one point Podkaminer under-emphasized was the excessively low price of services. From 1990 to

64 *The Political Economy of Reform in Poland*

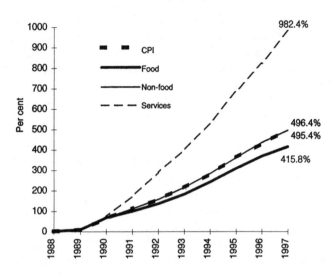

Source: Author's calculations from GUS data.

Figure 3.1   Cumulative price indices, 1988–1997

1997, the price of services rose at double the rate of other items, indicating that services prices were not just under-priced but also under-supplied, owing to the planned economy's emphasis on material production. But the apparently limited impact of services on the overall consumer price index suggests that food and other goods continued to constitute the bulk of the average Pole's consumption basket (Chapter 4). The relatively slower increase in food prices also suggests that rural opposition to market reforms was fuelled not only by lower than expected demand for food but also relatively lower prices for farmers' produce, both of which depressed farm income.[8]

Price indices and 'real' wages
Looking at recent statistics on income and GDP in Poland, the lasting effects of transition are clear. First, the 'j-curve' of Poland's recession and recovery are evident in the GDP data. Pensions have risen in real terms in every year since 1990, whereas real wages were quite flat between 1991 and 1994, and even fell slightly, before beginning to grow in 1996 (Figure 3.2).

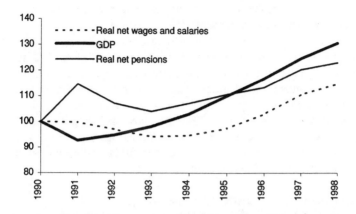

Sources: GUS, *Mały Rocznik Statystyczny* and *Biuletyn Statystyczny*, various issues.

Figure 3.2   Real net wages, net pensions and GDP (1990 = 100)

This figure does not show results for before 1990. Strictly speaking, the preceding pages give several good reasons why the data for before and after 1 January 1990 are not entirely comparable. However, the fact remains that people want to know what kind of impact transition had during these critical early months.

Using the available statistical data, GDP is estimated to have fallen by about 15% between 1989 and 1990, average real wages are calculated to have dropped by about 25%, but the average monthly pension fell by less than 10% in real terms.[9]

Given that 'real' wages and salaries fell by about a quarter between 1989 and 1990, it is often argued that average welfare must have fallen by a similarly large proportion.[10] This claim makes good political ammunition, but probably overestimates the problem. First of all, 'real' wages had risen much too quickly in the late 1980s, increasing 42.2% between June 1987 and the election month of June 1989 (Berg 1993, GUS data). Rising incomes fuelled the expansion of nominal demand (and the budget deficit which financed increases in state sector wages). However, the higher level of consumption demand was not matched by an increased supply of consumer goods (Bell and Rostowski 1995). Rather than boosting consumer welfare, this excess demand led to high levels of both open and repressed inflation, which aggravated macroeconomic disequilibrium.

For the population, the resulting shortages, longer queues and escalating inflation worsened living standards. [11]

Furthermore, payments in kind and special access to shortage goods undermined the accuracy of real prices as a measure of welfare during transition. Under shortages of consumer goods, the distribution of goods through non-market mechanisms (such as through payments in kind or privileged access to special shops) reduced or devalued the role of wages in consumption. Freeman (1993) notes how including the value of bonuses and other 'add-ons' reduced the percentage of the base wage in total pay, but these types of bonuses and benefits in kind were most likely largely missed by statistical measures.

Inconsistencies in statistical data gathering

An additional source of inconsistency in the statistical data occurred with the change in accounting procedures from Net Material Product to Standard National Accounts. It took time to adjust data collection methods on production and consumption during this time of rapid change, the result being a larger than usual gap between aggregate supply figures and consumption data. In one instance, official statistics showed that the *aggregate supply* of butter in Poland *fell* 16% in 1990, but household data indicate that *consumption* of butter *increased* by 4%, the gap not explainable by the pattern of imports and exports (Berg 1993).

GUS provides several specific reasons not to compare aggregate national accounts figures on private consumption with household survey expenditure data. For example, the national accounts data include social transfers such as rent subsidies in its disposable income data, while only the Household Budget survey (HBS) includes transfers or gifts between households. On the consumption side, the HBS covers only food consumed at home, whereas the macro data include meals eaten in restaurants, schools, workplace canteens and so on.[12] There is also an acknowledged and consistent non-random error in households' underestimation of tobacco and alcohol consumption. Alcohol accounted for 10.1% of aggregate consumption expenditure but just 2.7% of households' reported consumption in 1989; in 1993, alcohol made up 6.8% of total aggregate consumption expenditure, but only 1.2% of household expenditures (*Rocznik Statystyczny*, various issues).

To summarize, three keys to understanding income and consumption data include:

- that price indices which span the pre- and post-liberalization period should be interpreted with caution, and that time series given in monetary values should be supplemented with complementary data based on quantities or relative prices;
- that because comparisons of one pre-transition year with a post-transition year can lead to misrepresentation of the relative influence of liberalization versus socialist-era distortions on living standards, it is better to use complete trend data where possible; and
- that generalizations about the impact of economic transitions based on aggregate data can disguise important consequences of reform across various segments of the population.

Finally, one of the key differences between incomes under the socialist economy and under the market is that wages and salaries went from being very reliable sources of income to being more variable across occupations and less predictable in times of unemployment and fluctuating growth rates domestically and in Poland's export markets. Under the socialist system, the shortage of workers meant that even negligent employees ran little risk of being fired, and even if they were, another job could be found relatively easily – especially for low-skilled manual workers. Subsidies on goods and services boosted the consumption possibilities of lower income households, while the upper end of the income distribution was flattened by the lack of opportunities to earn income on capital (for example interest on savings accounts, certificates of deposit and other financial instruments, or portfolio investment). Now, there is not only increased uncertainty and variation in income, but also a tendency to rely on multiple sources of income. In 1992, 46% of households relied on one major source of income, but 42% relied on two sources, and 12% on three (Beskid *et al.* 1995, p. 21). A 1994 survey found that 17.2% of respondents said they had worked *na czarno*, or in the second economy.[13] In the same year, the Gdańsk-based Institute for Market Economics estimated that one in three Poles worked in casual jobs, earning 1.6 million extra złoty per month for each average household (Grabowski 1995).

Income Distribution

During the later years of Poland's planned economy, the wages paid for different types of jobs were relatively evenly distributed. Atkinson and Micklewright (1991) describe five factors explaining why income inequality was constrained: (1) the high level of job mobility and the frequency of voluntary resignations; (2) the restrictions on geographical labour mobility resulting from the endemic housing shortage; (3) the dominance of large enterprises in the economy; (4) officially legislated minimum wages and equal wages for men and women; and (5) the statutory right to work and the primacy of the goal of full employment.

However, when measured by standard indicators, income distribution patterns in socialist-era Poland were not very different from those found in market economies. While the Gini coefficient for all social groups in Poland in 1980 was 0.23, in the United Kingdom in 1989 the Gini was also 0.23 and in the United States 0.33 (Redor 1992, p. 56). The real difference between the western and eastern markets comes through the distribution of wealth rather than income, opportunities for wealth creation being much more limited under socialism. Gini coefficients[14] for the first three years of reform show that income inequality across all Poland's households actually decreased slightly (Table 3.1). Because the decile data needed to calculate the Gini coefficient are no longer published in the statistical yearbook, we have to look for clues about changing income distribution in alternative measures.

Table 3.1   Inequality measures by household groups, 1987–1992

	1987	1988	1989	1990	1991	1992
Gini	0.235	0.236	0.258	0.246	0.237	0.250
Atkinson (e = 2)	0.169	0.177	0.210	0.210	0.177	0.189
Piero	16.48	16.56	18.11	18.11	16.64	17.76

Source: Górecki and Wisniewski (1995, p.3).

Relative changes in nominal income

Comparing monthly incomes can give a good idea of how different groups are faring, but the data themselves may not tell the observer why proportions are changing. A widening or narrowing gap may mean one group's income is rising, another group's is falling, or both, or both groups may experience rising income but with one growing faster than the second. Consider, for example, Figure 3.3, which compares the

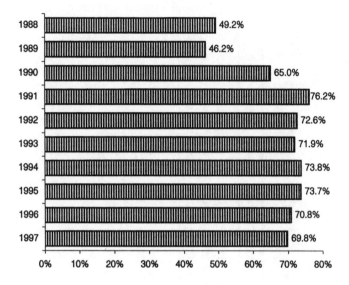

Figure 3.3   Relation of average retirement pension to the average net wage

nominal, net value of the average old-age pension with the average monthly wage in the state sector for the years 1988 to 1997.[15]

The ratio between the average pension and the average state sector wage rose dramatically between 1988 and 1993, and then decreased gradually. Yet it cannot be deduced from the figure alone whether this is because of an increase in the real value of pensions or a deterioration in the average wage in the state sector. Or, perhaps state sector wages grew at a faster rate than pensions. If the first reason is true, then there has probably been an improvement in the living standard of the average pensioner. If wages have fallen, we still cannot tell whether pensions have risen or fallen in terms of purchasing power. More information is needed to answer these questions.

Table 3.2 compares annual indices of nominal growth of pensions and salaries with the consumer price index. From this table, we can see that nominal pensions lagged behind wages in the late 1980s, increased

Table 3.2   Indices of nominal net pensions, state sector wages and annual CPI

	1988	1989	1990	1991	1992	1993	1994	1995	1996	1997
Pension	100	364.2	590.4	196.2	134.9	131.7	136.9	132.0	122.5	121.9
State sector wage	100	391.8	498.0	170.6	138.9	131.3	132.9	131.8	126.7	122.9
CPI	100	351.1	685.8	171.1	142.8	135.2	132.3	128.0	119.9	115.1

Note: Preceding year = 100
Source: Mały Rocznik Statystyczny, 1995, pp. 99, 110 and 132.

at a more rapid rate than either state wages or inflation in 1991, with a narrowed but variable rate thereafter.

An interesting story of politics underlies these shifts. Because of rising political tensions in 1988, the communist-led government allowed an increase in real wages (most people being directly or indirectly state employees), which boosted pay to unsustainably high levels. By the next year, even before the start of the transition programme, there were already signs that real wages were moving downwards. In 1990, a combination of high inflation, the excess wage tax (*popiwek*), fiscal austerity, falling demand and cautious behaviour from managers depressed wages further. Wages held steadily at this low level through the recession and through the first two years of growth, more because of tight monetary policy than the excess wage tax (Coricelli and Revenga 1992). From 1995, falling unemployment and a competitive labour market, especially among skilled workers and the professions, produced renewed upward pressure on wages, but because wage rises actually lagged behind productivity gains, they were economically sustainable.

Whereas wages experienced a fall in their real value during the first years of transition, the first post-communist governments increased the real value of pensions, which were very low. Partly, this was to counteract the transition from the socialist system, under which the low monetary value of pensions was augmented by subsidized social provision of basic goods and services, to the new system of primarily cash transfers. Also, the cost of living rose faster for pensioners than for other social groups from early 1990 because of these households' smaller size and associated consumption patterns. The 1991 reform of Labour Minister Kuroń caused real pensions to rise by another 26%. The increase in pension benefits prevented even more pensioners from falling into severe poverty, but the rapid rise in the number of early retired persons caused state pensions to become a serious threat to fiscal balance.[16] The total pension bill grew from 8.2% of GDP in 1989 to 12.2% in 1991 and 15.8% in 1994 (Golinowska 1996, p. 20). The state pension system became reliant upon subsidies to cover payments; by 1997, 20% of total budget expenditures were allocated in subsidies to cover the gap in running expenses of the Pension Fund.

However, the effect of linking pensions to the CPI rather than the average wage became apparent only when real wages began to increase more rapidly. In 1995, real pensions increased by 3.3%, and real wages grew by a strong 6.1%. Real wages have continued rising, but the

SLD–PSL and the AWS–UW governments both resisted accelerating the rise in real pensions. However, with the introduction of the three pillar system in 1999, in the future the real gap will be between those who can and those who cannot make significant contributions to the voluntary third pillar.[17]

Therefore, we can conclude from Table 3.2 that *the rise in the ratio between pensions and wages reflects the joint effect of an increase in pensions from a very low relative level and the fall and stagnation of real wages until 1995.* The subsequent, moderate decline in the ratio since 1995 reflects rising real wages more than the relatively lower rate of the real increase in pensions.

This kind of gap existed not just between earned incomes and income from social benefits. What was truly different about wages in the socialist economy was the inequality in income across sectors. In 1990, the average wage paid to workers employed in the extractive sector was about 30% higher than the average wage in finance and insurance, and 50% higher than in education.[18] But even at this early date, wages in the foreign trade sector were more than twice the national average.

Regional gap in incomes
Another source of inequality in Poland is the persistent gap in incomes across the country's regions. As in most countries, average per capita income in large cities and the capital tends to outstrip incomes in more remote regions, and particularly those more dependent upon agriculture and traditional livelihoods. Table 3.3 provides a measurement of the dispersion in average monthly income in Poland's 49 districts (in use prior to the 1999 state administration reform), for each year in which a national election was held. The table shows that the gap between rich and poor regions in Poland has been widening over time, whether

Table 3.3   Disparities in average monthly per capita income across Poland (49 regions)

	1990	1991	1993	1995	1997
Variation (st dev/avg)	0.0723	0.078	0.098	0.110	0.114
Max/min	1.472	1.413	1.520	1.575	1.700

Source: Górecki and Wyśniewski (1995, p. 3).

measured in terms of the richest versus the poorest regions, or in terms of the dispersion of income. As shown in the next section of this chapter, the uneven distribution of growth is also reflected in regional disparities in unemployment (more in Chapter 4).

3.2 UNEMPLOYMENT IN POLAND

As Poland's transition programme took hold, the labour market shifted radically. One of the most immediate changes was the rapid shift from a tight to a very loose labour market. As Figure 3.4 illustrates, the unemployment rate increased rapidly over the first four years of transition. The total percentage of the adult labour force registered as unemployed increased from negligible levels in early 1990 to 6.5% at the start of 1991, 12.1% in 1992 and 14.2% at the start of 1993, before peaking at 16.9% in July 1994 (GUS data). The Labour Force Survey rate, which is measured via a panel survey using ILO methodology, has tended to reflect the same trends over time.

After the steep increase in unemployment between 1990 and 1994, joblessness finally began to head downwards in 1996–1997, as Poland's strong growth rates worked through into job creation and a steady decline in the registered and the Labour Force Survey rates. However, a jump in the number of registered unemployed during the latter half of 1998 caused the public's confidence in the resilience of the Polish economy to waver. Unemployment at the end of 1998 was half that of its mid-1994 maximum, but another upturn in 1999 (11.9% in February) and 2000 (13.9% in February) reversed much of these gains.

Part of the increase in early 1999 can be attributed to the reform of Poland's health system. In order to qualify for free coverage, individuals had to be registered with the labour office as being unemployed. This is akin to the phenomenon observed in 1990 of an increase in the number of unemployed due to benefit eligibility criteria.

At the start of Poland's transition, virtually all Poles over the age of 15 who were neither working nor in full-time education were eligible to claim unemployment benefits for an indefinite period. However, this policy was not only fiscally unsustainable, but arguably it also provided incentives for those not previously unemployed to register with the Labour Office and start claiming benefits (Góra 1996). This excessive

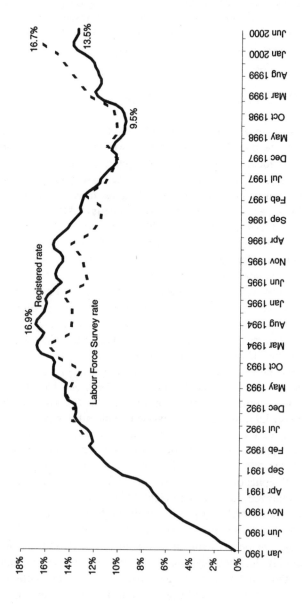

Figure 3.4 Registered and LFS unemployment rates

registration was encouraged not only by loose eligibility requirements for benefits, but also by the fact that access to other social services was linked to unemployed status. The bulk of claimants using unemployment as a means to other social benefits consisted primarily of long-term unemployed women, especially those with children. Until November 1992, access to free health care depended upon being registered as unemployed. Since this link was severed, there has been a convergence of the Labour Force Survey and GUS unemployment figures.

Within the first few years of transition, eligibility criteria were tightened. Within the first year, benefits could be claimed only for one year under most circumstances. As of October 1993, school leavers could no longer claim unemployment benefits. However, the combination of tighter criteria and rising long-term unemployment contributed to an increasing share of the unemployed who were unable to claim unemployment benefits (Figure 3.5).

However, in 1999, it can be expected that the increased enrolment revealed more of the 'true' level of unemployment, capturing those who had not bothered to register with the labour offices, owing to ineligibility for benefits or because they were discouraged job-seekers.

In 1999, about seven out of ten registered unemployed were not eligible to claim benefits (Figure 3.5, middle line). In 1998 and 1999, the parallel movements among the total number of unemployed and the subset of those out of work but ineligible for unemployment benefits suggest that the sharp jump in the number of registered jobless in December 1998 and January 1999 were among this latter group. Another negative development is that since late 1995, the total number not entitled to unemployment benefits has been slowly rising.

A surprising development, also shown in Figure 3.5, is that the impact of redundancies and labour shedding in total unemployment peaked in 1993 and has since been relatively low. Redundancies never accounted for more than a quarter of the total number of registered unemployed (24.5% in May and October 1992), and by December 1996 accounted for fewer than one in ten (8.5%). This is not to say that they were not previously working; 1999 data show that three out of four registered unemployed had held jobs; another one in five are market entrants. We can surmise that many of these are long-term unemployed; however, school-leavers, other market entrants, and those with insufficient work records and contributions to the social security system also do not qualify for benefits. Rising ineligibility may

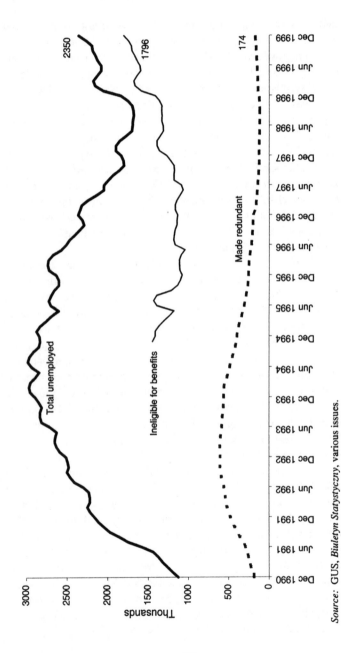

Source: GUS, *Biuletyn Statystyczny*, various issues.

Figure 3.5 Unemployment, ineligible and redundant

therefore be linked to high job turnover, particularly among the young and less-skilled. Data on the reasons for inflows into and out of unemployment suggest that there is a fair degree of movement from joblessness to short-term or contract employment (short enough not to gain the worker eligibility for unemployment benefits) and back into unemployment.[19] But the share whose positions were destroyed for economic or downsizing reasons has been relatively low.

High as the rise in unemployment was during the early years of reform, it was still outpaced by the rate of economic contraction. Conversely, during Poland's economic recovery the rate of job creation has been slower than the rate of growth of output.[20] Thus, as the full impact of transition on unemployment took time to unfold, so a proportion of the unemployed have yet to be reintegrated into the labour market.

This is important for the longer-term social impact of transition, because the longer it is before unemployed individuals are reabsorbed into the workforce, the more difficult it becomes for these individuals to find work. In advanced market economies, long-term unemployment (defined as joblessness lasting a year or longer) has been recognized as a problematic residual of economic restructuring; often the long-term unemployed are concentrated in depressed regions, and they may possess skills which are less in demand in the current economy.

Official registration data on long-term unemployment in Poland show that, in the autumn of 1994, half (46%) of all those registered as unemployed had been out of work for a year or longer (Figure 3.6). By the second half of 1999, long-term unemployment had decreased both in numbers (at 775,000, it was half that in September 1994) and as a proportion of the total unemployed (37%).

Although a third of Poland's unemployed have been out of work for more than a year, it is encouraging that a significant proportion of unemployment in Poland during the 1990s did in fact turn out to be transitional. By mid-1988, the total and long-term unemployed numbers had been halved from the peak levels of 1992 and 1994. However, within two years it had risen back to a total of about 2.5 million. While previous experience suggests that these unemployed could be reintegrated into the work-force, this will depend on whether the economy can restart its dynamic expansion, which in turn depends not only upon the course of enterprise restructuring and growth in the domestic economy, but also upon trends in the European and international economy.

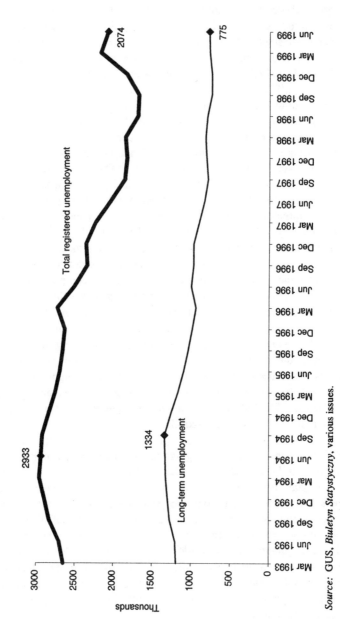

Source: GUS, *Biuletyn Statystyczny*, various issues.

Figure 3.6 Long-term unemployment

Mismatch in the Labour Market

Like other market economies, after liberalization the Polish labour market developed a 'mismatch' between the types of unemployed workers available to start new jobs and the types of jobs being offered in terms of either the skills needed to perform the job or the part of the country where the jobs are located.

Educational attainment, and especially post-secondary education, is one of the most important factors in attaining success in the job search. A high proportion of the unemployed have a basic or secondary vocational education. The Labour Force Survey (LFS, based on ILO methodology) found that in August 1998 slightly less than 4% of those with university or other third-level education were unemployed, one-third as high as among those with a secondary education or less (between 12% and 14%).[21]

Not only are the better-educated less likely to become unemployed, but those who do become jobless are more likely to be hired again. A World Bank report on poverty in Poland (1995) found that the 1993 monthly exit rates from unemployment were three times higher for people with post-secondary education (22%) than for those with only primary education (8%). Góra (1996) and Kudrycka (1993) have also reached similar conclusions about education and exit rates.

However, the employment benefits of education do not extend equally to both sexes. Educated women appear to have a harder time finding work than similarly educated men.[22] Young women with basic vocational education tend to have the highest unemployment rates, and rural women with a high-school education also have higher than average jobless rates. In 1995, unemployment rates were declining relatively quickly except for women in rural areas with primary or vocational education, for whom unemployment continued to rise.

At the end of the 1990s, however, youth unemployment was still higher than average. In 1992, 85–90% were under 44 years of age; between one-quarter and one-third of men and women aged between 18 and 24 were unemployed (Coricelli *et al.* 1995, p. 77). In August 1998, the Labour Force Survey found that those aged 15–24 had a national unemployment rate of 22%, considerably higher than among those aged 25–34 (11%), 35–44 (9%), or over age 44 (7%).[23] While middle-aged Poles have a lower overall unemployment rate, research from the mid-1990s found that new entrants and school leavers tend to leave the unemployment rolls quite quickly, although this is increasingly into short-term and contract work. In comparison, those over 45 have tended to spend a longer time finding new work, and the duration of their unemployment tends to be longer. Góra (1996) found that people over 55 were much less likely to re-enter employment once they had been made jobless. There is little to indicate that much has changed in this respect in recent years.

Young Poles have responded to the rise in demand for skilled and educated people on the labour market. Between the 1990/91 and the 1994/95 academic years, the number of students enrolled in tertiary education increased by nearly 70%, and it has kept on rising (Table 3.4). Fewer students are enrolling in vocational secondary schools, which probably reflects high unemployment among this educational group. By contrast, students have been enrolling in greater numbers in both technical secondary schools and more academically-oriented high schools.

Table 3.4   Students enrolled in education (in thousands)

	1990/91	1991/92	1992/93	1993/94	1994/95	1995/96	1996/97	1997/98
Elementary	5287	5311	5313	5278	5196	5104	5013	4896
High school	445	500	556	602	649	683	714	758
Technical secondary	634	672	709	765	812	864	869	899
Vocational secondary	814	806	793	770	746	722	691	661
Tertiary or university	404	428	496	584	682	795	928	1092
No. of graduates	56	59	61	64	70	89	116	143

Sources: Mały Rocznik Statystyczny 1994, p. 153; *Mały Rocznik Statystyczny 1998*, p. 187.

Apart from individual characteristics, unemployment in Poland has been marked by sizeable regional differences (Table 3.5). The rate has consistently been much lower in Warsaw and regional centres such as Cracow and Katowice, and much higher in rural and more remote areas such as Suwałki as well as depressed, industrial regions like Olbrzych. Small towns with fewer than 20,000 residents have been worst hit by unemployment, often because of the failure of a large state enterprise

Table 3.5 Labour market mismatch: województwo *unemployment rates*

	Standard deviation	Variation (st dev/mean)
November 1990	0.0210	0.2994
November 1991	0.0411	0.3029
September 1993	0.0518	0.3050
November 1995	0.0498	0.3004
November 1997	0.0415	0.3493

Source: Author's calculations from GUS data.

that was the main employer in the area. The lack of demand for services in more rural areas has been made worse by depressed incomes in agricultural households. Regional concentrations of high unemployment have been aggravated by impediments to regional mobility in post-communist countries, resulting not only from a traditional reluctance to move but also from the lack of efficient household markets and the physical shortage of places to live.

It can also be shown graphically. Figure 3.7 plots the registered unemployment rate for each of Poland's pre-1999 regions (*województwa*), ranked left to right from the lowest to highest 1994 average unemployment rates. This graph shows the scale of regional variation in joblessness, and it also shows how, after initial surges in unemployment in 1990, there was a generally parallel increase up to 1994.

Figure 3.8 looks at the regional unemployment rate from 1994 to 1997. It shows how the overall decrease in the unemployment rate, shown in Figure 3.4, has happened more incrementally than its increase. Also, the figure suggests that unemployment has fallen more quickly in regions including Gdańsk, Łódź, and Piła, but has remained stagnant in regions such as Radom, Jelenia Góra, and Włocławek.

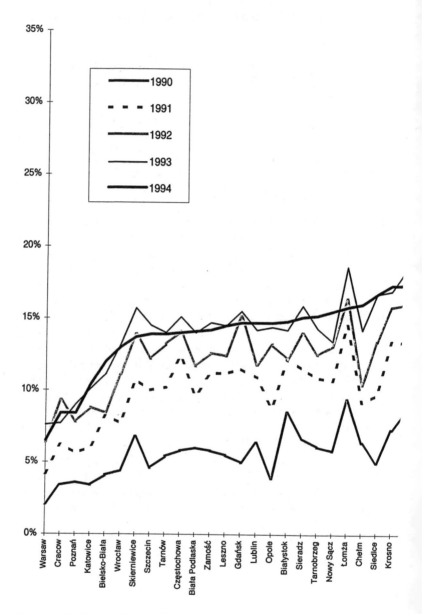

Figure 3.7   Regional unemployment rates: Poland 1990–1994

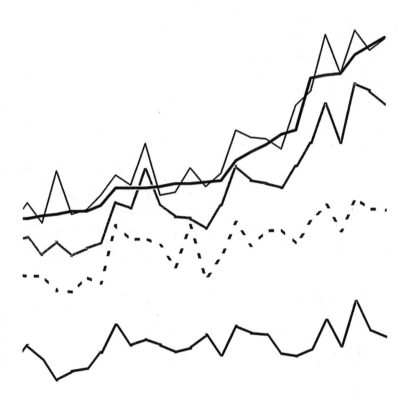

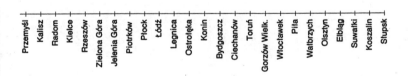

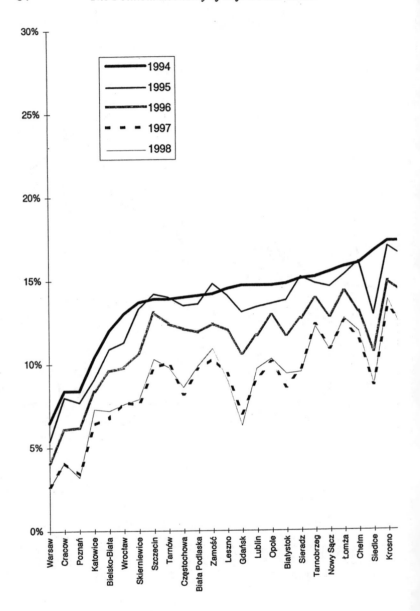

Figure 3.8   Regional unemployment rates: Poland 1994–1998

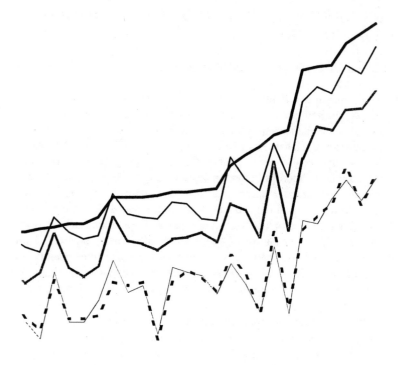

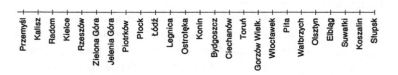

3.3   INCOME, UNEMPLOYMENT AND VOTING IN POLAND[24]

Economic Performance and Voting in Theory

As discussed in Chapter 1, one of the most prevalent approaches used to explain and predict election results is through the impact of economic performance on voting behaviour. Economic growth improves an incumbent's chances of being re-elected, while a slowed economy benefits the challenger.[25] Higher growth, larger incomes, and lower inflation in the months before an election tend to boost popular support for the serving government, party, or candidate. However, the exact mechanism between the economy and voting, and which indicators are most important for which voters, are topics of continuing debate. Some use fluctuation in short-run variables, while others, such as Tufte (1978), have used short-run economic performance, the incumbent's advantage or disadvantage on issues other than economic ones, and the incumbent party's long-run strength or 'normal vote', to look at national election outcomes.

But one common aspect of this general approach, rooted in public choice theory (for example, Mueller 1989), is the *rational voter hypothesis*, which assumes that the individual voter behaves the same way in the polling booth as in the marketplace – rationally and in pursuit of his or her own self-interest. Rational self-interest can be calculated either retrospectively (on the basis of past economic performance) or on future expectations. The voter considers the competing policy platforms, and then calculates which candidate or party would be likely to deliver the highest 'streams of utility' once elected (Mueller 1989, p. 349). Whether the perspective is retrospective or future-oriented, the calculation of potential benefit is usually assumed to be self-centred, with the voter only taking his or her own welfare – past, future or both – into account.

For more than thirty years, scholars have debated whether personal experience of unemployment and stagnating real wages affects individual voting behaviour more than wider social preferences. Kramer (1971) argued along the lines of Downs (1957) that short-run fluctuations in personal income, rising inflation and higher unemployment do affect (aggregate) voting behaviour in US Congressional elections.[26] If this theory is accurate, the relation between price, income, unemployment and voting should be expressed in a multivariate analysis through *positive coefficients for real and nominal income, and negative coefficients for price and unemployment variables.* Kramer found significant connections between voting and price and income variables, but with a positive sign for the unemployment variable, possibly because the unemployed are usually less likely than others to vote.[27] Despite this, the assumption that individual financial and employment conditions influence voting behaviour has permeated much research into the political economy of elections.

However, the connection between personal incomes, unemployment and voting has been seriously challenged. Criticizing Kramer's model for not providing sufficiently consistent results, Kinder and Kiewiet (1979) also examined voting in US Congress elections, but in their influential study did not find that individual or 'pocketbook' concerns were the key to explaining voting behaviour.[28] Rather, they argued that general 'collective judgements' about economic issues at the national level were more important for party identification and election outcomes than 'personal economic grievances'. General trends such as the business cycle, national economic issues and the parties' competence in managing the macroeconomy had a greater influence on voting than voters' perceptions of their own financial situation. The micro-level 'pocketbook' relations found via aggregate data were not evident in survey data, in which they found little evidence of consistent and predictable voting patterns by employment status or satisfaction, or even among the working class and other groups who are vulnerable to policy shifts. If Kinder and Kiewiet's thesis holds, then *there should not be a significant relationship between personal income and unemployment* at the aggregate level.

However, the split between personal and social interest may not be so sharp. Moreover, the assumptions about the behaviour being observed should in some way reflect the nature of the data which will be used in the analysis. Mueller and Murrell (1987, p. 89) propose a utility function which aims to incorporate these considerations, in that the voter seeks to maximize:

$$O_i = U_i + \theta \Sigma U_j$$
$$i \neq j$$

where θ equals 0 for the selfish voter and 1 for the altruistic or socially-oriented voter. Aggregate data can mask shifts and distributions of the weights of these utility functions in the overall set of preferences. Yet it seems realistic to work on the assumption that, given the poor quality of information about macroeconomic performance during most of the first decade of the post-communist system, much of people's assumptions about overall economic performance and welfare to some extent reflect personal experience and observations of the local economy. This chapter works from the assumption that θ < 0.5, meaning that average voters weigh personal experience more heavily than social welfare into their utility function. Voting behaviour is therefore a combination of both self-interest and socially oriented voting, but with the weight on the former being greater.

A simple macroeconomic model of voting
The first two sections of this chapter showed that, although there have been significant changes in income and unemployment in Poland, these have been far from uniform across the country or across the public. In this section, some common approaches to economic politics will be used to see whether the basic relationship between party support and economic conditions holds in Poland. However, because of the special circumstances surrounding Poland's political system, some adaptations of methods and the questions being asked have been made.

Because of the short time-span and low number of national elections conducted in Poland since the fall of communism, it is not appropriate to try to use the kind of time series employed in Kramer (1971) and that type of political economy study. Instead, one of the most interesting relationships in Poland over the past decade has been the level of disparities at the local level. Early in the transition, it became common-place to talk of a more prosperous and advantaged 'Poland A' and a more backward and less developed 'Poland B'. During the transition, regional inequalities in income and unemployment appear to have become entrenched. Coupled with this, an examination of voting data shows persistent clusters of party support across Poland's regions (*województwa*).

For these reasons, Poland's voting results are examined at the regional level, and related to regional income and unemployment. Actual data and not rates of change in income and unemployment were used to compare voting patterns in richer and poorer regions. Also, because unemployment is largely a phenomenon of the transition period, and so it is of interest to compare regions more and less affected by unemployment. The indicator used here is similar to that used in Parysek *et al.* (1991) and in Gibson and Cielecka (1995) for similar purposes.

Going back to Mueller's utility function and the dataset used here, regional data may express some relationships which do not emerge from the national data, just as cross-sectional data can reveal aspects which are not visible in time series data. Individuals may attach more importance to the welfare of people close to them, whether in their family, town or *województwo*, than to the welfare of the country as a whole.[29] This may be especially true of unemployment: in areas of high unemployment, even people who are still employed may perceive a higher probability of losing their own job in that environment or they may consider high unemployment to lower the entire community's welfare. Survey data from 1993 found that eight out of ten Poles (80%) blamed poverty on unfavourable conditions in the local, domestic region.[30] For these reasons, we can expect a greater preference for parties and candidates promoting redistributive or pro-employment policies in high unemployment regions.

Voting functions can incorporate a wide range of economic and non-economic data, such as rate of GDP, personal income growth (or both), recent trends and levels of popularity in public opinion polls, the exchange rate, incumbency and so on. In this chapter, a simple multi-variate model is used to analyse how well per capita income and unemployment rates explain voting patterns in Poland. Research into voting in the US often uses aggregate macroeconomic indicators to explain the dependent variable of the vote distribution across several decades of elections (for example, Fair 1996). However, Poland has had only two presidential and three freely contested parliamentary elections since 1990, and so any regressions based on four observations would be patently unreliable.

Instead, I will use a technique which is not only better suited to the available data, but which will allow us to continue our investigation into the politics of the distribution of economic costs and benefits. The simple equation is as follows:

$$V = b_1 + b_2 I + b_3 U$$

where V is the share of the vote gained by the designated candidate in each of 49 *województwa, I* is average per capita monthly income (on an annual average) in the *województwo*, and *U* is the province's unemployment rate. This regression uses per capita income for the year as a whole, as this is the format available in the *Rocznik Statystyczny* for total per capita income, not just average wages in industry or construction. However, each of Poland's post-communist elections was held in the latter part of the third or in the fourth quarter of the year, and so this is an adequate proxy for incomes on the day of the election. Also, for rural households it is preferable to use annual income data because of seasonal variations in income and outlays.

This chapter considers whether a relationship exists between aggregate macroeconomic indicators and voting patterns in national elections from 1990 to 1997. *Województwo*-level figures for per capita income and unemployment will be related to election results from the same region.[31] After testing for correlations and covariance, OLS regressions are performed on the impact of unemployment and per capita income on voting in Poland's regions. Of all the possible economic variables which could be used to try to explain voting, the two classic models of self-interested and sociotropic voting discussed above agree that unemployment and changes in real income are the most politically salient factors, because of the very real social costs they impose. People's most basic economic concerns, after all, are ensuring a source of income and the level of that income in absolute and relative terms.

1990 Presidential Elections

This part of the chapter focuses on national elections for the presidency and for the Sejm (the lower house of parliament). The 460-member Sejm plays the predominant role in policy making, and its proportional representation system makes it a more interesting case than the 100-seat Senate (distributed across 49 electoral districts).

Starting with the 1990 presidential election (Table 3.6), the overall impact of personal income and unemployment is perhaps less telling than the sign and significance of each variable for candidates' levels of support across the regions. Regional patterns of support for the eventual victor, Solidarity candidate Lech Wałęsa, show a negative relation with income and unemployment. Wałęsa finished more strongly where there was lower unemployment but also lower per

Table 3.6 First round of 1990 presidential elections

	R^2	Adj. R^2	Unemployment (significance)	Income (significance)
Wałęsa (Solidarity)	0.1711	0.1351	-1.5818 (0.0090)	-0.3676 (0.0378)
Tymiński (Ind.)	0.4017	0.3757	1.8852 (0.0000)	0.3521 (0.0019)
Mazowiecki (ROAD)	0.2615	0.2294	-0.7546 (0.0866)	0.3836 (0.0043)
Bartoszcze (PSL)	0.3208	0.2913	-0.1036 (0.7814)	-0.3860 (0.0000)
Cimoszewicz (SdRP)	0.1335	0.0958	0.6030 (0.0141)	-0.0014 (0.9847)

Sources: Author's calculations from GUS and PKW data; Parysek *et al.* 1991.

capita incomes. These can be thought of as regions where there are more working poor: regions with state enterprises, typically employing low-skilled industrial workers whose wages fell in real and in relative terms during 1990.

The surprise second-place finisher, Stanisław Tymiński, received more support from areas with higher unemployment. Tymiński finished better in 'Poland B': regions outside of the regional urban centres, such as Chełm, Elbląg and Legnica. His populist and redistributionist themes attracted protest votes, particularly among the newly emergent group of unemployed. Tymiński's libertarian and low-tax policies also appear to have gained support from some higher income areas, but this effect was weaker and somewhat less significant than unemployment. In the second round between Wałęsa and Tymiński, the independent variables explain about one-third of the total deviation from the trend, with again higher unemployment regions backing Tymiński and lower unemployment regions supporting Wałęsa.

By contrast, support for Mazowiecki shows a positive relationship to nominal income and a negative link to unemployment, indicating support in regions more able to profit from marketization. Mazowiecki's pro-reform manifesto appealed to electorates in Warsaw and the large regional centres, regions which have consistently displayed higher average income levels and lower joblessness rates. People with higher incomes and more secure employment – and, as Chapters 4 and 5 will show, the education and skills which make this status possible – are more likely to support market-oriented reform than more vulnerable groups, such as less-skilled industrial workers and farmers.

The candidate of the Polish Peasant Party (PSL), Roman Bartoszcze, appealed primarily to voters in rural areas. There is a strong link between support for Bartoszcze and lower per capita incomes. As mentioned above, rural regions of Poland have consistently demonstrated lower incomes than urbanized areas. However, unemployment rates are not significant, which indicates that the sector of employment (agriculture) is more important for this agrarian vote than registered unemployment.

Finally, Włodzimierz Cimoszewicz, the non-aligned candidate backed by the ex-communist SdRP, attracted almost one vote in ten. This surprised some observers nearly as much as the level of support for Tymiński. But in the 1989 semi-free parliamentary elections, candidates from the combined government list (PZPR, ZSL and SD) received 3.34 million votes, an electorate which in 1990 was mostly split into 1.176 million for Bartoszcze and 1.5 million for Cimoszewicz.[32] In the 1990 vote, Cimoszewicz received more votes in regions with higher unemployment rates. Income had little effect in explaining his support. The results suggest that in this election Cimoszewicz and Tymiński were competing for the votes of the unemployed. The disappearance of an overtly populist candidate or party in subsequent elections, and the strong link between high unemployment and social democratic voting, suggests the post-communists were better able to attract and retain these voters.

The pattern of votes between the first and second rounds also suggest that many of those who selected Mazowiecki in the first round were 'trapped' into supporting Wałęsa in the second, as did farmers, in response to the real threat of a victory by Tymiński. Despite the split in Solidarity's leadership, the shift of support from Mazowiecki to Wałęsa is logical, and indeed was crucial in the latter's victory.

1991 Parliamentary Elections

As recounted in Chapter 2, the first fully free parliamentary election in post-communist Poland took place during a time of economic and political upheaval. Although the number of parties running in this election weakens the overall strength of the analysis results, the patterns of voting support by unemployment and income display a consistency in sign and significance in line with the other national elections.

Similar to patterns of support for Mazowiecki in 1990, his party – the Democratic Union (UD) – also tended to gain more votes in regions with higher average income and lower unemployment rates (Table 3.7). The link between better economic status and support for the pro-reform UD indicates that this electorate is most likely to be in a position to benefit from (or, perhaps, to understand more fully) market and demo-cratic reform. That is, UD supporters are probably the most identifiable 'winners' of reform, or at least those who have lost less.

The KLD and its leaders even more strongly identified with a pro-market attitude, suggesting that their constituency will be even more strongly identifiable through higher income and lower unemployment rates than UD supporters, especially since UD retained a substantial social democratic wing (its most popular member being Jacek Kuroń). Overall, the income and unemployment variables explain more of the variation in KLD support than for any other of the important parties (adjusted $R^2 = 0.391$). As expected, regional support for the KLD displays a strong positive relation to income, and a negative, weaker dependence on unemployment rates.

In contrast to the UD and the KLD, patterns of support for the fragmented post-Solidarity centre-right are weaker in the income–unemployment regression. The Christian–nationalist coalition WAK shows regional variations in support to be similar to Wałęsa's in 1990, with a negative relationship to both income and unemployment. POC also tended to be higher in areas with less unemployment, but there is no significant relationship to income. The Solidarity trade union (NSZZ 'S') has positive but not significant relations to unemployment and income. Of the election contestants descended from Solidarity, only PL, the peasant party based in Rural Solidarity, produces a measurable link to these indicators: stronger support in areas of higher unemployment and lower income, a pattern conceivably consistent with regions with

Table 3.7   Regression results for 1991 Sejm elections

	R^2	Adj. R^2	Unemployment (significance)	Income (significance)
UD	0.1948	0.1590	-0.0185 (0.8940)	1.6434 (0.0021)
SLD	0.1084	0.0688	0.3112 (0.0255)	0.3034 (0.5406)
WAK	0.0591	0.0173	-0.1255 (0.5135)	-1.1198 (0.1146)
POC	0.0973	0.0572	-0.2456 (0.0342)	0.0153 (0.9704)
PSL	0.1169	0.0758	0.0982 (0.5880)	-1.4757 (0.0303)
KPN	0.0474	0.0051	-0.1513 (0.1441)	0.0056 (0.9879)
KLD	0.4179	0.3911	-0.0339 (0.6731)	1.6254 (0.0000)
PL	0.3008	0.2675	-0.4432 (0.0279)	-2.6763 (0.0004)
NSZZ 'S'	0.0494	0.0019	0.0480 (0.5727)	0.4224 (0.1778)
PPPP	0.2842	0.2465	0.0760 (0.0063)	0.2854 (0.0052)

Source: GUS, Panstwowa Komisja Wyborcza (1991).

mixed economies, dependent upon both small-scale private farming and regional industries, which in more remote regions tended to be harder hit by economic contraction.

The post-communist peasant party, the PSL, similarly gains more votes in poorer regions with lower per capita income, but with less of an impact from regional unemployment rates. The R^2 for the PSL is very low, suggesting that more detailed analyses are needed to explain this party's electorate (the local importance of employment in agriculture and in other economic sectors for party support is explored in Chapter 4).

The post-communist SdRP and its electoral coalition SLD show, as did Cimoszewicz in 1990, a discernible boost in regions with higher unemployment. However, this relationship was enough to explain only about one-tenth of the total variation in support for the former communist party. The coefficient for income is also positive, but is not highly significant.

Finally, even peripheral parties can be analysed through this technique. As the name implies, the Polish Friends of Beer Party (PPPP) started out as a publicity stunt, but over the course of the semi-free Sejm they became identified with a pro-market, low-tax platform. Although relatively weak, support for PPPP varied positively with both higher income and higher joblessness, suggesting that the PPPP was an interesting variation on a protest party, having attracted not only a proportion of the unemployed, but, one assumes, a proportion of maverick entrepreneurs as well. The ideological basis of support for other, smaller, and often more radical parties is indicated by the lack of any measurable link between regional economic factors and voting results. KPN is the most notable example of this effect in 1991, with little sign that its electoral support is based on economic issues.

September 1993 Parliamentary Election

Within two years, however, the public's displeasure with the chaos of the parliament elected in 1991 and the effects of the 1993 electoral reform stimulated a process of political party consolidation in Poland. Generally speaking, the regression results are higher and more significant for this election than for the preceding one.

Compared with 1991, unemployment and income explain more of the regional variation in support for the SLD, the party which gained the most votes in the 1993 election (Table 3.8). SLD support is stronger in areas with higher unemployment, but this effect is outweighed by the coefficient and significance of the unemployment variable. Once again, the SLD vote is higher in regions more seriously affected by job losses. Furthermore, the increase in total support for the SLD suggests that this party's support increased under conditions of rising unemployment.

Voting patterns for the other winner in the 1993 election, the PSL, are similar to its 1991 results, with a comparable R^2 and, again, a negative relationship to both income and unemployment – although income had a much stronger effect than unemployment. However, low income

Table 3.8   Regression results for 1993 Sejm elections

Variable	R^2	Adj. R^2	Unemployment (significance)	Income (significance)
SLD	0.2619	0.2284	0.5153	0.3547
			(0.0003)	(0.0753)
PSL	0.1253	0.0855	-0.0402	-0.9164
			(0.8759)	(0.0190)
UD	0.2204	0.1850	-0.1625	0.4151
			(0.1495)	(0.0129)
UP	0.1481	0.1094	-0.1217	0.0756
			(0.3579)	(0.0330)
Ojczyzna	0.1550	0.1166	-0.1974	-0.2703
			(0.0221)	(0.0325)
BBWR	0.0975	0.0582	-0.0926	0.0418
			(0.0663)	(0.5669)
NSZZ 'S'	0.0660	0.0235	0.0676	0.1269
			(0.5726)	(0.0854)
PC	0.0473	0.0040	0.0042	0.0705
			(0.9011)	(0.1564)
KLD	0.1816	0.1444	0.0132	0.2140
			(0.7835)	(0.0039)

Source: GUS, Panstwowa Komisja Wyborcza (1993).

and unemployment levels are probably more indicative of the agri-cultural constituency of this party rather than being primary causal factors.

The 1993 vote was disastrous for post-Solidarity groups and parties: the parties which led the previous coalition, the UD and the KLD, were ousted from government. Overall, regional backing for the UD shows a greater total link to the two economic factors, but with a slightly lower level of significance for income but a more distinguishable pattern of lower support in high-unemployment regions. The KLD shows poorer overall results in 1993 compared with 1991, in part because of its low level of support in the election. However, regional support for the KLD remains linked to high income regions. Unemployment rates have less of an effect, but the sign indicates more support in regions with less joblessness, primarily the Gdańsk region and large cities.

Of the post-Solidarity parties, the UD and the KLD were joined in the Sejm by only the BBWR and the UP, and only the BBWR gained a substantial number of seats. It ran on a pro-economic reform but socially conservative platform, and its vote share displays a negative and significant relation to unemployment but not to income. *Unia Pracy*, which attracted its supporters from the social democratic wing of the 1989 Solidarity coalition, attracted more votes in areas of higher per capita incomes and lower unemployment rates – primarily Warsaw and the urban centres of western Poland. Rather than being a typical blue-collar labour party, the UP appears to have a more ideologically driven, white-collar electorate (Chapter 5). Furthermore, the UP's chronic problem is that the number who vote for this party is consistently lower than the proportion who in public opinion surveys express a preference for this party. Other studies have found signs that the UP loses as a result of strategic voting, as its supporters are more likely to switch their vote to their second-favoured party (whether the UW, SLD, or AWS) if the second choice is in a close race for the lead.[33]

In the 1993 parliament, however, about three votes in ten were not represented. Mostly this was because of the failure of the anti-communist centre-right to pass the 5% and 8% thresholds. Over time, the PC, ZChN and Solidarity's political wing became more clearly identified with a conservative social stance (pro-Church, anti-abortion), anti-communism (continuing to push for lustration laws), and a more interventionist economic stand, at least concerning employment policy and pensions. Yet the composition of the centre-right electorate is suggested by the strong, high coefficients for lower incomes and lower unemployment in regional voting for the Solidarity trade union and the Christian–nationalist *Ojczyzna* coalition, which implies support from the working poor in more urban as well as more rural regions.

1995 Presidential Election

Both rounds of the 1995 presidential election were mainly a contest between the incumbent, Wałęsa, and the SLD-backed challenger, Aleksander Kwaśniewski. Although the overall results of the regression are moderate at best, some interesting continuities do emerge.

Wałęsa continues in the trend whereby the centre-right fares better

in the low income, low unemployment regions (Table 3.9). Kwaśniewski's electorate is apparently more dispersed, but there is a high
and significant link to high unemployment regions. However, another
recurring factor is the split between the supporters of these two candidates. Regions which supported one candidate tended to give lower
shares of their votes to the other (correlation –0.32). In the second
round, unemployment looks to have been a decisive factor. Although
higher regional unemployment rates are linked to support for Kwaśniewski, income is also positive but much less important, suggesting
that a wide range of income groups, and therefore social groups, voted
for the SLD candidate.

*Table 3.9   Regression results for first round of presidential election,
1995*

	R^2	Adj. R^2	Unemployment (significance)	Income (significance)
Kwaśniewski (SLD)	0.0684	0.0279	0.5273 (0.0773)	0.0833 (0.6791)
Wałęsa (Ind.)	0.2318	0.1984	–0.9667 (0.0006)	–0.1866 (0.3042)
Kuroń (UW)	0.2456	0.2128	0.1573 (0.0272)	0.1787 (0.0005)
Olszewski (ROP)	0.1414	0.1040	–0.2205 (0.0090)	–0.0799 (0.1563)
Pawlak (PSL)	0.1866	0.1512	–0.2278 (0.0884)	–0.2882 (0.0024)
Gronkiewicz-Waltz (Ind.)	0.1762	0.1404	–0.0172 (0.3360)	0.0284 (0.0235)
Zieliński (Ind.)	0.3032	0.2729	0.0437 (0.0452)	0.0650 (0.0001)
Korwin-Mikke (UPR)	0.2782	0.2468	–0.0054 (0.7987)	0.0540 (0.0005)

Source: Państwowa Komisja Wyborcza (1996); author's calculations from GUS data.

Results for the candidates who did not survive beyond the first round in 1995 show similar relations to those found for these candidates and their allied parties in previous elections. An exception is Kuroń, whose patterns of support differ from those of the UD and the UW in other elections in that it is related to *higher* unemployment. Although he was one of Poland's most popular and respected politicians, concerns about Kuroń's health damaged his chances.[34]

While Pawlak received less than 4% of the total vote, the regression reveals a considerably strong relation to both lower unemployment and lower income, typical of rural *województwa*. Pawlak's poor showing reflects the decline in public support for the PSL, whose participation in the coalition government was marked by political patronage, as well as a protectionist, anti-privatization and pro-agrarian policy stance.[35]

Apart from Wałęsa, the results for the centre-right and right-wing candidates were mostly inconclusive, mainly because of the low vote shares attained by each across Poland. Gronkiewicz-Waltz and Korwin-Mikke both show a negative relation to unemployment and a positive relation with income, but at insignificant levels. Olszewski has a better relation with lower unemployment rates: a 1% drop in regional unemployment is related to a 0.22% rise in his support.

1997 Sejm Elections

The results from the 1997 election indicate the deepening consolidation of the party system and, interestingly, an apparent solidification of the divide between supporters of post-communist and post-Solidarity parties. Between them, the two largest coalitions in the 1997 election – the AWS and the SLD – gained six out of every ten valid votes cast. However, the regional divide in support for these two groups was deeper in 1997 than in any other post-communist election. Regions which favoured the AWS tended to give low support to the SLD and vice versa (correlation = –0.83). Moreover, regions which voted for Wałęsa in 1995 tended to give their votes to the AWS in 1997 (0.89), and the same holds true (to a lesser degree) for regional backing for Kwaśniewski in 1995 and the SLD in 1997 (0.49).

As in years past, the SLD's vote share is better in regions with higher unemployment and higher income, but the latter displays a poor level of statistical significance (Table 3.10). Areas worst affected by unemployment, which include north-eastern and central-western

Table 3.10 Regression results for 1997 Sejm elections

	R^2	Adj. R^2	Unemployment (significance)	Income (significance)
AWS	0.1106	0.0720	-0.6659 (0.0333)	-0.0856 (0.2745)
SLD	0.1838	0.1484	0.7431 (0.0057)	0.1042 (0.1177)
UW	0.1003	0.0594	-0.2938 (0.0371)	0.0125 (0.7225)
PSL	0.0204	-0.0252	0.0111 (0.9561)	-0.0473 (0.3526)
ROP	0.0014	-0.0486	-0.0163 (0.8435)	0.0022 (0.9111)
UP	0.1292	0.0421	0.0835 (0.1725)	0.0134 (0.3009)

Source: GUS data, Państwowa Komisja Wyborcza (1997).

regions with a high concentration of socialist-era enterprises, provide higher levels of support to the SLD.

The eventual victors, Solidarity Electoral Action (AWS), joined together the centre-right. Despite fears about whether the coalition could hold once in power – and indeed maintaining unity has been difficult – this federation of centre-right parties gains more votes in regions with less unemployment (as indicated by the high coefficient and good significance level), and there is a negative but rather weak link to average income.

Similarly, the regression results for the UW fall within the established pattern. Support for the UW rises in regions less affected by unemployment; the relation is significant although the coefficient is lower than for the AWS. As with the previous two parties, the relation with income is small, almost non-existent, thereby emphasizing the role of employment issues as one of the defining economic cleavages in Polish politics.

This regression has very little explanatory power for the two other parties which received representation in parliament. Regression results for the PSL and ROP are insignificant, and lack any explanatory power. In previous elections, the sign of the coefficient for the PSL's share of the vote has fluctuated, and is really significant only in 1995; the income level has been negative although also with poor significance levels. This suggests that the PSL constituency is based on other factors, mostly dependence upon agricultural employment, as shown in the next chapter. For the ROP, as well, the regression results also indicate little, suggesting that other, non-economic factors were critical in gathering this support. *Unia Pracy*, which just missed crossing the 5% threshold, shows again that their support tends to come from the urban centres, indicating again a stronger ideological than economic motive for these voters.

Unemployment Matters for Elections

As the results presented above indicate, from the first year of Poland's transition there were identifiable variations in political preferences according to regional levels of income and unemployment, the latter being the more significant factor. Areas which sustained greater job losses during transition gave a falling share of their votes to those candidates most closely identified with radical, market-oriented reform. As unemployment rose, so did levels of support for candidates running on more redistributive platforms. Likewise, people in *województwa* less affected by unemployment or falls in real income have been more likely to support liberal parties. Furthermore, the data suggest a concentration of support for agrarian parties in the low income regions where small-scale agriculture is central to the local economy. In contradiction to Kabaj and Kowalik (1995), we can conclude that interest-based voting models along the lines of those used in advanced market economies can be applied fruitfully to Poland.

This can be shown in a concise form (Table 3.11). For each of the elections discussed in this section, candidates and parties are divided into four groups: peasant parties, the post-communist SdRP and SLD, the liberal post-Solidarity parties (UD, KLD, UW) and the post-Solidarity centre-right, plus a residual category. Each candidate or party is listed along with a sign indicating whether the income–unemployment regression provided a positive or negative coefficient for each variable. In other words, the sign indicates whether votes for the specified candidate or party were positively or negatively related to

Table 3.11 Relation between regional variations in unemployment and votes

	1990	1991	1993	1995	1997
Peasant	Bartoszcze –	PSL–PL + PL –**	PSL – PSL–PL –	Pawlak –*	PSL +
Post-Communist	Cimoszewicz +**	SLD +**	SLD +***	Kwaśniewski 1 +* Kwaśniewski 2 +***	SLD +**
Liberal	Mazowiecki –	KLD – UD –	KLD – UD –	Kuroń +**	UW –**
Centre-right	Wałęsa 1 –** Wałęsa 2 –***	POC –** WAK – 'S' +	PC + 'S' –* Ojczyzna –** BBWR –*	Wałęsa 1 –*** Wałęsa 2 –*** Gronkiewicz-Walz – Olszewski –**	AWS –** ROP –
Others	Tymiński +***	KPN – PPPP +*	KPN –** UP –**	Korwin-Mikke – Zieliński –**	UP +

Note: Significance levels (one-tail test): * = 0.10 ** = 0.05 *** = 0.005.
Sources: GUS data, Państwowa Komisja Wyborcza (1990, 1991, 1993, 1995); Bell (1997a, 1997b).

regional variations. The asterisks in the table cells designate the level of significance of the coefficient.

Each of political tendencies in Table 3.11 has a consistent – and in half of these a statistically significant – relationship to unemployment levels. This is true both for the post-Solidarity groups, who gain more support in areas with lower unemployment, and for the SLD, which attracts relatively more votes in areas affected by higher joblessness. For other parties, such as the PSL, ROP and UP, other factors or variables must be more important. For the PSL, party support is linked not just to the rural population, but also to central and western more than south-eastern regions. The UP electorate appears more closely tied to ideological, leftist preferences than to working-class status. The ROP, by contrast, also gains its support from ideological preferences, but in this case from nationalists and social conservatives.

CONCLUSIONS

Interpretation of these data can be made at two levels. The first way is to read it only as an analysis of regional dispersions of voting patterns. It is well known that there are persistent regional differences in party preferences, with the south-east between Bielsko-Biała and Przemyśl strongly favouring the centre-right (and regions east of Warsaw moderately so), central regions and the 'recovered territories' to the west leaning towards the post-communist SLD, and more liberal forces favoured in the trade and commerce centres of Warsaw, Gdańsk, and Poznań. In addition to regional differences in economic structure, there are also strong cultural trends behind these long-standing allegiances. Żukowski (1997) linked these patterns not only to the borders of the 1797 partition of Poland between the Russian, Prussian and Austro-Hungarian empires, but also to the post-Second World War migrations of Poles from L'vov to Wrocław, and the concentration of communist-era state farms in the western regions.

However, the data also seem to indicate some apparent relationship between political attitudes and socioeconomic status. One interesting conclusion is that the party system in post-communist Poland is definable along economic cleavages dating from the outset of political mobilization (as in Lipset and Rokkan 1967). However, the influence of these cleavages may be waning in favour of – or may have consolidated along lines roughly equivalent to – the divide between the post-communist and post-Solidarity political blocs.

But the motives appear more complex than simple pro- or anti-reform reactions, in Poland as in other transition countries. For the 1993 Russian elections, Whitefield and Evans (1994) asked whether the loss of electoral support for the most pro-reform parties should be understood as a protest vote or as part of an iterative progression towards interest-led voting. A protest vote would indicate that the electorate has accepted democratic and market principles but nevertheless votes to express a general dissatisfaction with the manner in which reforms have been enacted. On the other hand, if democratization involves a learning process on the part of both voters and politicians, a greater diversification of the vote may indicate that voters who were initially ignorant of the implications of radical economic reform have gained experience and gradually come to identify their interests and learnt how to vote accordingly. Whitefield and Evans predict that as part of an iterative process, Russian voters will continue to support economic reform but of a less radical variant.

The interpretation of politics as a learning process led to some realistic conclusions for the case of Poland. Changing economic conditions can shift electorates. Evans and Whitefield propose that more competent governments may increase support for reform. For Poland, Gibson and Cielecka (1995) predicted that economic growth would reduce the share of the vote going to the SLD.

However, economic growth between 1993 and 1997 did not lead to a reduction in the SLD's vote. In 1997, the fourth year of strong GDP growth, the SLD actually increased its electoral support in comparison with 1993. The regressions in this chapter suggest that a shift in voting will occur when GDP growth leads to growth in employment, but I would argue that two outcomes, not mutually exclusive, may emerge. As the rate of job creation picks up, and if economic growth absorbs more unemployed labour, then the current success of the AWS may potentially be translated into a stable electorate. Yet the SLD may not lose either, being supported by professional sectors who credit the SLD with the economic recovery and by the more vulnerable segments of society who look to the SLD to advocate redistribution policies. Also, the resurgence of unemployment and slowed economic growth in

1998–1999 has apparently caused public discontent with the current AWS–UW government.

In the longer run, the Polish political scene will most likely continue to centre upon the AWS and the SLD as the two main blocs with a fairly stable electorate. A small number of more specialized parties with relatively volatile electorates will inhabit the political spaces between the AWS and the SLD. In particular, the decline of the PSL is not attributable simply to the poor campaign the party ran in 1997: it may also be indicative of political modernization, given that agrarian parties have mostly disappeared from European democracies.

This raises the question of whether the more important dynamic for election outcomes is an evolving identification or 'crystallization' of interests (given relatively stable groups), or whether it is that people are moving from net losses to net gains and vice versa in substantial enough numbers to affect election outcomes. While there are ideological, historical and political factors behind the formation of party electorates in Poland, economic interests are especially strong – and are to a great extent not at all incompatible. For instance, we could ask how movement into and out of different labour market statuses (for instance, from employed to unemployed, then to either economic inactivity or back into employment) affects political preferences. Another important topic is the rural vote, which appears to be the floating vote in Polish politics. Finally, the longer-term trends in growth and the extent to which it does or does not translate into job creation and income growth may also have considerable and not necessarily positive political consequences for popular support of continued sectoral reform and also EU accession.

NOTES

1. See Gomułka (1993) and Calvo and Coricelli (1993).
2. 'Poverty stalks the losers', *Financial Times*, 18 March 1994.
3. Shapiro and Granville (1995) have written on the mysterious formulation of the Russian RPI and CPI from a knowledgeable perspective, and emphasize the distortive effects of erroneous price indices for indexed contracts and wages.
4. The OECD now publishes purchasing power parities for Poland in its *Short Term Economic Indicators* series.
5. This section draws from Bell and Rostowski (1995).
6. Kornai (1992, Chapter 8, especially Sections 8.7–8.9).
7. See, for instance, GUS, *Rocznik Statystyczny 1994*, Table 22(715), p. 565.

8. J. Gomułka (1995) used price indices to estimate shifts in demand for different goods within aggregate categories such as food, housing and clothing. Nine price sub-indices were calculated by aggregating price indices for 252 categories of goods over the years 1989–1991, with monthly and then quarterly tables using both the Laysperes (last period quantity weights) and Paasche (first period quantity weights) indices. Comparison revealed changes not only in relative prices but also in the kinds of goods being consumed, especially across different kinds of food. Also, energy prices are shown to have risen at twice the overall price index.

9. GUS, 1993, *Rocznik Statystyczny 1992*, pp. xxvii, 191, 169, 203.

10. As in Kabaj and Kowalik (1995).

11. The welfare effect of the price shock seen in the first months of 1990 was probably more deleterious for the population's well-being than a gradual decline in the real value of wages, as would happen under a high but steady inflation rate. This is referred to as the 'Pazos–Simonsen mechanism' in Dornbusch and Simonsen (1988).

12. See the Final Remarks in the Methodological Notes of *Budżety Gospodarstw Domowych w 1994 r.* (Warsaw: GUS 1995, p. xxxii).

13. 'Polak oszukuje [The Pole Cheats]', *Polityka*, 8 November 1994.

14. The standard measure of income inequality, the Gini coefficient, measures the deviations of the distribution of incomes from total equity. Instead of using the Gini coefficient, official Polish statistics used the Pietra ratio (the coefficient of deviation, equal to half the mean deviation divided by the mean). Graphically, where the Gini coefficient is equal to the area between the Lorenz curve and the line of equal distribution, the Pietra ratio is equal to the maximum distance between the Lorenz curve and the line of absolute income equality. This 'Robin Hood Index' estimates the share of total income which would have to be taken from those with incomes above the mean and redistributed to those below the mean to bring about equal income distribution.

15. *Mały Rocznik Statystyczny*, various issues.

16. This, in turn, led to the three-pillar system introduced on 1 January 1999.

17. Office of the Government Plenipotentiary for Social Security Reform, *Security Through Diversity: Reform of the Pension System in Poland* (Warsaw: Ministry of Labour and Social Policy, 1997).

18. GUS, 1993, *Rocznik Statystyczny 1992*, p. 190.

19. GUS, 1998, *Registered Unemployment in Poland, III Quarter 1998*, Information and Statistical Papers, pp. 5–6.

20. For more information on unemployment, benefit criteria and employment dynamics, see Mickiewicz and Bell (2000), especially Chapters 1 and 5.

21. GUS, 1998, *Aktywność Ekonomiczna Ludności Polski w 1998 roku: Sierpień*, p. xxv.

22. In 1996, 42% of unemployed women had a secondary or higher education, compared with only 23% of unemployed men: 'Kobieta szuka pracy', *Życie Warszawy*, 16 October 1996.

23. GUS, 1998, *Aktywność Ekonomiczna Ludności Polski w 1998 roku: Sierpień*, p. xxiv.

24. This section uses material originally published in Bell (1997a).

25. See Chapters 2–3 of Keech (1995) for an overview of models of 'economic politics'.

26. Often, these types of models relegate to a catch-all 'error term' other factors that figure prominently in the 'pure' political science literature, such as the effects of incumbency, the 'coat-tail effects' of a preceding presidential election on mid-term

elections, campaign tactics and the like. The error term, also called a disturbance, is 'a random (stochastic) variable that has well-defined probabilistic properties. The disturbance term ... may well represent all those factors that affect [the dependent variable] but are not taken into account explicitly': Gujarati (1995), p. 5.

27. It can be argued that, because unemployment was such a new phenomenon in Poland compared with advanced market economies, the unemployed in Poland may be more politically mobilized than their counterparts in other countries.

28. They worked from the null hypothesis that people dissatisfied with their own financial situation should vote against the incumbent, and that the unemployed should also prefer the opposition to the incumbent.

29. Alternatively, voters may take local and regional performance as a proxy for national performance. This would also result in regional variation in preferences, although from different bases of understanding. However, national figures for leading indicators are widely publicized, enabling comparison with local performance to be made.

30. CBOS, 1993, 'Społeczna definicja biędy w Polsce', Report 997/93, April.

31. Fidrmuc (1997) also reaches a similar conclusion, that 'high unemployment decreases support for parties associated with the reform and increases support for left-wing parties', from his study of voting in the Czech Republic, Hungary, Poland and Slovakia.

32. A. Kublik and P. Pacewicz, 'Nasza wyborcza szesciolatka', *Gazeta Wyborcza*, 1 December 1995, p. 2.

33. M. Subotic, 'Twardzi i miękcy w kampanii', *Rzeczpospolita*, 7 August 1997, p. 4.

34. Not to mention the recurring theme of anti-Semitism.

35. For instance, the controversies over the PSL's connections with the BGZ in both the recapitalization programme and the PSL renting office space from the BGZ at absurdly low rates; the PSL's constant blockading of any progress in privatization, its constant lobbying for protection and tax breaks for the sole benefit of peasant farmers, and so on.

4. Regions

As shown in the previous chapter, regional patterns of party support display repeating associations with regional levels of income and unemployment for each of Poland's freely contested national elections. From these regional patterns, some speculations were made about the relationship between income and unemployment and the characteristics of these regions' economies and the people who live in them. But rather than relying on these conclusions, the ideas proposed in the last chapter can be investigated through the extensive sets of data available on economic and social structures at the *województwo* level. For instance, data are available on the percentage living in urban and rural areas, on employment in broadly defined economic sectors, on numbers of pensioners and those receiving social benefits, and on industrial production.[1] Using the same regression analysis approach as in the last chapter, factors such as agriculture, urbanization and employment in the trade and retail sector are shown to have an impact on regional voting patterns, even from the first year of transition. But in general, the most significant factors concentrate on farming and rural regions on the one hand, and on trade and the private sector on the other. Although this analysis focuses on the socioeconomic basis of party support, this does not imply that other, non-economic issues do not affect voters' decisions – issues covered in more depth in Chapter 5.

SELECTING THE VARIABLES

Even the brief selection of regional income and unemployment data presented in the previous chapter gave an idea of the gap between Poland's most and least developed regions, using the 49 *województwa* which were in existence prior to the 1999 administrative reform. Data are available not just for standard economic figures including unemployment and employment, average income, and demographic data, but also for variables such as the proportion of hospital beds, nursery school places and shops relative to the local population, which provide more detailed information on the quality of living standards in the local community.

As in Chapter 3, the dependent variable in the following regressions is the percentage of the vote for each candidate, measured in each province. The independent variables which were selected concentrate on the socioeconomic variables discussed in Chapter 3, with attention also given to the precedent of other research and also to the language of political debate on the economy. The approach is most similar to those used by Parysek *et al.* (1991), Gibson and Cielecka (1995), and Wade *et al.* (1995). In Parysek *et al.* (1991), regressions use varying combinations of the strongest variables,[2] while Gibson and Cielecka use eleven independent variables in seven categories.[3] In the former paper, the strongest and most appropriate variables are selected from the many sets of available data, while in the latter study, the variables focus on key political constituencies directly affected by the economic reform process.

As in the previous two chapters, the choice of data requires some consideration. To illustrate how choices can be made in the selection of regional data, some comparisons are made with the variables used in Gibson and Cielecka (1995). The purpose is to show how different research aims can necessitate different approaches to data selection, with two key examples related to retirement and state sector employment. First of all, Gibson and Cielecka (1995) found that the size of the over-65 population had a positive, significant relationship to SLD and BBWR election results in 1993. This is good for investigating generational differences in voting. But if the relationship in question relates to pensioners as a voting block, with entitlement to government transfers rather than just age as the most important factor, then it is better to use the regional concentration of pensioners. One reason is that many pensioners are under 65. An important consequence of transition was the early surge into early retirement, which not only increased dramatically the number of people receiving pensions, but pushed down the average age of pensioners. Although the over-65s probably include poorer pensioners, the potential interest group which could be mobilized in favour of pensioners includes all recipients, and especially younger ones. In any case, the proportion of pensioners turned out not to be a significant factor (except for the SLD and *Ojczyzna* in 1991). There may be some basis for this result. Prior to the 1997 election, two pensioners' parties were formed (one aligned with SLD and the other, aligned with AWS, formed to draw votes away from it), but each received only about 2% of the total vote.

Gibson and Cielecka also used a variable estimating state sector employment, but their weighted number of state enterprises is not necessarily representative of the total number of employees. First of all, in 1989 and 1990 many state enterprises hived off their profitable and unprofitable sections, split into several units, or set up new activities, potentially increasing the number of state enterprises but with the absolute level of employment remaining the same. Second, from 1991 enterprise restructuring picked up steam. State-owned enterprises which remained in operation were shedding employees, some state-owned enterprises went bankrupt and others were privatized, with each action potentially changing the relationship between enterprises and employees. Gibson and Cielecka also calculated non-farm state employment by subtracting their estimates of employment on state farms from total public employment. This is probably as close as is possible to the actual number, but it is still too imprecise, leaving the compilation of a consistent indicator of state sector employment as problematic.

All variables used in this section were cross-checked for correlation; the strongest relations were between income and farming and urban residence and income.[4] As suggested in the last chapter, agricultural regions have lower per capita income than urban regions, where private sector growth has been strong and where professional jobs and people with higher education tend to be concentrated. These relations suggest that there are underlying, identifiable factors at work. Following the political blocs outlined in Chapter 3, for each of the four main political groupings certain regional variables repeatedly emerge as the most significant for explaining voting patterns – unemployment first of all, followed by farming and trade. The latter two are correlated, but each has greater explanatory power for different political blocs. A number of other variables were also tested,[5] but these turned out not to be significant for most parties and elections.[6]

THE POST-SOLIDARITY CENTRE-RIGHT

The economic and structural patterns of support for the post-Solidarity centre-right show that this a far from homogeneous group, particularly when fragmented as in 1991 and 1993. When this electorate unites behind a single candidate or party (as in 1990, 1995 and 1997), the patterns are more evident. Generally, the centre-right receives more support in areas of lower unemployment but average rather than high average incomes, as shown in Chapter 3 (Table 4.1). In the 1990 and 1997 elections, support for the centre-right is higher where the trade sector is less developed. Of the smaller parties, *Ojczyzna* in 1993 was distinguished by its appeal to pensioners. Yet the most significant factor in 1997 was not economic or structural, but rather turnout, a result not evident in earlier elections. The AWS fared better in regions where voter turnout was higher, indicating that last-minute and less committed voters came out intentionally to support the AWS in their close run against the SLD. The 1997 result is particularly interesting because in the 1991 and 1993 elections higher turnout benefited parties of the *left* (Wade *et al.* 1995).

Over time, there is a tendency for a negative correlation in regional support for centre-right and post-communist parties which is stronger than each of these parties' relationships to other parties. In 1990, support for Wałęsa is negatively correlated with that for Cimoszewicz (–0.50).[7] SLD regional support is also negatively related to centre-right parties in 1991 (WAK –0.25, p = 0.09) and 1993 (Wałęsa –0.32, p = 0.02), and in the 1995 presidential race (Kwaśniewski–Wałęsa: –0.32, p = 0.02). In 1997, however, regional support is even more strongly related than before (SLD–AWS –0.82).

THE POST-COMMUNIST LEFT

As in Chapter 3, regional voting patterns for the PZPR successor party, the SdRP,[8] and the SLD reveal stronger support in areas of higher unemployment in all but the first round of 1995 and the 1997 election (Table 4.2). In 1991, there was greater support in regions with a higher concentration of pensioners, and in 1993 and the first round in 1995, urban regions were particularly prominent.

Table 4.1   Regressions for centre-right candidates and parties

	1990 Round 1	1990 Round 2	1991	1991	1993	1993	1993	1995	1997
	Wałęsa	Wałęsa	POC	NSZZ S	BBWR	Ojczyzna	PC	Wałęsa	AWS
R^2	0.3297	0.3350	0.0972	0.1528	0.0910	0.3724	0.0729	0.2138	0.7950
Adj. R^2	0.3005	0.3209	0.0776	0.1321	0.0716	0.2568	0.0523	0.1970	0.7814
Independent variables (significance)									
Constant	0.7153	0.8902	0.1159	0.0741	0.0666	0.0822	0.0303	0.4555	-0.0473
	(0.0000)	(0.0000)	(0.0000)	(0.0000)	(0.0000)	(0.0002)	(0.0000)	(0.0000)	(0.4446)
Unemployment (%)	-1.5227	-0.2514	-0.2460	*	-0.1011	*	*	-0.8577	*
	(0.0042)	(0.0000)	(0.0310)		(0.0352)			(0.0008)	
Trade (% total employment)	-0.0252	*	*	*	*	*	*	*	-1.5309
	(0.0002)								(0.0001)
Farming (% total employment)	*	*	*	-0.0608	*	*	*	*	*
				(0.0096)					
Urban residents (% population)	*	*	*	*	*	-0.0702	0.0207	*	*
						(0.0081)	(0.0664)		

112

Pensioners (% population)	*	*	*	*	*	0.1495 (0.0099)	*
Benefit recipients (% population)	*	*	*	*	*	-0.1428 (0.0176)	*
Industry (% employment)	*	*	*	*	*	*	-0.5413 (0.0000)
Turnout (% eligible)	*	*	*	*	*	*	1.5182 (0.0000)

Source: Author's calculation from GUS and PKW data.

Table 4.2 Regressions for SLD

	1990	1991	1993	1995 Round 1	1995 Round 2	1997
	Cimoszewicz	SLD	SLD	Kwaśniewski	Kwaśniewski	SLD
R^2	0.1335	0.1838	0.4144	0.2077	0.3015	0.7438
Adj. R^2	0.1150	0.1476	0.3877	0.1733	0.2866	0.7205
Independent variables (significance)						
Constant	0.0533 (0.0022)	-0.0428 (0.4900)	0.0389 (0.2022)	0.5324 (0.0000)	0.3276 (0.0000)	0.2491 (0.0051)
Unemployment (%)	0.6043 (0.0098)	0.3959 (0.0056)	0.1582 (0.0003)	*	1.3157 (0.0000)	*
Per capita income	*	*	*	-0.5378 (0.0175)	*	*
Pensioners (% population)	*	0.5762 (0.0380)	*	*	*	*
Urban residents (% population)	*	*	0.4639 (0.0002)	0.3538 (0.0000)	*	*

Trade (% total employment)	*	*	*	*	*	*	1.3599 (0.0009)
Industry (% employment)	*	*	*	*	*	*	0.6853 (0.0000)
Turnout (% electorate)	*	*	*	*	*	*	-0.8342 (0.0000)

Source: Author's calculation from GUS and PKW data.

In 1997, the regional profile of the SLD vote changed, with unemployment playing a lesser role but trade (a factor associated with urban areas) playing a stronger one. As mentioned above, an important element in explaining the 1997 regression is the strong result where the SLD gained a smaller share of the total vote in areas where turnout was higher, although the effect was weaker for the SLD than for AWS support. Although turnout in 1997 (46.1%) was slightly lower than in 1993 (49.8%),[9] the dynamics of the 1997 election campaign point to the same explanatory factor as that proposed by Wade *et al.* (1995): that the SLD's electorate is a more disciplined group which can be counted on to come out and vote. But whereas in the run-up to the 1993 election it looked as though the centre-right parties would finish ahead, the neck-and-neck contest between the AWS and the SLD, along with the chastening effect of the preceding two elections, mobilized anti-communist voters.

THE POST-COMMUNIST LIBERALS

Apart from the two largest political groups, the centre-right and the social democratic left, one of the smaller but most readily identifiable electorates is the pluralist, mostly economically liberal segment stemming from the Solidarity opposition. Along with the PSL, the liberal parties attain some of the strongest results for regional patterns across the five national elections. The last chapter showed that this bloc consistently received a greater share of the votes in regions with a lower unemployment rate, the exception being Kuroń's finish in the first round in 1995. Yet Kuroń's social democratic views have been less dominant in the UD and subsequently the UW than a more liberal line, particularly under Leszek Balcerowicz's leadership of the UW. These liberal parties have also tended to do better in areas with a higher proportion of employment in the (mostly privately operated) trade sector (Table 4.3).

A very strong negative relationship is found between support for liberal parties and farming employment. Since the start of transition, the farming sector has been critical of the liberal reforms – particularly those introduced under both of Balcerowicz's tenures as finance minister. Liberal voters tend to live in areas of higher employment rates

Table 4.3 Regressions for UD, KLD and UW

	1990	1991	1991	1993	1993	1995	1997
	Mazowiecki	KLD	UD	KLD	UD	Kuroń	UW
R²	0.8134	0.5413	0.6852	0.3806	0.6206	0.8046	0.7551
Adj. R²	0.8053	0.5314	0.6784	0.3668	0.6033	0.7961	0.7439
Independent variables (significance)							
Constant	-0.0805	0.1092	0.1961	-0.0082	0.1924	0.1192	0.2085
	(0.0066)	(0.0000)	(0.0000)	(0.3150)	(0.0000)	(0.0000)	(0.0000)
Unemployment (%)	-0.7318	*	*	*	-0.2493	0.0659	-0.2182
	(0.0011)				(0.0013)	(0.0462)	(0.0034)
Trade (% total employment)	0.0338	*	*	0.3252	*	*	*
	(0.0000)			(0.0000)			
Farming (% total employment)	*	0.1484	-0.2457	*	-0.2024	-0.1382	-0.2067
		(0.0000)	(0.0000)		(0.0000)	(0.0000)	(0.0000)

Source: Author's calculation from GUS and PKW data.

and a stronger economy, one less reliant upon agriculture – a description which most closely describes Warsaw and the more prosperous regional cities, where the labour market is stronger, with more and better jobs and higher pay.

Like the inverse relationship in regional support for social democratic and centre-right parties, regions which give more support to liberal parties give very little backing to peasant parties, a relationship stronger and more consistent than that to either the centre-right or the social democratic parties. Consistently, the regional vote for liberal and peasant parties is strong, significant and negative, from the presidential votes in 1990 (Bartoszcze–Mazowiecki -0.75) and 1995 (Kuroń–Pawlak -0.76), to the parliamentary votes in 1991 (UD–PSL -0.56; KLD–PSL -0.55), 1993 (UD–PSL -0.64; KLD–PSL -0.68), and 1997 (UW–PSL -0.74).

PEASANT PARTIES

The conclusion drawn from the regressions in Chapter 3 – a weak relationship to unemployment but a negative relation to income levels – correctly identifies the agricultural sector as the main source of support for the peasant parties, particularly the PSL. The rural vote is important not only because of its size (in 1997, 38% of the population lived in rural areas, mostly in towns of 5,000–10,000 inhabitants, and 24% of the active workforce was employed in agriculture),[10] but also because of the critical stance taken by the PSL leadership towards economic reform. Although the total share of votes gained by the PSL rose from 1990 to 1993 and sharply declined thereafter, a great deal of the regional variation in support continues to be attributable to concentrations of employment in farming (Table 4.4). However, the declining coefficient after 1993 indicates that this election saw a peak in farmers' support for the PSL. Indeed, the socioeconomic data presented in the next chapter show that, while nearly all PSL votes come from farmers, only a minority of Poland's large class of private farmers supports the PSL.

Table 4.4 Regressions for PSL

	1990	1991	1991	1993	1995	1997
	Bartoszcze	PSL	PL	PSL	Pawlak	PSL
R^2	0.6877	0.4220	0.5948	0.5501	0.7055	0.7252
Adj. R^2	0.6811	0.4088	0.5834	0.5401	0.6993	0.7124
Independent variables (significance)						
Constant	-0.0089	0.0328	-0.0325	0.0395	-0.0205	0.1102
	(0.4007)	(0.0482)	(0.0474)	(0.0797)	(0.0156)	(0.0115)
Farming (% total employment)	0.2820	0.2371	0.3262	0.4622	0.2383	0.2788
	(0.0000)	(0.0000)	(0.0000)	(0.0000)	(0.0000)	(0.0000)
Turnout (% eligible)	*	*	*	*	*	-0.2296
						(0.0098)

Source: Author's calculation from GUS and PKW data.

OTHER LEFT- AND RIGHT-WING PARTIES

While the grouping of these parties into one table is not meant to imply that they are the same, what these parties do share is an 'outsider' status *vis-à-vis* the two main Solidarity and post-communist blocs. Also, the weak relation with economic variables indicated that this electorate is more motivated by ideology, rather than the interests of a particular socioeconomic group.

For instance, in 1990 support for Tymiński was most closely related to the emerging problem of unemployment; the data in Chapter 3 suggested that his electorate was largely composed of those fearful of and disaffected by the radical reform programme. Olszewski and the ROP tend to attract a constituency rather similar to the centre-right parties to which they are closest on the political spectrum. However, the ROP's stronger views regarding Polish nationalism distinguish it from the parties currently included in the AWS structure. Earlier in the transition, patterns of support for Moczulski's KPN – which was established independently of Solidarity – were not definable by these social and economic variables. Even more than for the ROP, attitudinal differences are the base of this electorate. *Unia Pracy*, which has striven to build a social democratic party independent of the former PZPR structure, is actually less easily described by the economic variables than is the SLD. In fact, in 1993 the UP received greater support in areas of *lower* unemployment (Table 4.5). Again, the socioeconomic and demographic composition of the UP's electorate, and their attitudes towards the economy, are most similar to those of the SLD; the difference lies in UP supporters' anti-communist outlooks and positive orientation towards democratization.

HISTORICAL INFLUENCES ON REGIONAL VOTING

In addition to the economic diversity across Poland's regions, there are well-established regional patterns based in historical experience. Although there is a general pattern of urban–rural and high–low unemployment regions and party preferences, regions with similar demographic and economic profiles can have widely varying political patterns. For instance, looking at the regional distribution of the

Table 4.5 Regressions for other parties

	1990	1995	1997	1990	1993	1993	1997
	Tymiński	Olszewski	ROP	Moczułski	KPN	UP	UP
R^2	0.2610	0.5019	0.3229	0.1241	0.1008	0.1314	0.2463
Adj. R^2	0.2453	0.4802	0.3069	0.1055	0.0808	0.1121	0.2104
Independent variables (significance)							
Constant	0.1317	0.0647	0.0992	0.0276	0.7477	0.0743	0.1073
	(0.0000)	(0.0000)	(0.0000)	(0.0000)	(0.0000)	(0.0000)	(0.0001)
Unemployment (%)	1.5540	-0.1839	*	*	-0.1282	-0.1373	*
	(0.0002)	(0.0021)			(0.0297)	(0.0123)	
Farming (% total employment)	*	0.1079	*	-0.1134	*	*	*
		(0.0000)		(0.0130)			
Industry (% employment)	*	*	-0.1567	*	*	*	*
			(0.0001)				
Turnout (% electorate)	*	*	*	*	*	*	-0.1217
							(0.0160)

Source: Author's calculation from GUS and PKW data.

vote for the 1990 presidential election, Wałęsa received twice as high a share of the vote in the southeastern region of Nowy Sącz (62%) as in the central region of Leszno (25%). Yet both these regions are rural and agricultural, with below-average unemployment (5.8% and 5.5%, against 7% nationally) and below-average per capita income.

In general, the anti-communist parties have consistently gained greater support in the south-eastern regions of Poland, which have traditionally been Solidarity strongholds. Some attribute the strong anti-communism of the region to the legacy of the political activism of Galicia under the relatively lenient Austro-Hungarian rule. It can also be attributed to the prevalence of small-scale farming and the self-sufficient people of the mountain regions. In western Poland, where social traditions are weaker owing to the post-Second World War migrations into and out of the 'recovered territories', there tends to be stronger support for the post-communist parties.

Wade *et al.* (1995, pp. 421–422) divide Poland into political regions along a line which extends from between Suwałki and Białystok in the northeast, to the west of Warsaw and Łódź, to the south-west corner of Poland just below Wrocław; they also include the concentration of priests per capita as a cultural measure of the presence of the Catholic Church in each region. Weclawowicz (1996, Chapter 9) also discusses the political geography of Poland in terms of rural–urban and east–west regions. Żukowski (1997) examines the 1995 and 1997 results along the borders of the nineteenth-century partition of Poland. In effect, the cultural and traditional divide across Poland's regions in some ways puts a cross-tension on the economic factors. But in others, the industrial concentration in the west and the predominance of small, private farms in the more remote eastern regions reinforces these trends. However, the differences are more apparent when structurally similar regions produce very different voting results.

NOTES

1. The main source from GUS being the annual *Rocznik Statystyczny Województw.*
2. Farming, urban versus rural population, the ratio of women to men, the percentage of working age and post-working age in the population, the proportion of people with secondary or higher education rather than vocational training, and the ratio of state-owned to private farmland.

3. The percentage unemployed in September 1993; weighted percentage change in industrial and construction sales, weighted percentage change in the number of state enterprises; percentage of employment on state farms, percentage of employment on private farms, percentage of non-farm private employment; percentage of population receiving social benefits; percentage of population aged 20–29, percentage of population aged 65 and over; percentage of working population with higher education. The central concerns for Gibson and Cielecka are the effects of privatization, growth and unemployment on electoral support for liberal parties. In particular, their assumptions are based on the Hayekian idea that growth of the private sector (and, implicitly, the middle class) will increase support for pro-reform parties. Another key idea tested by their regression is the link between the number of social benefit dependants and support for the redistributive platforms of the SLD and PSL.

4. Some of the relevant variables show high levels of correlation, including a positive relation between urban population and employment in the trade sector, a negative relation between farming and both urbanization and trade sector employment, as well as positive relations between the share of the public receiving benefits and the unemployment rate, and between employment in the non-agricultural private sector and employment in the retail and trade sector, the area of the highest job creation during the first years of transition. However, proper care was taken not to skew the regression results by including closely related variables in the same equation.

5. Variables tested but not found to be statistically significant include: the percentage of those employed in agriculture including private farmers, the percentage of the workforce employed in the trade sector, the registered unemployment rate, average monthly per capita income, the percentage of the population receiving social benefits, the share of pensioners in the total population, average monthly pension, the share of employment in industry, the percentage of employment in the non-agriculture public sector, the economic activity rate (percentage of population employed), and the vacancy rate.

6. Exceptions include social benefits, which showed a relation to the vote for Bartoszcze in 1990 (coefficient: 0.297), the PL in 1991 (0.392), and the SLD in the 1993 election (0.183, all significant at the 90% level). Gibson and Cielecka (1995) also received only one significant result for percentage of benefit recipients, a coefficient of 0.59 for the SLD in 1993.

7. In correlations, p = 0.000 unless otherwise noted.

8. Which was dissolved in spring 1999, and reconstituted into the SLD which had changed its party constitution to become a political party in its own right. This was widely believed to have been a tactic to avoid the long-delayed repayment of debts to the state linked to the PZPR's communist-era property.

9. *Mały Rocznik Statystyczny 1998*, pp. 84.

10. *Mały Rocznik Statystyczny 1998*, pp. 72 and 114.

5. Households During Transition

So far, we have seen how the voting choices made by people in Poland's regions interact with employment and income, and the underlying structure of the local economy. In particular, higher unemployment is associated with greater support for social democratic parties. Since the preceding chapters examined the aggregate level, it is also useful to consider voting patterns within specific social and occupational groups (the subject of this chapter) and at the individual level (the subject of the next chapter). Before considering how political preferences vary across different social and economic groups in a transition society, this chapter first outlines empirical measures of change in living standards across the main socioeconomic groups – the factors behind gains and losses in living standards which are often thought to underlie political choice. Then, the chapter looks at corresponding data on voting and political preferences.

It is a long-standing tenet of political economy that in market economies, people's sensitivity to inflation and unemployment (as well as to the effects of reforms such as trade liberalization or privatization) will vary across classes and occupations. In the transition economy, account needs to be taken of the very rapidly changing environment. During the stabilization phase of transition, lower income groups tend to be more susceptible to inflation than wealthier ones because of their dependence on indexed pay and benefits, and their lack of access to hard currency or foreign financial instruments, and because inflationary shocks can wipe out the value of domestic currency savings (Shapiro and Granville 1996). As the economy moves from stabilization to the stage of transitional restructuring, the threat of unemployment grows, especially for low-skill workers, employees in 'sunset' industries, and households in economically depressed regions.

5.1   CHANGING SOCIAL STRUCTURE

Even given the problems posed by using price and income data during
transition, the income and unemployment data in Chapter 3 indicate
that class and social group play a substantial part in explaining the gap
in living standards. The main source of data used here is the Household
Budget Survey (HBS – in Polish, *Budżety Gospodarstw Domowych*).[1]
Income and consumption data are given for six socioeconomic household types: employees,[2] worker-farmers, farmers, pensioners and, since
1993, self-employed and benefit-dependent households.

While indicators on GDP and average wages show Poland's recession and recovery at the aggregate level, at the micro-level there has
been a more complex pattern of gains and losses. Panel data from the
Polish Central Statistical Office's Household Budget Survey show that
the losses and benefits of transition have weighed unequally across
society. Since this and following chapters make extensive reference to
the socioeconomic groups used in the HBS, Table 5.1 provides a breakdown of the number of households and average number of individuals
within the sample population for 1997.

*Table 5.1   Structure of socio-demographic groups in Household Budget
Survey*

	Number of households	%	Average number per household	Projected share of population in sample (%)
Employees	13,188	41.5	3.50	45.2
Employees with farms	3,057	9.6	4.55	13.6
Farmers	1,691	5.3	4.25	7.0
Self-employed	1,978	6.2	3.78	7.3
Pensioners	1,0821	34.1	2.22	23.5
Benefit dependent	1,041	3.3	3.34	3.4

Source: GUS, *Rocznik Statystyczny 1998.*

In the 1997 sample, the two largest household groups received most
of their income from either paid employment or pensions. The proportion of households which rely on agriculture or a combination of

employment and small-scale farming may underestimate the weight of farming in total *employment* (not population), which largely because of job shedding rose from 20% in 1990 to 24% in 1997. Households which earn most of their income from self-employment make up a relatively small but prosperous group, while households which rely most on social benefits and other unearned incomes (excluding pensions, referred to as 'benefit-dependent households') are also numerically few, but they are the most impoverished and vulnerable group of the six.

Representativeness of Statistical Data

There are specific quirks affecting the figures on household income and consumption, most significantly the inconsistencies from the early stages of transformation when data-gathering methods failed to keep pace with rapidly changing economic conditions and behaviour. Although all the national statistical agencies in Central and Eastern Europe have adapted their methods to improve the representativeness and reliability of the data, as with any statistics direct comparisons of essentially different measurements should be avoided.

Through self-reported income and expenditure records, the household budget surveys profile the activities of an 'average' household,[3] but social change has altered what 'average' means. Over the past decade, private sector employment grew dynamically, as did open unemployment. Consequently, the four original socioeconomic groups of the socialist-era household budget survey quickly became less representative. Górecki and Wiśniewski (1995) estimate that 12% of the population was excluded from the surveys as early as the end of the 1980s.

In response, the panel for these surveys was widened in 1993. The 'employee' group incorporated employees in the private as well as the state sector; on average, however, the wage differential between the two sectors is not great. New categories were introduced to include self-employed households and those maintained from non-wage income, the latter category covering households where the main income source is neither earned income nor retirement or disability pensions. Primarily, these households depend upon unemployment benefits, alimony, income support and other social benefits, and also aid from family and from charity – but most of these households' heads qualify as unemployed (World Bank 1995). For purposes of simplicity, the 'non-wage income' group can be understood as primarily composed of unemployed adults and their dependants, predominately children.

5.2 HOUSEHOLD INCOME

Widening Gap Between Household Incomes

Although the average incomes of different social groups are often compared with one another, it is not always clear whether a widening or narrowing gap has resulted from one group's income rising or one's falling, or both changing but at different rates. Figure 3.3 (p. 69), for instance, compared the average, nominal monthly pension with the average monthly wage from 1998 to 1997.

The ratio between the average pension and the average state sector wage rose dramatically between 1988 and 1991, levelled off, and then decreased slightly. Yet it cannot be deduced whether there was an increase in the real value of pensions or a deterioration of the average wage in the state sector, or whether state sector wages grew at a faster rate than pensions. If the first or even the second reason is true, there may well have been an improvement in the average pensioner's available income. Even if average wages fell, pensions may have risen or fallen in terms of purchasing power. To answer these questions, Table 5.2 compares annual indices of nominal growth of pensions and salaries with the consumer price index. Nominal pensions lagged behind wages in the late 1980s, and increased at a more rapid rate than either state wages or inflation in 1991, with a narrowed but variable rate thereafter.

We can conclude that *the rise in the ratio between pensions and wages reflects the joint effect of an increase in pensions from a very low relative level and the fall and stagnation of real wages until 1995*. Before 1990, these shifts mostly occurred because of policy decisions. In response to rising political tensions, the communist-led government increased real wages in 1988 (most people being directly or indirectly state employees), boosting pay to unsustainably high levels. By the next year, even before the start of the transition programme, real wages were already moving downwards. In 1990, a combination of high inflation, the excess wage tax (*popiwek*), fiscal austerity, falling

*Table 5.2　Indices of nominal net pensions, state sector wages and
annual CPI*

	1988	1989	1990	1991	1992
Pensions	100	364.2	590.4	196.2	134.9
State sector wage	100	391.8	498.0	170.6	138.9
CPI	100	351.1	685.8	171.1	142.8

	1993	1994	1995	1996	1997
Pensions	131.7	136.9	132.0	122.5	121.9
State sector wage	131.3	132.9	131.8	126.7	122.9
CPI	135.2	132.3	128.0	119.9	115.1

Note:　Preceding year = 100
Source: Mały Rocznik Statystyczny, 1995, pp. 99, 110 and 132.

demand, and cautious behaviour by managers depressed wages further.
Wages held steady at this low level through the recession and the first
two years of growth, but more because of tight monetary policy than
the excess wage tax (Coricelli and Revenga 1993). The subsequent,
moderate decline in the ratio since 1995 reflects rising real wages more
than a lower rate of real increase for pensions. From 1995, falling
unemployment and a competitive labour market, especially among
skilled workers and the professions, produced renewed upward pressure on wages, but because wage rises lagged behind productivity
gains, they were economically sustainable.

Whereas real wages fell during the first months of transition, the
Mazowiecki government increased the real value of pensions, in part to
counteract the low value of pensions which under the socialist system
were augmented by subsidized basic goods and services. Also, the cost
of living rose faster for pensioners than for other social groups because
of these households' smaller size and associated consumption patterns.
Under Kuroń, Labour Minister at the time, the average real pension
rose by 14.5% in 1991. This prevented more retired persons from
falling into severe poverty, but the rapid rise in the number of people

taking early retirement caused the state pension system to become a serious threat to the fiscal balance.[4] The total pension bill grew from 8.2% of GDP in 1989 to 12.2% in 1991 and 15.8% in 1994 (Golinowska 1996, p. 20). The state pension system became reliant upon subsidies to cover payments; by 1997, 20% of total budget expenditures were allocated in subsidies to cover the gap in running expenses of the Pension Fund. However, the advantage of linking pensions to the CPI rather than the average wage became apparent only when real wages began to increase more rapidly. In 1995, real pensions increased by 3.3%, and real wages grew by a strong 6.1%. Both the SLD–PSL and the AWS–UW governments have resisted accelerating the rise in real pensions, and the 1999 introduction of the three-pillar system means that there will probably be a future income gap between those pensioners who were able to contribute to the voluntary third pillar and those who were not.[5]

Nominal Income across Household Groups

Large shifts in the average monthly per capita income[6] for the six socioeconomic groups (Table 5.3) give an initial impression of relative gains and losses. Farmers appear to be among the greatest relative losers: in 1989, their average per capita incomes were one-third greater than pensioners' and 15% greater than employees' incomes, but just two years later farmers had the lowest per capita income of the four Household Budget Survey groups. Worker-farmers, who combine paid employment with running a small farm,[7] also went from a relatively comfortable to an impoverished situation. But by 1995, households dependent upon 'non-wage incomes' were falling further behind all other household groups, including pensioners and farmers. By contrast, pensioners and self-employed households both appear to have made substantial gains in income during transition, even more than the moderate gains made by employees since 1991.

Even more in pensioners' households than in, for instance, self-employed households, the rather positive income result in this group – even considering the higher pension:wage relationship, the smaller average household size of pensioners, and the lower average age of the new cohort of early retirees – may well obscure a widening income gap between the poorest and more affluent pensioners. However, if the bulk of pensioners have at least held their ground, if not made gains in their

Table 5.3   Nominal per capita incomes by socioeconomic group (PZL)

	Employees	Worker-farmers	Farmers	Pensioners	Self-employed	Unemployed
1987	1.87	1.88	2.18	1.73		
1988	3.33	3.51	4.10	2.82		
1989	11.60	12.45	13.45	8.45		
1990	56.30	59.63	57.73	49.34		
1991	97.90	93.02	82.39	94.59		
1992	142.83	129.36	117.33	126.58		
1993	176.61	145.37	157.72	185.71	218.85	95.33
1994	234.69	194.56	205.18	245.86	297.69	125.87
1995	301.26	260.80	282.35	319.68	386.13	155.89
1996	395.25	321.40	343.16	402.37	487.81	200.37
1997	458.53	368.55	379.28	477.14	564.52	227.31
1998	546.35	419.36	406.78	552.96	655.11	299.20

Note: Pre-1995 prices are rescaled into current PZN values (1 PZN = 10,000 PZL).
Sources: Rocznik Statystyczny, Biuletyn Statystyczny and *Mały Rocznik Statystyczny,*
various issues.

material situation, this would contradict the conventional wisdom that pensioners in general have fared worse than others over the course of transition.[8] Additionally, while employees as a whole fared relatively well during the transition, employees in different skill levels and sectors have faced varying circumstances. Employment in the budget sector remained more stable than employment in state-run enterprises and farms, and greater disparity appeared in wages for blue- and white-collar workers.[9]

Despite the lack of pre-1993 data for either self-employed or benefit-dependent households, the available income figures strongly suggest that these are the most identifiable winners and losers of transition, a finding which strongly echoes the opinion data (Chapter 6). Self-employed households have the highest average income, about one-quarter higher than in employees' households (24% in 1993, 28% in 1995, and 23% in 1997) and more than twice that in unemployed households. Estimates from the early 1990s suggest that the true income levels in the self-employed sector may be even higher.

Kudrycka (1993) calculated that private sector incomes were under-estimated by 80%, and that the unemployed reported their incomes as half of their true level. Wiśniewski (1996) cites a 1990 GUS survey of small enterprises, in which wages and salaries in companies with fewer than four employees (which were not required to keep accounts) were cited as only 20% of those in enterprises with five or more employees which were obliged to meet accounting standards.[10] Even despite the risk of starting a small business and the acknowledged tendency to under-report private sector income, self-employed households are, on average, relatively prosperous.

Even taking into account the number of caveats on the use of price deflators during the transition, Figure 5.1 indicates the widening income disparities between household groups between 1987 and 1988, when farmers benefited most, to the narrowing of income differentials at a considerably 'lower' level subsequent to the initial impact of 'shock therapy'. The greatest impact occurred in early 1990, but in general it did not lead to a prolonged slide in incomes. The adjustment related to stabilization was concentrated in the first months of transition; further income changes should be attributed to other causes, whether shifts in terms of trade, collapse of the CMEA, drought,

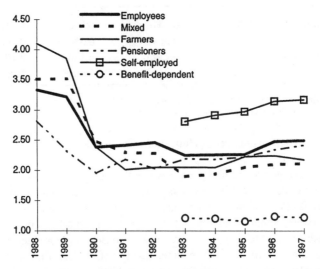

Figure 5.1   Average monthly household incomes (in constant 1988 prices)

changing benefit eligibility criteria, altered indexation of pensions, and so on.

A decade on, the situation is very different: employees' wages are rising in real terms. Average per capita incomes for agricultural house-holds are still lower than all others except those on non-wage incomes. Again, the agricultural sector appears to be a loser of transition, as its relatively privileged position under socialism disappeared, while employees and pensioners faced a more moderate cost. For pensioners, real incomes were 12% higher in 1994 than in 1990, despite a relatively higher increase in the cost of living for this group. Workers' real wages stabilized soon after liberalization, grew at about 6% annually in 1996–1997, but slowed in 1998 (up 3.8%).

Furthermore, farming incomes were much more volatile during the initial years of transition, implying not only the greater seasonal variation which characterizes farm incomes, but a also greater unpredictability over time (Table 5.4).[11]

Table 5.4   Variation in sources of income, 1987–1994

	Employees	Worker-farmers	Farmers	Pensioners
Hired work	0.1543	0.2416	0.2704	0.2190
Own farm	0.1940	0.3642	0.5300	0.1604
Social benefits	0.2131	0.1525	0.1864	0.1901
Other	0.9521	1.2162	1.4669	1.1008

Note: Variation equals standard deviation/mean.
Source: Author's calculations from GUS data.

Income Distribution across Household Groups

Not only did greater overall gaps between the rich and the poor appear, but these trends have different causes depending upon the main income source. Workers in state enterprises went from a situation in which wages were administratively set to one where market conditions, the push for profitability, and hard budget constraints would suddenly change the distribution of income. Even before the first year of transition passed, the correlation between higher wages and profita-bility strengthened (Schaffer 1991). Liberalization of economic activity expanded the possibilities for skilled and educated individuals to choose from a range of more lucrative employment, while households dependent upon less-skilled work in uncompetitive sectors came under greater threat of poverty because of lower wages or unemployment.

Until 1992, the Household Budget Survey data included income deciles for the four main household types. In the first three years of transition, the ratio between the highest and lowest deciles among employees and pensioners widened (for pensioners, this was mostly to the advantage of the middle deciles rather than the highest groups) (Table 5.5). Agricultural households experienced less change in income inequality, but this is largely because of a decrease in incomes at the higher end of the scale which levelled incomes towards the lower end of the scale.

Table 5.5   Ratio of income in highest and lowest decile groups (D10/D1)

	1988	1989	1990	1991	1992
Employees	4.13	4.63	5.02	4.93	5.17
Worker-farmers	4.67	4.79	4.74	4.26	3.73
Farmers	9.16	11.13	8.47	7.00	6.75
Pensioners	4.23	4.51	4.43	5.05	5.54

Source: Rocznik Statystyczny, various issues.

The Gini coefficient, introduced in Chapter 3, shows more moderate changes in inequality over the first two years of transition (the period for which data are freely available) (Table 5.6). Workers' traditionally equitable income distribution became more polarized; other research has emphasized the growing numbers of working urban poor (Milanovic 1993). Again, for both farmers and worker-farmers, a more even income distribution points to the overall decline in this sector's real income. Moreover, the average number of people in the worker-farmer household grew (from 4.72 in 1991 to 4.88 in 1993), but the number of people earning incomes fell (from 2.55 in 1991 to 2.33 in 1993). And as Kudrycka (1993, p. 152) points out, before 1989 farming households received the highest average incomes but farmers were twice as likely as workers to have incomes in the lowest decile group.

Table 5.6   Gini coefficients for main socioeconomic groups

	1987	1988	1989	1990	1991
Employees	0.25	0.24	0.25	0.26	0.26
Worker-farmers	0.24	0.24	0.25	0.25	0.23
Farmers	0.34	0.34	0.36	0.34	0.31
Pensioners	0.20	0.20	0.22	0.20	0.22

Source: Górecki (1994).

5.3   CONSUMPTION OF FOOD AND GOODS DURING THE TRANSITION

Living standards depend not only upon what people earn, but also on how much they spend and what they spend it on. In market economies, consumer spending is a key indicator for monitoring confidence, demand and overall economic performance. In transition economies, actual consumption levels and people's expectations of improved living conditions under the new system have had a political importance and a social urgency as strong as, or stronger than, in market economies. Consumption figures allow a straightforward way to look at living standards across different occupational and demographic groups, and to avoid some of the problems encountered with income data. Yet distortions can still creep in regarding the points in time over which comparisons are made. For instance, Kabaj and Kowalik (1995) used consumption data as evidence that Poland's 'big bang' transition programme caused a dramatic drop living standards; the table from their article is reproduced below (Table 5.7).

From this table, it appears that there was a dramatic fall in average consumption of these basic food items, implying a substantial drop in living standards. However, two important points are obscured. First, these data are only for households where the main income source is from paid employment; the consumption patterns in other household types covered in statistical surveys are quite different, as is shown in this chapter. Second, the side-by-side comparison of data for each year

*Table 5.7   Average monthly per capita consumption in Poland
(kilograms)*

Food item	Consumption		Change
	1989	1994	(%)
Flour	1.14	0.95	−16.7
Bread	6.92	6.90	20.0
Potatoes	8.01	6.84	−14.6
Vegetables	5.06	5.00	−1.2
Fruits	3.00	3.39	13.0
Meat	5.01	4.51	−10.0
Fish	0.46	0.42	−8.7
Oil and fats	1.58	1.41	−10.8
Butter	0.73	0.33	−54.8
Milk (litres)	7.26	5.53	−23.8
Cheese	0.92	0.72	−21.7
Eggs (units)	15.80	12.74	−19.5
Sugar	2.06	1.66	−19.4

Source: Kabaj and Kowalik (1995).

between 1989 and 1994 (Figure 5.2; the horizontal line marks total consumption in 1989) indicates that it is difficult to attribute lower consumption in 1994 to the 1990 liberalization programme.

Unlike in Table 5.7, only foods measured in kilos are included (eggs and milk are not). As the numbers show, 1994 consumption was lower than 1989 levels. But during the peak of the economic crisis, between 1989 and 1991, average consumption of bread, potatoes, vegetables and fruit *increased*, and meat consumption was relatively consistent. There was another increase in total consumption in 1993, but in 1994 consumption of staples including potatoes, vegetables and fruit declined. If this reduced consumption was simply an effect of the liberalization programme, one would expect it to have occurred several years earlier. Rather, this decline is more probably related to contemporary events, including a 1993 agricultural price stabilization scheme which effectively *increased* retail food prices, and a drought during that spring and summer. But lower quantities may not equal reduced

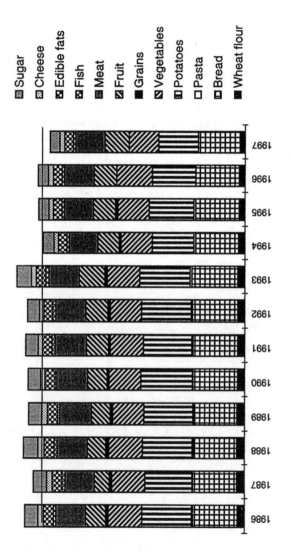

Legend:
- Sugar
- Cheese
- Edible fats
- Fish
- Meat
- Fruit
- Grains
- Vegetables
- Potatoes
- Pasta
- Bread
- Wheat flour

Years: 1986, 1987, 1988, 1989, 1990, 1991, 1992, 1993, 1994, 1995, 1996, 1997

Figure 5.2   Average per capita monthly consumption of basic foodstuffs: worker households, in kilos

welfare. Concentrating on the volume of food intake ignores the potential for improved quality and variety of Polish diets, as well as consumers' voluntary reallocation of expenditure away from food and towards consumer goods.[12]

Consumption data provide an insight into living standards not dependent upon prices and deflators, which are particularly prone to the distortions of the socialist economy (Berg 1993). Under the shortage economy, household consumption was often deflected into queuing, forced substitution or forced savings (Kornai 1992, Chapters 12–13). The prices rarely reflected either demand or even costs of production. Whether one was part of a queue for meat or had access to the special shops for the *nomenklatura*, access to and consumption of goods and services was often a function of neither income nor impersonal rationing, but of politics.

As with incomes, the switch from artificial to market-set values requires consumption data to be interpreted within context. Starting from the socialist-era literature on the welfare costs of the shortage economy, significant welfare gains were argued to have resulted from economic liberalization.[13] One school of thought argues that *in general*, living conditions and the material situation in Poland improved compared with the situation under real socialism (Sachs 1995), partly because liberalized imports eased supply constraints. Critics of reform – such as Kabaj and Kowalik – responded that Polish reforms were 'unduly cruel', with the hardships experienced by farmers and pensioners being *a result of the unforeseen costs of stabilization.*

Income data reveal emerging inequalities in society, but it is not always clear what this means for people dependent upon different income sources and earning different incomes. Starting from Engel's Law, per capita consumption of selected foodstuffs can be used as a bottom-line indicator of well-being. Considering the level of development of the socialist countries and the historical aspirations of Polish society, it is useful to examine the stock and flow of consumer durable ownership. While food consumption can indicate basic shifts in welfare, an analysis of durable goods consumption can explain why falling consumption of quantities of food may not be as disastrous as it first appears, mostly because of the end of shortage-related substitution effects (Bell and Rostowski 1995). As Kornai stated, 'if people cannot spend their money on housing, they go to the butcher and try to get more meat.'[14] Once other goods become available, people may choose to reduce excess spending on food and increase spending on other things.

Over the first few years of transition, both household survey data and aggregate trade data show a large accumulation of durable goods, including cars and home electronics – across socioeconomic and income groups and largely in the absence of consumer lending. Moreover, this reorientation of expenditure did *not* occur at the cost of greatly reduced food consumption. On the contrary, overall consumption patterns arguably came to resemble what would be expected from an *increase* in income. The combination of changing prices and supplies of consumer goods with shifting income patterns led to a complex adjustment of consumer behaviour across all socioeconomic groups, and not all of it negative. Rather, a more accurate picture of changes in material living standards must take a differentiated approach across social groups and types of consumption behaviour.

Households where the main income comes from either paid employment or pensions have fared relatively well under transition, showing somewhat moderated food consumption but increased ownership of consumer goods. The clear winners of transition are again the self-employed and the losers those dependent on 'non-income sources' (primarily social benefits). As a class, farmers and rural-based mixed households are largely worse off than before, and households dependent upon employment largely are better off. For some, housing costs and utilities are taking a larger chunk of monthly spending. Farmers, households combining farming income with paid employment, and pensioners spend about two-thirds of their monthly outgoings on the 'essentials' – food, housing and fuel – with little left over for discretionary spending on leisure. However, compared with western societies, housing and particularly rents still account for a relatively small share of total expenditure. Household type is not the only factor at work, but, as previous and subsequent chapters show, these groups provide an illustrative way of understanding complementary factors which affect material living standards, including labour market status, household size and so on. In the next few sections, we will look at material living standards through expenditures and bulk measures of consumption across the different household types.

5.4 PRICES AND EXPENDITURES

Household Savings

Under the socialist economy, households accumulated often quite large stocks of savings, whether in (negative-interest bearing) domestic currency savings, in hard currency or in cash. In the socialist economy, forced saving was a method by which the investment ratio could be increased, thereby freeing resources for industrial investment. At the macroeconomic level, the high savings rate was really 'excess demand', as wages and other incomes paid to the public exceeded the stock of goods available at administered prices and quantities (leaving aside for the moment the effects of the black market). To a large extent, high savings rates represented 'forced savings' or frustrated consumption demand. In a shortage economy with repressed inflation, the real value of money stocks is analytically considered to be less than their nominal value.[15] As there is a shortfall of goods and services on which the consumer can spend his or her money, a stock of savings accumulates. Artificially high savings do not automatically turn into improved living standards because the money is not convertible into purchases at the official prices. But they do cause an inflationary shock. Price liberalization causes a jump in the price level, deflating away 'excess' savings and allowing prices to rise to equilibrium levels.

At the individual level, households also kept considerable amounts of money on hand because of the high transaction demand for cash under the shortage economy, to finance large purchases in the absence of household credits or to cover search costs. When goods were scarce, one common practice was to carry relatively large amounts of cash and a foldable shopping bag. If one happened upon desired goods for sale, sufficient stocks could be bought to cover present and future consumption. As the economy slipped into accelerating inflation rates, people had to dedicate a larger proportion of income to maintaining the real value of savings, especially as deposit interest rates did not keep up with inflation.

But it is likely that most people understood the value of their savings to be equal to potential consumption at the controlled prices. That is, someone might have saved enough to buy a small car, if one was available. The inflating away of savings might represent a theoretical loss for academics, but one which was quite real in the minds of the population. If this were not the case, people would have been indifferent between either buying goods at state prices after queueing or buying them at black market prices.[16] One reason for early disenchantment with reform could be this *perceived* wealth effect, where people's sense of economic security was inflated away with their savings.

From 1989 to 1990, the 'real' value of the stock of the population's savings deposits fell by 30%.[17] The stabilization plan aimed to reduce real net domestic assets by 28% over the first six months of 1990 and 24% for the year as a whole, curbing real income growth to less than the rate of inflation and reducing the real value of money stocks. Positive interest rates for deposits were also introduced.

The złoty was devalued in January 1990, different exchange rates unified, and the currency pegged at a rate of 9,500 PZL to the US dollar, which held for nearly a year and a half. While the real złoty value of *foreign exchange money holdings* of the population fell by half from 1989 to 1990, the value of domestic currency savings in dollar terms rose from $4.2 billion to $5.7 billion – a rise of 35.7% (Milanovic 1993, p. 24). By 1994, total złoty personal deposits held with banks had grown 4.9%, mostly in time deposits with a maturity of one year or less.[18] As in stabilization programmes in Latin America and other parts of Central and Eastern Europe, the increase in the dollar value of wages in relation to the pre-unification parallel rate constituted a wealth effect on the consumption side.

Table 5.8 shows savings rates for 1987–1998 as a percentage of nominal income. Of course, since this is a percentage of a smaller 'real' income level after 1989, this should only be understood as the share of total income that households were able to save.[19] In 1988–1989, 20% or more of incomes in economically active households were not spent. But there were few investment options for households, who often resorted to buying hard currency, making savings account deposits, or stocking up on goods. Pensioners have been spending nearly all they receive in transfers and other income, with withdrawal of savings even more severe for unemployed households. These limited data point to four possible conclusions about the role of savings during transition:

- In 1989–1990 there were high levels of forced savings.
- Sustained high levels of savings in the initial phase of transition

Table 5.8 Savings rates (% monthly nominal income per capita)

	Employees		Farmers	Self-employed		
		Worker-farmers		Pensioners		Unemployed
1987	13.4	22.7	22.1	6.0		
1988	17.2	30.1	26.9	5.7		
1989	19.6	30.5	22.2	1.9		
1990	13.2	23.8	11.8	1.5		
1991	10.1	21.1	8.0	2.4		
1992	13.6	23.0	11.8	-0.6		
1993	4.9	4.5	3.9	-2.2	1.1	-12.3
1994	7.6	5.8	9.1	0.6	4.4	-6.5
1995	8.7	14.5	16.9	2.8	7.0	-3.9
1996	10.1	12.7	13.2	3.4	8.0	-2.3
1997	6.4	6.7	8.6	1.9	5.0	-9.7
1998	5.3	9.3	9.3	-0.9	3.4	-13.5

Source: Author's calculation from GUS data.

could indicate precautionary behaviour in an uncertain environment.

- As the life cycle theory suggests, households withdrew their savings during the recession of 1991–1992 in order to preserve living standards, with the expectation that their incomes would soon recover.
- Uncertainty regarding the złoty exchange rate also influenced savings, with expected depreciation spurring higher conversion to dollars, and gradual appreciation increasing the appeal of accumulating savings in domestic currency.

Public opinion surveys have found that very few Poles have had any savings during transition. A 1995 Demoskop survey[20] reported that only 30% of Poles had accumulated savings or some sort of financial reserves, and pensioners had virtually nothing saved.

Allocation of Consumption Expenditure

As mentioned above, the liberalization of private trade quickly eased shortages of consumer goods. However, liberalization also changed the consumer market through changing price signals, increased competition among sellers, and rapidly shifting consumption patterns. Podkaminer theorized that the exaggerated demand for food would be diverted to purchasing more, higher priced consumer goods and services. Moreover, the effects of exchange rate liberalization on the consumption of domestic and imported or importable goods would also predict a shift of consumption behaviour from domestically produced staple goods (most importantly food) to imported consumer goods, including home electronics, cars, appliances and so on. Certainly, there was a pent-up demand for durable goods by the end of 1989. If this were strong enough, even low income groups might divert spending power from food or savings to durable goods. Larger stocks of durables, and not just the flow of new accumulation, implies greater utility for the household (Górecki 1994). The household budget surveys allow a direct examination of changing consumption patterns for each of the defined household types.

Table 5.9 deflates household expenditures to 1988 prices, to give an

Table 5.9 Real monthly per capita expenditure (in PZL, 1988 prices)

	Employees	Worker-farmers	Farmers	Pensioners	Self-employed	Benefit-dependent
1988	27,582	24,487	30,001	26,623		
1989	25,888	24,421	29,989	22,831		
1990	20,699	18,955	21,073	19,242		
1991	21,713	18,147	18,530	21,338		
1992	21,261	17,580	18,070	20,404		
1993	22,516	19,011	20,531	21,936	28,067	12,073
1994	22,598	19,408	20,483	21,836	29,099	12,013
1995	22,645	20,533	22,264	22,216	29,696	11,515
1996	24,779	21,017	22,418	23,399	31,447	12,334
1997	24,932	21,104	21,735	24,170	31,673	12,178

Source: Author's calculations from data in *Rocznik Statystyczny*, various issues.

approximate measure of spending in constant terms. The table shows that 'real' consumption expenditure began to decline in 1989, by 6% for workers and 17% for pensioners but less so for farmers and worker-farmers. In 1990, there were substantial falls of about 20% across the board. Real consumption expenditures remained fairly steady between 1990 and 1995, then rose moderately in 1996–1997. Agricultural households spend less per head than urban and pensioner households. Although price indices probably caused some distortion, a cautious conclusion is that most of the fall in 'real' consumption occurred in 1989 and 1990, especially for pensioners and workers (Figure 5.3). Agricultural households, on the other hand, experienced a further fall in 1991 and still have not managed to recover to 1990 levels.

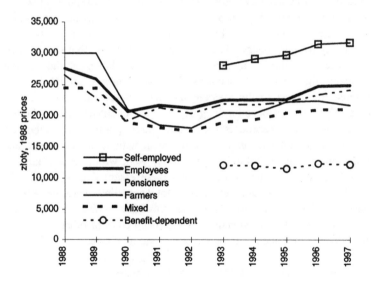

Source: Rocznik Statystyczny, various issues.

Figure 5.3 Real monthly per capita expenditure (1988 prices)

Considering the problems with real income data, consumption data provide a complementary estimate of the effects of the 'big bang' reform programme on living standards. In Tables 4.3 and 4.4 (pp. 117 and 119), real consumption expenditure in 1990 was between 19% and 42% lower than a year earlier. However, the reliance on price indices to calculate these figures suggests that they may be liable to the same sources of distortion as income data. This further re-emphasizes the role of quantitative indicators for determining real changes in economic welfare.

Budget shares

Greater detail about who was spending how much on what is available through a breakdown of total per capita monthly spending. Table 5.10 breaks down total spending into the types of goods and services purchased, with a rough estimate of basic living standards given by the proportions spent on the 'essentials': food and housing (including rents, utilities and maintenance). Between 1987 and 1990, essentials took up a moderately greater proportion of total household expenditure. Moreover, the necessities of life became relatively more expensive, especially for pensioners. On one level, the relatively high shares spent on basic expenditures in farming and benefit-dependent households indicates tightened circumstances. But the numbers should be considered in respect to the average income and spending levels across each of these socioeconomic groups. For benefit-dependent households, especially, essentials took about three-quarters of a relatively much smaller total income. In comparison with them, employee and self-employed households fared relatively well, with between half and two-thirds of spending on other than these essential goods. Essential goods are taking up a smaller share of total spending over time, even in the most deprived groups. However, this may indicate not so much increased discretionary spending as the rising costs of other previously subsidized goods such as transport, fuels and medicines.

Food as a Percentage of Total Domestic Spending

Table 5.11 shows that across all household types, most of the rise in essentials spending between 1989 and 1990 went towards food (from 38–48% of total monthly expenditures in 1989 to 48–58% in 1990). These figures are high for industrialized economies, and are at levels normally associated with very low incomes. After 1990, food accounted for the same share of worker-farmer and farmers' household spending, but less for employees and pensioners. Historically, pensioner households spend proportionately more on food than the three other

Table 5.10 Essentials as a percentage of total per capita consumption expenditure

	1987	1989	1990	1991	1993	1995	1996	1997	1998
Employees	53.8	58.1	61.1	58.1	58.2	58.0	56.4	51.0	50.9
Worker-farmers	58.9	63.1	66.2	64.2	64.5	61.6	61.3	55.0	55.2
Farmers	59.5	64.4	67.5	65.5	65.5	63.2	61.7	59.8	60.2
Pensioners	65.3	70.9	73.1	68.6	66.5	65.2	64.7	61.5	62.0
Self-employed							49.8	44.7	45.7
Non-income							66.6	63.5	59.9

Note: 'Essentials' equals food, housing, and utilities.

Source: Author's calculations from GUS data.

Table 5.11   Food as a percentage of total expenditure

| | Worker-farmers | | | Pensioners | Self- | Benefit- |
	Employees	I	Farmers	I	employed	dependent
1988	38.1	40.9	39.0	48.0		
1989	45.8	46.7	45.3	58.7		
1990	48.0	50.8	51.8	57.8		
1991	42.0	46.9	50.3	48.2		
1992	39.0	45.5	49.2	45.5		
1993	37.2	45.8	46.8	44.1	34.0	54.8
1994	34.8	42.7	43.4	41.3	30.9	50.5
1995	37.4	46.3	47.2	41.3	32.3	48.8
1996	36.8	45.7	46.5	41.7	33.3	48.1
1997	34.2	42.5	46.7	39.8	30.7	44.4
1998	31.8	42.1	47.4	37.7	28.4	39.4

Note: Monthly per capita expenditure on food as percentage of total spending on consumer commodities and services.
Source: Biuletyn Statystyczny, various issues.

panel groups, but now consumption patterns are more like employees' households. If a high share of food in total expenditure indicates low living standards, pensioners and employees appear to be faring relatively better than under socialism. Those dependent at least partly on farming tend to spend more, probably because of measurement techniques which include consumption of home-produced goods at market prices, but farming and worker-farmer households are still spending more on food than any group except the benefit-dependent.

While aggregate spending in 1990 fell by about 15%, the volume of food consumed at the household level remained fairly steady. In addition, utilities and energy charges account for a rising share of total housing costs. Spending on transport and communications increases with income (especially among self-employed households), indicating that these are 'normal goods'.[21] As shown below, there was a gradual increase in spending on durable goods (from 2.5% of private consumption in 1985 and 1989, to 3–4% in 1994).[22]

5.5 CONSUMPTION IN QUANTITIES

Food

Data on households' spending on food and other goods provide a general estimate of living standards, but the amount that is spent on food provides no real perspective on how much people were buying of what goods. Did diets improve or worsen during transition? Data on the average per capita consumption of specific foodstuffs, measured by weight or in units, give a more tangible look at households' living patterns. Moreover, these data are gathered in the same Household Budget Surveys as the income and expenditure data referred to above.

While falling calorie intake and a rising level of carbohydrates in the diet can indicate deteriorating economic conditions, it cannot be assumed that more is always better. After the Communist takeovers, Central Europeans ate relatively generous quantities of food, but it was not the healthiest diet. A disproportionate amount of nutrition came from potatoes and bread, foods normally considered to be inferior goods. There were chronic shortages of fruit and meat in the socialist economy, and quality was often substandard. The shift in consumption patterns – guided by availability, price and choice – therefore reveals as much about living standards as do changes in physical quantities.

Appendix Table 5A.3 presents average per capita consumption of basic food items across household types for the years 1986–1989 and 1990–1995. Appendix Tables 5A.4 to 5A.8 provide annual data from 1986 to 1998. Comparing averages for the latter half of the 1980s and the first half of the 1990s, it is clear that Polish households across demographic categories tended to have more fruit in their diet and slightly less bread and potatoes after the start of transition. Meat consumption was stable, except for pensioners, who bought more. The consumption of those staple goods which make up the bulk of the Polish diet – bread, potatoes, vegetables, fruit and meat – has been remarkably stable before and after 1990. Poles are eating fewer eggs and drinking less milk, but for most household types the amounts are still generous. In addition, lower consumption of some goods such as milk may not necessarily be negative: before 1990, milk was of poor quality and spoiled quickly; pasteurization and the introduction of UHT milk meant less wastage. Thus, lower measured milk consumption may not adequately reflect the improved quality of milk and dairy products (Szamuely 1996).

It appears that for most social groups in Poland, neither the January 1990 stabilization nor the subsequent transformational recession resulted in a serious deterioration in diets across society. But food consumption continues to be affected by both policy and environment. As noted above, the consumption of many foods fell for most demographic groups in 1994. Probably because of a combination of drought during the growing season and the government's price intervention policy, the annual price rise in 1994 for food (32.9%), which in the first four years of transition was outpaced by the rate of price increases for other goods and services, drew level with annual price rises for non-food goods (32%) and services (32.5%) (GUS 1995, p. 132). Market research also finds, perhaps to an even greater extent, that Poles are changing their food preferences. While more processed foods are being bought, the volume levels are still much lower than in Western Europe. For example, in 1994 sales of fruit juices and juice drinks doubled, but at 3.5 litres per person each year Polish consumption of juices is much less than the 40 litres consumed annually in Germany.[23]

Important differences in food procurement and consumption continue to exist across the socioeconomic groups. Pensioners tend to consume the greatest per capita volume of food (followed by farmers' households). Production for own use also remains important, particularly for households which combined paid employment with a smallholding. In 1992, these 'worker-farmer' households produced 45% of their food themselves, as measured by value,[24] and there has been a high and rising ownership rate of refrigerators and freezers in this group. For farming households, own production provided 53% of the total value of consumed food in 1992, compared with only 5% among employees' households. One-tenth of pensioners' food was home produced, this being more important for lower income pensioners.

The inclusion of the self-employed and unemployed from 1993 provides an interesting observation. Their total volumes of food consumption are quite similar, and are both less than in employees' households; but self-employed households not only eat more of the better goods such as vegetables, fruits, meats and fish, but they also consume more cream, cheese, eggs and sugar.

Typical of poorer households, unemployed people consume more flour, bread, potatoes and fats. This is the one group whose eating patterns are noticeably affected by low income. These households are more reliant upon staple starches, and consume less meat, fruit and vegetables per capita than other household types. This group contains relatively more children than other groups, so it may be expected that less food would be needed, but still the lower average intake of milk, fruits and vegetables provides grounds for concern. If we imagine that some of these unemployed households were formerly employed, then unemployment could potentially lead to a serious fall in basic nutrition. However, worker-farmers who lost their jobs may have had at least this aspect of economic security somewhat mitigated through production of their own food.

Consumption of Durable Goods by Volume

Previous sections referred to how the 1990 exchange rate devaluation lowered the cost of imported durable goods relative to złoty incomes. Although the household survey data do not differentiate between imported and domestically produced items, since 1990 there has been an explosion in the ownership of durable goods, which were for many years unattainable luxuries. This suggests that the impact of Poland's transformation recession on living standards was at least partly dampened by a surge in personal consumption of durable goods, even in 1990. As the transition progresses, people are replacing basic consumer goods with more sophisticated items. For instance, colour televisions are replacing black and white sets, more people have access to cable and satellite transmissions, and videocassette recorders are permeating the market. Poland has been reported to have the fourth highest density of cable television subscribers in Europe.[25] Automatic washing machines are replacing basic washing machines and spin dryers, but there are fewer sewing machines as there is now little need to make one's own clothes. Car ownership is rising and motorcycle ownership falling (bicycles, however, are undergoing a resurgence for recreation rather than just transport). Dishwashers are the one home appliance which not many households have acquired, but which are becoming more common in new and remodelled homes.

Another aspect of the social implications of this accumulation of goods is how different social groups have participated in the benefits of transition. Self-employed households have showed the most rapid acquisition of these goods, with nearly all these households possessing a car, an automatic washing machine, a VCR and colour television, and one in five having a CD player or personal computer. Employees' households have also accumulated basic and more sophisticated goods, although at marginally lower rates; there is about one car for every two employee households. Employee households includes blue-collar and white-collar workers, and a larger and wider range of the total population than the self-employed group. Most pensioner households – including lower income ones – have important labour-saving devices, including cars, but there is slower accumulation of more technological goods such as computers and CD players.

The situation in non-wage income (or, benefit-dependent and unemployed) households is rather a mixed bag. Car ownership is lower than all but pensioner households, probably because of the costs of maintaining and running a car. They also have the lowest number of colour televisions, but much greater access to satellite and cable television than farmer households, as urban households have more access to communal cable and satellite services than rural ones. Vinton (1993) quotes a 1992 Labour Ministry report which found that, of the 12.3% of Polish families which received income support, one-third owned colour televisions, one in four owned a videocassette recorder and one in five owned a car, which in 1992 was still a luxury. In the early years of transformation, ownership levels in unemployed households most probably reflected purchases made when there was a steady income source. But as time passes, this group is apparently falling further behind in terms of income and consumption.

Farmers' households have acquired durable goods, but at a slower rate than non-agrarian households and with an emphasis on more utilitarian goods. There are two cars for every three farming households; rural residents cannot always rely on public transport. There are also greater numbers of sewing machines and freezers, reflecting the importance of home-produced goods in the rural economy.

Other sources of information confirm these patterns. But as Table 5.12 shows, it makes a difference whether durable goods ownership is measured by the number of goods per 100 households, as the GUS data do now, or the percentage of households owning at least one item in each class of goods, as in a 1992 CBOS survey.[26] This helps explain why the GUS figures tend to be higher than the CBOS ones. Yet both sources show that, just two years into the transition, employees'

Table 5.12 Ownership of selected consumer goods, 1992

	State workers		Worker-farmer		Farmer		Pensioner	
	GUS	CBOS	GUS	CBOS	GUS	CBOS	GUS	CBOS
Refrigerator	99.9	98	100.9	96	98.5	90	96.3	89
Colour television	91.4	82	65.4	56	48.9	39	52.7	49
Sewing machine	57.1	60	74.9	61	67.5	51	55.6	46
Automatic washing machine	69.7	62	37.4	25	28.5	21	39.5	30
Automobile	41.4	44	49	42	41.7	35	15	14
Freezer	30.3	32	55.7	41	56.6	43	16.3	18
VCR	53.4	45	27.7	22	15.5	12	13.5	12

Note: Goods per 100 households for GUS data; percentage of households owning good for CBOS data.
Sources: CBOS 1992, 'Ekonomiczny wymiar życia codziennego', pp. 100–101; *Rocznik Statystyczny* 1993, pp. 243–244.

households possessed more electronic goods including colour televisions and VCRs, while farmers' households owned more refrigerators and freezers. Pensioners had fewer consumer durables overall, and substantially fewer cars. By contrast, the CBOS data record that 65% of self-employed households had at least one car and 90% had a colour television set; more than one in five had a computer.

Furthermore, the quantity of goods bought on credit has been rising rapidly since about 1994, during which year consumer credit rose 60%.[27] The goods most frequently bought on credit include televisions, videocassette recorders, computers, and also bicycles and cars. As Poland during the 1990s was still largely a cash economy, the expansion of consumer credit means that consumption can now be linked to future as well as current income, reflecting increasing confidence in the economy, or less uncertainty about the risk of lending to certain segments of the public. Finally, it is worth noting that consumption patterns in Poland are still not exactly like those in, for instance, European Union countries. Poles are buying cars at astonishing rates: there were nearly 7 million cars in Poland in 1995, with an estimated 10 million expected to be owned in 2000 and 15 million in 2010. However, during the first decade of transition, the vast majority of cars were purchased second hand, although new car purchases are rising as a percentage of the whole.

5.6   WHO ARE THE WINNERS AND LOSERS OF POLAND'S TRANSITION?

The first conclusion we can draw is that *self-employed households exhibit the highest living standards* of the socioeconomic groups examined. The private sector has become the engine of growth and innovation in Poland's transition to the market. Between 1992 and 1995, economic growth was almost completely accounted for by the private sector. By 1994, 96% of agriculture, 89% of retail trade, 86% of construction, 43% of transport services, 38% of manufacturing and most of Poland's foreign trade were in private hands (Bossak 1995). The number of self-employed people tripled between 1985 (575,000) and 1991 (1.63 million).[28] Taking the 1997 Household Survey panel as a guide, households in the self-employed sector account for about 7% of the population, a group far smaller than that of employees. But these figures are not absolute, and observation in the towns of Poland suggests that this group is in fact establishing a Polish 'middle class' in the more west European (economic rather than intellectual) sense of the term. Certainly, across a range of indicators self-employed households exhibit the best living standards of the six socioeconomic groups. However, there is still an inherent risk to entrepreneurship: 1993 World Bank estimates found that 8.9% of self-employed households were poor (World Bank 1995, p. 16).

Second, *living standards in benefit-dependent households are much lower than other groups and falling further behind*. This is not a large group; for 1993 the World Bank (1995) calculated that they total slightly more than 2% of all households, and in the 1997 Household Survey they formed 3% of the sample. Most of these households have been affected by unemployment. In total, 1.8 million people were registered as unemployed in December 1997, just after the last parliamentary election, and of these 70% (3% of the total population) did not qualify for unemployment benefits.[29] The concern about the benefit-dependent arises over the poor living standards and poverty in this group. Durable-goods ownership suggests that many unemployed households have relatively recently entered sub-poverty expenditure levels. A surprisingly low proportion of the unemployed *appeared* to have substantial outside earnings. A Gallup poll conducted in September 1994 found similarly low figures: in this case 9.2% of respondents had claimed unemployment benefits and worked at the same time.[30]

The World Bank poverty report (1995) suggested that job creation would make substantial inroads into alleviating this situation. At rates of job creation current at that time, it was thought that the poverty rate could have been reduced to 5% of the population by the year 2000. At present, however, various statistical sources suggest that the problem will be harder to eradicate. The number of unemployed without the right to unemployment benefits has remained persistent even though the total number of unemployed has dropped. The knock-on effects from the 1997 emerging markets crisis caused an upswing in unemployment in 1998–1999, potentially raising the poverty rate again. Although fewer in number now than in 1993, the real losers of transition continue to be the unemployed and people dependent on social transfers other than pensions.

Third, more optimistic news comes from the *relatively advantageous position of pensioners and retired persons* in the post-communist economy. Before 1989, monthly pension benefits were extremely low. During the 1990s the real value of pension payments was preserved or increased, even though the number of claimants rocketed during the first few years of transition. On average, pensioners increased their consumption of food and consumer goods and improved their income even in relation to pre-1990 deflated incomes. The difference is especially striking in comparison with the non-wage income group. Because pensioners form an important political lobby through their sheer numbers, the Polish government decoupled pension levels from other benchmarks such as the minimum wage, unlike in Russia, and so has been able to preserve or increase these payments. However, this should not overshadow the more unequal income distribution among the retired, as shown by income inequality indicators from 1990 to 1992.

Fourth, *employees are doing fairly well, but farmers have fared rather poorly.* The broad-ranging group of households dependent upon paid employment improved their material living standards over the course of the decade, but there are signs of widening gaps in labour market status. As Chapter 3 showed, there is an increasing benefit to having education and skills, conveyed through higher wages and

through fewer and shorter spells of unemployment. By contrast, farmers have suffered from a combination of factors including increased
competition from imported (and often subsidized EU) produce,
increased input prices, shifting consumer demand, rising interest rates
and several droughts, all of which have made it difficult for the small
and inefficient agricultural sector to adjust and restructure. Income in
farming households fell by more than that for employees or pensioners,
and remains highly volatile. Few farming households have increased
their ownership of advanced consumer goods as many employee and
entrepreneurs' households have done, indicating a more basic living
standard. Regional data also show a persistent income and unemployment gap between urban and rural areas of Poland, to the countryside's
disadvantage. Some farmers have carried their complaints to street
demonstrations, and, although the main peasant party, the PSL, is in a
state of disarray, the rural lobby still carries political weight.

Public Opinion on the Winners and Losers of Transition

As discussed in Chapter 2, public opinion can be used to examine
perceptions of the gains and losses associated with transition, including
asking people to evaluate their own living standards. In addition to
considering attitudes at the individual level, we can also examine
attitudes within certain demographic groups. In 1988, prior to the state
of transition, workers and pensioners expressed the most dissatisfaction
with their material situation, while skilled workers and technicians were
the most satisfied.[31] Similar patterns emerge the following year, when
unskilled workers, pensioners, the unemployed and those with elemen-
tary education were most likely to evaluate their own material living
situation as 'bad'.[32] There is a calculable benefit to skills and education, and the disadvantages of being in a lower-skill job, older and
(later on) out of work are clearly understood. They feel more vulnerable
to transition and the market economy because they are.

The same holds true, more or less, for transition's winners. Over the
1990s, Poles have tended to see private business owners as the main
winners and farmers as the main losers of transition. In 1991, three out
of four (76%) thought owners of private firms were better off
compared with two years earlier, but many also thought that former
oppositionists (52% better, 16% same, 8% worse), 'Solidarity' activists
(47% better, 23% same, 12% worse), and workers in the central state

administration (43% better, 28% same, 11% worse) were advantaged.[33]
The public perceived the greatest losers compared with 1989 to be
farmers (86% worse), unskilled workers (81%), teachers (78%) and
skilled workers (63%).

These patterns also emerge in the views of whether life is better or
worse among respondents in various demographic and professional
groups. Although these breakdowns create groups with relatively small
numbers, general patterns can be determined. First of all, between 1992
and 1999 an increasingly positive outlook appears among those best

Table 5.13   *'In general, life is better or worse' by demographic
groups (%)*

	1992		1999	
	Better	Worse	Better	Worse
Education				
Primary	28	54	32	60
Secondary	35	54	47	46
Higher	50	35	67	21
Age				
18–24	35	53	53	33
25–34	41	52	61	33
35–44	26	61	48	45
45–54	24	62	41	54
55–64	41	48	31	59
65 and older	43	33	35	57
Occupation				
White collar	44	44	66	26
Skilled labourers	29	60	51	42
Unskilled labourers	17	67	27	60
Farmers	26	63	32	64
Pensioners	38	44	35	57
Housewives	31	55	33	55
Students	67	19	65	28
Unemployed	17	75	29	64
Total	34	52	45	47

Source: Office of Research 1992, 1999.

placed to take advantage of the opportunities offered by transition: those with third-level education, people 45 years old and younger, and people in white-collar jobs (Table 5.13). The apparent link between education, age and attitudes towards transition can be explained to a large extent by individuals' relative positions in the labour market. The young and well-educated, especially those living in larger cities, are more optimistic about the benefits of the market, while those older, out of work, less-educated, and dependent on social benefits are understandably more sceptical. Those with a primary education, those over age 45, as well as unskilled workers, farmers, pensioners, housewives and the unemployed, are more negative. The case of pensioners is more interesting. Six out of ten pensioners say they are worse off now than they were under communism. Other polls show that the general public also thinks that pensioners live less well than the rest of society (for example, 70% in a 1993 CBOS poll).[34] However, the income and consumption data suggest that pensioners have generally benefited under the current system.

5.7   PARTY PREFERENCE AND SOCIOECONOMIC GROUPS

Since there is a connection between these demographic characteristics and attitudes towards the costs and benefits of transition, we can predict that there will be a similar pattern of social groups and support for political parties. For instance, the relationship of higher income and lower unemployment with support for the liberal post-communist parties suggests that these parties do better in regions with a higher concentration of professional, high-wage jobs and young people – perhaps a university town. Likewise, the low-wage region in which the peasant party gains most of its support will tend to be dominated by agriculture. Both the SLD and Solidarity parties attract support from workers, but the impact of restructuring as well as regional cultural differences may also play a part in the sharp division in support across regions. Although these patterns could apply to a fraction within each social and occupational group, it may be enough for the trend to emerge and be significant. But other factors apart from objective socioeconomic indicators such as occupation, education, class[35] and income have an impact on forming political preferences, and so this chapter looks at party preferences through more subjective questions on attitudes towards economic reform, religion and evaluations of citizens' own financial well-being.

Although there are obvious problems in using data gathered at the regional level to draw conclusions about individual behaviour, the results from analysis of thesse data can lead to some hypotheses about the socioeconomic composition of these groups. In this section, the socioeconomic composition of the parties' electorates is further tested via a range of public opinion survey data, to look for these differences at the individual level. But with a standard sample size of 1,000, the sheer number of political parties in Poland can lead to very small subsets for each party's supporters. For this reason, only the strongest relationships are reported, and even these are taken as being indicative of overall trends. For the same reason, the smaller parties such as the UP, KPN, ROP and UPR are not included. In this section, the main comparison is between the post-Solidarity parties on the one hand, and the post-communist parties on the other, but we will look for differences within both of these groups as well as between them.

The Post-Solidarity Parties

Starting with data from a series of five Office of Research surveys, as in earlier chapters it is difficult to make distinctions in support for centre-right parties in the 1991 and 1993 elections because this bloc was so fragmented (Table 5.14). In general, the post-Solidarity organizations whose deputies formed the core of the 1991–1993 coalition gained support from both urban and rural voters. These voters share an essentially positive attitude towards economic and political reform, welcome foreign investment, and accept unemployment as an 'inevitable' effect of reform. They are divided between those who prefer the public rather than private ownership of businesses, whereas the post-communist voters prefer state ownership for large firms (see below). These potential centre-right voters are satisfied with the course of political reform and with the development of democracy in Poland – more so than SDP and PSL supporters but not as much as liberal voters.

Is the centre-right based on a common constituency with interests beyond religious conservatism and anti-communism? Looking across the available economic variables, although the electorate was still

Table 5.14 Socioeconomic patterns of support for the centre-right (%)

	1990 Wałęsa	1991 PC	1991 'S'	1993 BBWR	1993 'S'	1993 ZChN	1995 Wałęsa	1997 AWS
Total	40	4	5	3	4	3	20	31
Higher white-collar	37	4	2	2	0	4	18	19
Lower management	n/a	n/a	n/a	2	2	0	18	18
Clerical, white-collar workers	42	3	1	0	6	2	n/a	32
Skilled workers	39	7	0	5	5	1	17	34
Unskilled workers	35	0	4	3	5	3	20	33
Farmers	49	0	0	0	0	2	21	29
Pensioners	42	5	2	3	5	6	25	36
Unemployed	n/a	n/a	n/a	3	3	3	13	31
Elementary	44	4	2	2	4	5	25	36
Secondary	39	5	5	3	4	2	19	32
University	31	6	3	3	1	2	32	18
Male	39	4	5	3	4	3	19	33
Female	40	5	4	2	3	3	20	30
Urban	41	6	5	n/a	n/a	n/a	20	33
Rural	40	1	3	n/a	n/a	n/a	19	30

18–24	29	5	3	0	5	3	14	29
25–34	38	3	3	4	4	2	14	26
35–49	42	5	5	3	2	0	20	31
50–64	38	5	5	2	5	3	23	34
Over 65	52	4	6	4	5	9	35	37
EU membership for/against	n/a	n/a	n/a	84/17	78/10	60/11	n/a	84/6
NATO membership for/against	n/a	n/a	n/a	42/ 4	65/10	63/0	87/5	83/7
Economy now better/worse	n/a	n/a	n/a	67/29	55/42	41/37	72/22	68/18
Free market economy right/wrong	n/a	n/a	n/a	54/46	55/39	37/44	53/24	53/26
Radical or gradual economic reform	33/46	9/87	24/71	n/a	n/a	n/a	n/a	n/a
Private/state ownership	46/41	45/52	33/65	46/50	48/48	44/44	50/46	24/67
Foreign investment good/bad	39/41	67/24	59/35	58/38	39/48	33/30	48/40	44/45
Unemployment inevitable/preventable	n/a	43/55	22/72	30/71	52/45	59/38	n/a	n/a
Political system better/worse	n/a	n/a	n/a	71/21	64/17	69/12	71/25	67/20
Importance of God in daily life	74/19	n/a	n/a	n/a	n/a	n/a	n/a	n/a
Church too involved in politics	n/a	62/36	65/28	63/38	55/42	22/74	48/48	50/47
Number	395	46	42	24	31	27	193	294

Source: Author's calculations from Office of Research data.

Table 5.15   Socioeconomic patterns of support for UD, KLD and UW (%)

	1990 Mazowiecki	1991 UD	1993 UD	1993 KLD	1995 Kuroń	1997 UW
Total	16	11	11	3	6	18
Higher white-collar	25	26	28	10	11	33
Lower management	n/a	n/a	8	2	0	34
Clerical, white-collar workers	9	15	13	5	n/a	24
Skilled workers	32	6	11	3	5	14
Unskilled workers	5	9	16	0	13	15
Farmers	3	0	0	0	2	7
Pensioners	13	9	8	3	6	12
Unemployed	n/a	6	9	4	13	22
Elementary	8	5	6	1	7	9
Secondary	16	10	11	4	5	19
University	37	34	24	6	8	33
Male	16	11	10	4	8	15
Female	15	11	11	3	5	19
Urban	19	15	82	100	7	21
Rural	10	5	18	0	6	14

18–24	18	10	11	3	8	22
25–34	14	11	12	6	6	24
35–49	16	12	13	3	6	18
50–64	18	13	9	5	6	14
Over 65	6	9	8	1	4	10
EU membership for/against	n/a	n/a	95/3	89/3	n/a	87/7
NATO membership for/against	n/a	n/a	94/2	79/7	78/10	72/13
Economy now better/worse	n/a	n/a	68/24	45/41	47/50	82/12
Free market economy right/wrong	n/a	n/a	71/26	66/31	48/28	69/17
Radical or gradual econ reform	40/48	23/74	n/a	n/a	n/a	n/a
Private/state ownership	44/51	55/43	62/37	55/41	37/58	40/53
Foreign investment good/bad	50/37	60/31	64/34	52/41	43/52	63/32
Unemployment inevitable/ preventable	n/a	35/60	31/69	31/65	40/60	n/a
Political system better/worse	n/a	n/a	75/22	79/21	63/27	80/13
Importance of God in daily life	61/30	n/a	n/a	n/a	n/a	n/a
Church too involved in politics	n/a	83/16	69/32	76/21	75/22	70/25
Number	155	113	78	17	60	164

Source: Author's calculations from Office of Research data.

161

fragmented in 1993, there is a fairly consistent relationship with higher employment rates but (to a lesser extent) lower income, and, excepting the POC electorate, an increased relationship with rural areas and agriculture, and also less support from the new private sector, represented by figures for the trade and retail sector. There are signs that there is an electorate open to nationalistic, protectionist and interventionist policies, among industrial workers in smaller towns and cities and among farmers. In general, centre-right voters can be divided into conservative and liberal factions. More centrist voters are concentrated in urban areas with average income. Those who prefer the more conservative parties including 'Solidarity' and the Christian nationalists are drawn from both city and country, the former with more male supporters and the latter more female.

By contrast, the liberal post-communist parties have not gathered as much popular support as many originally hoped. Over the past decade, their support has been concentrated among people who express a commitment to market reform, accession to European and international organizations, and political pluralism. This is one of the most clearly defined electorates in Poland. Support for these parties is nearly non-existent in the small towns and villages of 'Poland B', especially where unemployment has been higher than average. Demographically and normatively, UD and KLD supporters in 1991 and 1993 shared many characteristics, and after their merger in 1994 it appears that much of their core support was preserved. These parties attract primarily urban voters, white-collar workers and professionals, people with a university education, and those who are optimistic about their own economic situation (Table 5.15). Although white-collar voters give a proportionately greater share of their support to these parties, all occupational groups are represented to some extent. Other studies have found that support for the UW at the *gmina* level is strongly related to the number of new enterprises which are opened; support for the PSL is also negatively related to the entry of new firms.[36]

While their perspective on current economic performance is not any more positive than the overall public's, those who backed the liberal parties are strongly in favour of the market economy, foreign investment and the private ownership of most businesses. Split between those 'somewhat satisfied' and 'somewhat dissatisfied' with the course of market reform, the liberal electorate is somewhat more likely to accept some level of unemployment if it furthers economic adjustment. The democratic system is also rated more highly by liberal voters than by others, and they tend to be more socially liberal than those on the centre-right. More like SLD voters, those favouring the UD and the KLD were more likely to attend religious services 'a few times a year', in contrast to the more frequent practice among the centre-right and PSL voters. A large majority also reject nationalist statements and ideas. While not dogmatic in their views on economic reform, they were more confident in its main elements and more assured that they would soon benefit from the changes.

Comparing the two post-Solidarity blocs, it emerges that the centre-right parties were generally more successful than liberal parties among rural voters. Liberal parties attracted support from all age groups, but particularly the young, while centre-right voters tend over time to be older. By occupation, the centre-right has a higher than proportional share of skilled workers and pensioners, while the liberal parties attract more professionals and higher level white-collar workers. Despite the demographic differences between the supporters of these three parties, the public opinion data indicate that they share an essentially positive attitude towards economic and political reform. They are divided between those who prefer the public and private ownership of businesses (in contrast to supporters of post-communist parties, as shown below), but say that foreign investment can have a necessary and positive influence on development. A key difference within the group is based on social differences, with parties such as the WAK and Solidarity tending to gain the more socially conservative vote, but the POC and the BBWR taking a somewhat more liberal economic position. There are also varying levels of nationalist and pro-Catholic attitudes.

The Post-Communist Parties

Prior to the 1993 election, the number of respondents who declared their support for Cimoszewicz or the SdRP was so low as to make the results presented in columns 1 and 2 in Table 5.16 amount to little more than a straw poll. However, we can approach the data as indicative of trends rather than as statistically significant.

The SLD electorate is generally divided among urban and rural voters in proportions equivalent to the overall population, but with marginally more support from women – an electorate which the SLD particularly targeted in 1997. SLD supporters also had average income

Table 5.16   Socioeconomic patterns of support for SdRP and SLD (%)

	1990 Cimoszewicz	1991 SdRP	1993 SdRP	1995 Kwaśniewski	1997 SLD
Total	5	3	12	28	22
Higher white-collar	5	4	14	26	16
Lower management	n/a	n/a	23	23	28
Clerical, white-collar workers	3	4	16	n/a	18
Skilled workers	3	3	14	37	25
Unskilled workers	4	4	5	30	15
Farmers	5	1	2	19	17
Pensioners	6	1	10	25	21
Unemployed	n/a	4	8	31	19
Elementary	4	2	7	22	17
Secondary	4	3	15	30	24
University	7	5	14	32	23
Male	3	3	15	29	23
Female	6	2	9	27	21
Urban	4	2	n/a	30	22
Rural	5	3		25	21

18–24	6	2	12	24	20
25–34	3	2	9	36	23
35–49	5	3	15	27	21
50–64	4	3	15	30	25
Over 65	3	1	7	18	20
EU membership for/against	n/a	n/a	83/11	n/a	81/12
NATO membership for/against	n/a	n/a	72/23	79/11	83/9
Economy now better/worse	n/a	n/a	34/60	46/47	55/32
Free market economy right/wrong	n/a	n/a	55/34	54/29	59/29
Radical or gradual economic reform	20/76	0/77	n/a	n/a	n/a
Private/state ownership	20/64	15/81	23/71	38/59	21/73
Foreign investment good/bad	29/60	35/50	46/47	44/50	46/47
Unemployment inevitable/ preventable	n/a	4/92	46/54	60/40	n/a
Political system better/worse	n/a	n/a	64/26	51/38	50/41
Importance of God in daily life	55/27	n/a	n/a	n/a	n/a
Church too involved in politics	n/a	88/8	80/19	88/10	86/11
Number	45	26	101	273	204

Source: Author's calculations from Office of Research data.

Table 5.17 Socioeconomic patterns of support for PSL (%)

	1990 Bartoszcze	1991 PSL	1993 PSL	1995 Pawlak	1997 PSL
Total	4	2	23	5	6
Higher white-collar	1	0	17	5	3
Lower management	n/a	n/a	11	4	2
Clerical, white-collar workers	2	1	19	n/a	4
Skilled workers	3	0	23	3	4
Unskilled workers	4	0	18	3	3
Farmers	14	10	64	15	33
Pensioners	5	3	25	8	7
Unemployed	n/a	0	21	3	6
Elementary	8	4	29	9	11
Secondary	3	2	22	4	5
University	0	1	14	3	2
Male	3	2	23	5	6
Female	5	2	23	5	7
Urban	1	1	n/a	9	3
Rural	9	4	n/a	3	11

18–24	0	3	11	5	3
25–34	5	2	21	4	10
35–49	3	1	22	5	5
50–64	4	4	26	5	7
Over 65	6	3	27	10	7
EU membership for/against	n/a	n/a	79/11	n/a	71/18
NATO membership for/against	n/a	n/a	75/10	69/16	78/6
Economy now better/worse	n/a	n/a	36/59	28/53	44/44
Free market economy right/wrong	n/a	n/a	45/44	43/37	47/41
Radical or gradual economic reform	8/61	5/82	n/a	n/a	n/a
Private/state ownership	26/58	36/64	25/68	24/73	12/83
Foreign investment good/bad	18/58	50/46	36/53	24/65	34/54
Unemployment inevitable/preventable	n/a	9/82	54/46	n/a	n/a
Political system better/worse	n/a	n/a	61/30	41/45	41/42
Importance of God in daily life	76/16	n/a	n/a	n/a	n/a
Church too involved in politics	n/a	82/14	68/28	59/39	68/22
Number	38	22	103	51	59

Source: Author's calculations from Office of Research data.

167

levels, but often a higher than average educational attainment, and those who were employed were twice as likely than the overall sample to be employed in the public sector (or 'budżetówka'); another one in three were pensioners.

In terms of economic outlook, nearly half of SLD supporters said that the creation of a 'free market economy ... largely free of state control' was *wrong* for Poland's future. Large majorities preferred most enterprises to remain in state ownership, and said that the state should not allow unemployment, even at the cost of slowing aggregate growth. They were also slightly more negative than positive regarding foreign investment. They tended to be less satisfied with the course of economic reform, and more likely than the average to say that both Poland's economy and their own household's financial situation were 'bad'. In fact, more than eight out of ten said that the current economic situation in general was *worse* than that under communism. It can be assumed that a proportion of this negative reaction against the costs of reform, especially for older citizens who had more difficulties in adjusting to reform, was transferred into votes for the SLD.

While six out of ten Poles generally agreed that the current democratic political system was better than that under communism, SLD supporters were almost evenly split between those who thought it was better and those who considered it worse. People who backed the SLD were also more likely to be dissatisfied with the progress made towards democracy in Poland. People who favoured the SLD in the pre-election poll were also less likely to attend church more than a few times a year, and were more likely to disagree with nationalist statements such as 'Poland is only for the Poles'.

The other party consistently represented in parliament with roots in the communist political system is the PSL. Altogether, agrarian parties attracted 15% of all votes in the 1991 election (8.7% for the PSL; 5.5% for the PL, whose voters tended to be concentrated in regions sympathetic to Solidarity such as the south-east), but in 1993 the PSL worked to consolidate the farming vote and widen its electorate across the country, except in Warsaw, Łódź, Katowice, Białystok and Gdańsk.

Survey data show that three out of four PSL supporters in 1993 were rural residents, and were more likely to be male than female (Table 5.17). Most have below average household income and a primary or vocational education. Apart from a small minority who worked in the state sector, most others were private farmers or pensioners. On a number of economic issues – including approval of the market economy (half each for and against), evaluations of the current state of the economy (three out of four said it was 'bad'), and dissatisfaction with the course of economic reform (one in three satisfied, six out of ten dissatisfied) – the attitudes of PSL supporters were similar to those of the general public. However, they were slightly more likely than average to oppose open unemployment and foreign investment, more favourable to state over private ownership of firms, and more likely to say that the economy was worse than under communism (compared with the public in general, who have become more positive).

Regarding democracy, the PSL's electorate was less satisfied than supporters of post-Solidarity parties but more positive than SLD voters concerning the progress made towards democracy; more than half thought that the present political system was better than the previous one. Moreover, half (slightly more than the average) agreed with nationalist statements such as 'Poland is only for the Poles'. One of the most distinct characteristics of the post-communist electorate is a dissatisfaction with the progress made towards democracy in Poland, and an emphatic agreement that the Church is too involved in politics.

In some respects, such as attitudes towards private property, evaluations of future economic performance and attitudes towards democratization, supporters of peasant parties (primarily the PSL) are similar to post-Solidarity parties. In other respects, primarily attitudes toward micro-level economic policies, they are more interventionist. For instance, although most of these farmers clearly identified themselves as part of the private sector, like SdRP and SLD voters they tend to prefer gradual to radical reform, they preferred state ownership for the majority of businesses, and they were divided over the desirability of foreign investment. Similarly, PSL supporters were relatively more negative about the economy and their own financial situation, and said that the government should prevent unemployment from emerging (rather than accepting it as an inevitable consequence of reform).

One exception was that, like the three main centre-right parties, PSL supporters agreed that 'private property is necessary for economic progress' and that 'in the long run, everyone is better off' under the market economy – unlike a majority of SdRP supporters. Additionally, a sizeable majority of peasant party voters are closer to the post-Solidarity parties in their attitudes towards the democratic transition: a degree of satisfaction with the progress made towards democracy and with the political change in general. As the transition progressed, there appeared, first, to be a popularization of the party. Then, as non-farmers left for other parties, there was a focusing on a more radical agrarian agenda. Eventually, after the 1997 elections the PSL was left so divided and uninfluential that in early 1999 the political initiative had apparently passed to *Samoobrona*. Of some of the smaller parties, Moczułski's party, the KPN, ran on a strongly nationalistic and protectionist stance and received 7.5% of the total vote in the 1991 election. However, none of the given socioeconomic variables from the regional data produces robust results.

NOTES

1. The Central Statistical Office (GUS) gathers the data for this survey, via a quarterly rotation method between 1982 and 1992, and via a monthly rotating random sample since 1993. The sample is weighted to reflect the socio-demographic structure of the population. In 1993, disposable income was added to the income category. Full methodological notes are provided in the annual publication *Budżety Gospodarstw Domowych*.
2. Prior to 1992, this covered employees in state enterprises, cooperatives, social and political organizations and trade unions. From 1993, private sector employment was also included. The distortive effect of this is surprisingly not particularly large. First, this is because private sector wages did not greatly outpace state sector wages during the first three years of transition; in fact, it may have depressed total income. In addition, employee data are divided into blue- and white-collar workers in the original source.
3. GUS, 1993, *Budżety Gospodarstw Domowych w 1992 r.*, p. xxiii.
4. This, in turn, led to the three-pillar system introduced on 1 January 1999.
5. Office of the Government Plenipotentiary for Social Security Reform (1997).
6. Calculated as a straight average rather than in equivalent values.
7. *Chłopo-robotnicy*, who typically combined paid employment (that is, in a factory) with running a small, private farm. Under the socialist system, they did quite well. Davies (1984, p. 56) wrote: 'Many such families living in the fringe of the great industrial regions have the best of both possible worlds – a high cash income all the year round, a cheap supply of home-grown food, and an independent base. They are prosperous and relatively secure.'
8. Probably this stems from the increasing disparity in pensioners' incomes and the appearance of a group of very poor pensioners.
9. One way of measuring this gap is through the returns to education. In 1987, the ratio of wage disparity between university and primary education was 1.34. In other words, people with a third-level education earned about one-third more than manual workers. In 1992, the ratio was 1.56. In 1993, the return of university to primary education was 1.66 in the state sector and 2.13 in the private sector (World Bank 1995). Other studies (for example, Kudrycka 1993) confirm that education is the most important factor in explaining wage inequality among employees.
10. And these reported incomes were only half of the average state-sector wage.

11. Since 1993, data are also given on income from self-employment, including both income from work and imputed income from activities such as making repairs to one's own home.
12. Also, there is the factor of the change in the composition of the employee panel from 1993. See also a response to this paper focusing on the role of relative prices (Milanovic 1997).
13. Roberts (1993) proposed a quantification of these gains.
14. J. Kornai, panel discussion in A. Kelley *et al.*, *Modeling Growing Economies in Equilibrium and Disequilibrium* (Durham, NC, 1983), as quoted in Podkaminer (1987, p. 509).
15. For a description of how wage increases transfer into monetary overhang, see Sections 2.2–2.4 of Sahay and Végh (1995).
16. In Russia, both President Yeltsin and the Communist Party leader Gennadi Zyuganov endorsed campaign programmes to compensate people for savings eroded by inflation, presumably referring to savings before the January 1992 price liberalization (*OMRI Daily Digest*, Part I, No. 55, 18 March 1996).
17. *Rocznik Statystyczny*, 1992, table 25(248), p. 149.
18. National Bank of Poland, 1994, *Information Bulletin*, p. 71.
19. Data are not presented for 1993 and after because of methodological changes.
20. 'Polaków autoportret ekonomiczny', *Rzeczpospolita*, 1-2 July 1995, p. 4.
21. *Budżety Gospodarstw Domowych w 1994 r.*, 1995, p. 80.
22. *Rocznik Statystyczny*, 1990, p. 202; *Mały Rocznik Statystyczny 1994*, p. 118.
23. 'Wielkie Zakupy', *Wprost*, 14 May 1995, p. 37.
24. GUS, *Budżety Gospodarstw Domowych w 1991 r.*, 1992, table 7(24).
25. *Donosy*, 4 February 1997.
26. CBOS, 1992, 'Ekonomiczny wymiar życia codziennego', pp. 100–101.
27. 'Jak się żyje w rodzine i w regionach', *Rzeczpospolita*, 30 June 1995.
28. *Rocznik Statystyczny*, 1992, p. 96; *Mały Rocznik Statystyczny*, 1995, p. 330.
29. *Biuletyn Statystyczny*, 1998, No. 9 (491), October, pp. 20 and 49.
30. 'Polak oszukuje', *Polityka*, 8 November 1994.
31. CBOS, 1988, 'Zmiany w ocenach warunków życia', Report BDF/346, May, pp. 7-8.
32. CBOS, 1990, 'Opinie o standardzie życia ludności', Report 660/90, September, p. 12.
33. CBOS, 1991, 'Komu powodzi się lepiej a komu gorzej?,' Report 822/91, December.
34. Results from a 1993 CBOS survey, 'Aktualne problemy i wydarzenia', conducted 9-14 December 1993 from a representative sample of 1,239 adult Poles.
35. Obtained by grouping occupational categories into four groups: white-collar (white-collar workers, trade and service sector professional, professionals working in the cultural sector, civil servants, and students), skilled workers and artisans, unskilled workers, and those outside employment (pensioners, housewives and farmers). These groupings were first formed, then tested using disaggregated data, with the results confirming the voting patterns which characterize each group.
36. J. Hryniewicz, 1998, 'Bariery Dostatku', conversation with E. Cichocka, *Gazeta Wyborcza*, 9 October 1998, pp. 26–27.

6. Winners, Losers and Party Preferences

Public acceptance of Poland's move to the market economy and a democratic political system was assisted by the deep sense of crisis in the late 1980s. Although the subsequent transition has been more costly than expected, and although many have been critical of its costs, there is a growing public mood which sees that the present system has definite advantages over socialism. But not all groups in society have been equally affected by transition. Even prior to the 1990 'big bang', Poles perceived that farmers and low-skilled workers were most vulnerable to change, whereas highly skilled workers, professionals, entrepreneurs – and those with good connections – would be among the winners. The empirical data on income, consumption and unemployment reinforce this perception, while also showing that estimates using price deflators can overestimate the drop in living standards. At the level of the citizen, not only do individual perceptions of the net balance of wins and losses generally accord with the empirical status of different occupational and demographic groups, but there are identifiable and consistent patterns in regional and individual experience and party preferences.

This chapter reflects on the foregoing analysis to propose some thoughts on how the economy and ideology interact to influence voting behaviour. Do 'winners' and 'losers' vote differently, and if so, why? Having seen that there is consistency in public attitudes towards the present political and economic systems, the question now is how this affects people's behaviour in the polling booth. Some ideas about the dynamics of party support during transition are made, followed by conclusions.

6.1   THE SLD–AWS SPLIT: ECONOMIC OR IDEOLOGICAL?

The sharp and infrequently bridged divide between supporters of the post-communist party now organized under the Democratic Left Alliance(SLD) and the post-Solidarity centre-right currently gathered in Solidarity Electoral Action (AWS) is observable from a number of angles. At the regional and the individual levels, supporters of the centre-right are unlikely to back the SLD as their second choice party, and vice versa. Subotic (1997) reported how 74% of the SLD and 70% of the AWS electorates could be considered 'hard', and that their party choice was unlikely to change. Of the quarter or so who indicated that they might vote for another party, only 1% of AWS voters surveyed said they might vote for the SLD, and no SLD supporters said they might switch their vote to the AWS.

Furthermore, there is a distinct difference in attitudes towards transition among these two blocs' supporters. Individuals more critical of the impact of transition on themselves and on the economy at large tend to prefer post-communist parties, while those who are more positive about reform tend to favour the post-Solidarity parties. Observation of the political scene in Poland strongly suggests that these factors are interrelated, and that the key organizing idea in public perceptions is the ideological contest between the Polish variant of left and right.

An initial way of looking for this type of pattern is presented in Table 6.1, in which the strongest individual variables which emerged in the factor analysis (Appendix Table 6A.1) are used to examine AWS compared with SLD supporters. The focus is on this split because of the very limited overlap (see Subotic 1997), and because, as the two largest political groups in the current Sejm, they are the main competitors in the political arena. In this three-way cross-tabulation, individuals are grouped first by their views on whether life now is better or worse than under communism, and second by their opinion on the role of religious values in society. The columns show what percentage in each group support either the SLD or the AWS. To capture the SLD–AWS divide, a dummy variable was created of those who said they would be likely to vote for the SLD (0) and those likely to vote for the AWS (1). In the 1999 sample, 41% of respondents chose one of these two parties; supporters of other parties are omitted.

Table 6.1   Life now versus under communism

	Life is worse Religious values (%)				Life is better Religious values (%)			
	--	-	+	++	--	-	+	++
SLD	95.7	76.1	72.1	54.5	69.7	60.5	36.5	12.5
AWS	4.3	23.9	27.9	45.5	30.3	39.5	63.5	87.5

Source: Office of Research 1999.

In this selected group, those who say life is worse tend to prefer the SLD (75%) over the AWS (25%); the gap is narrower among those who say life is better (55% prefer the AWS, 45% the SLD). But a strong linear relationship also exists in the question of a greater role for religious values in society. There are more SLD than AWS supporters among those who say life is better but oppose a greater role for religion in society (70% versus 30%), and there are proportionately even more AWS backers among those who say life is better and favour more influence of religious values (88% against 13% SLD). Of those who say life now is worse and who oppose religious values in society, nearly all (96%) support the SLD over the AWS.

Another way of looking at the relationship between satisfaction with the present system and voting behaviour is through regressing party preference (AWS–SLD) as the dependent variable against the factor scores obtained through the factor analysis (Appendix Table 6A.1). Here, too, the main division between the post-communist left and the post-Solidarity right in Poland lies along the cleavage of self-defined winners and losers. Factor 1, comparing the present situation with that before 1989, is the strongest in terms of the coefficient, significance and fit. Again, AWS supporters tend to evaluate the present system as better than the previous one, whereas SLD supporters are more critical.

Religion (Factor 2) also plays an important role, with more support for religious values in public life associated with support for the AWS. SLD supporters are more secular minded. Furthermore, there is a divide between these two electorates, with the AWS demonstrating relatively less political alienation (Factor 4). Alienation is closely tied in to satisfaction with the present system (correlation = –0.61).[1] However, support for religious values is correlated with neither alienation (0.06,

$p = 0.23$) nor with life being better now (-0.04, $p = 0.44$). But religious values are correlated with support for AWS over SLD (0.36), which helps to explain why the 'religion' factor shows up as more significant than the 'alienation' factor in the regressions. In addition, the centre-right's more favourable attitude towards the European Union and NATO membership (Factor 3) also has an impact, but at a lower level of significance than the religious values factor.

The dependent variable can also be defined more widely, to include on the one hand the likely supporters of the two parties which participated in the previous coalition government, the SLD and the PSL (0), and on the other hand the two parties which governed together from the 1997 election until mid-2000, the AWS and the UW (1).[2] When this dependent variable is run in a logit regression, using the same factor scores as in the previous regression, the variable based on favourable attitudes towards the current situation versus socialism performs even more strongly than before (Appendix Table 2A.2). However, the widened electorate somewhat blunts the explanatory power of religion, although it is still strongly significant. The factors for life now and for accession to western organizations are stronger than for just the two parties alone, whereas the alienation factor weakens somewhat and the religious factor remains significant but with a lower coefficient. The electorates for the UW and the PSL will also fluctuate more than AWS or SLD support. This is shown in the survey results (Subotic 1997), where only half (54% UW; 53% PSL) of these electorates can be considered 'hard', with the remaining 'soft' electorate liable to switch their vote – UW to UP (18%) and AWS (14%), and PSL to ROP (14%), with smaller percentages distributed across most of the other national parties. Part of this is undoubtedly for strategic voting purposes, but also the narrower appeal of each party may make it harder to retain new support as economic conditions change.

6.2   VOTING PREFERENCES UNDER UNCERTAINTY

Given this extensive evidence on actual voting behaviour and declared party preferences, how can we conceptualize the decision making that goes into this choice? This section introduces one approach to thinking about voting behaviour in circumstances of uncertainty about the true state of the economy and the optimal set of policies to advance. First, however, it is useful to consider the two main cleavages in Poland's party structure in greater detail.

It is widely agreed that the main divisions in the Polish party system are into (1) the (post-Solidarity) right and the (post-Communist) left, and (2) a socioeconomic split between market advocates and those favouring a larger role for the state in the economy. Although these are far from uniform blocs of either politicians or voters, enough characteristics emerge to allow a number of cleavages (Catholic and secular, nationalist and pluralist, critical and accepting of the past system) to be covered by this divide. Markowski (1997, p. 231) finds that, although religion, economics and national questions influence left–right placement, the effect compared with that in other Visegrad countries appears blunted by the polarization between Solidarity and post-communist forces. Jasiewicz (2000, pp. 112–113) likens the ideological repolarization of politics in 1997 to Sartori's 'polarized pluralism', where too many parties are separated by a 'significant ideological distance'.

Overall, the evidence points to a consistent – although not unanimous – tendency for this split to be echoed in the fundamental attitudes towards reform: is the economy better or worse, is the political system better or worse, are living standards better or worse, and how has your own household been affected? The ideological component does not contradict the economic divide, and although there is not a complete overlap and while it can be difficult to define the four main blocs as pro-market or interventionist, there is some consistency in attitudes among those individuals and social groups which are better or worse prepared to cope with the changes of the past decade.

The regressions in Chapters 3–5 analysed income, unemployment and other economic influences on voting behaviour, because, as discussed in Chapter 1, the assumption is that support for reforms is linked to individuals' welfare. 'Winners' will support reforms while 'losers' will ask for reforms to be slowed down or interventionist actions to be taken to reduce or level the costs of transition. The main mechanism for the political expression of each group's preferences is voting.

Persson and Tabellini (1994) define three main purposes of elections for voters. The first is to control the behaviour of elected policy makers: if the incumbent's performance turns out to be disappointing, then he or she will not be re-elected, thus losing the value which politicians derive from being in office. Second, elections enable voters to choose the most competent policy makers, for instance as in political business cycle models by linking pre-election expansionary policies with competence: expansion would be too costly for an incompetent politician who would be unable to reverse the policy after the election, and thus incompetent politicians are unlikely to expand the economy prior to the election (Rogoff 1990). The third purpose of elections is to enable the public to choose a policy maker with ideological preferences closer to those of the majority.

A complicating factor is that Poland's multi-party parliamentary system makes strictly defined models of the median voter type difficult to apply, if the model depends on a yes-or-no choice – whether or not to adopt a reform – as embodied in two competing parties. There are various ways of approaching this issue. Lopez Murphy and Sturzenegger (1994) have parties display different strategic behaviour, with ideological and pragmatic preferences given varying weights, but in this case voting entails a mode of decision making rather than a political orientation.

During the early to mid-1990s, a lack of crystallization of economic interests because of the rapidly changing and highly uncertain environment was targeted as one of the causes for the confusing and frag-mented party structure and the public's lack of affiliation to any one party. Models assume that reforms are welfare-improving in the long run. In the real world, if carried out effectively, this also holds true. But in addition to the improbability of accurately forecasting the depth and duration of the recession associated with transition, uncertainty also arises from the *distributive* consequences of reform. This lack of certainty over the post-reform distribution of costs and benefits is identified in the political economy literature as an important factor in the generation and maintenance of support for reform. In Alesina and Drazen's 'war of attrition' model (1991), interest groups resist stabili-zation until the burden of necessary fiscal reform falls on another group. Policies which are known to be unsustainable can none the less be continued for a long time if no single group is able to transfer the costs of reform to another group. Delays arise as each group tries to wait out the others. Stabilization will be achieved only when one groups concedes and assumes a disproportionate share of the costs of reform. In addition, polarized groups tend to feed off each other, as the higher the degree of political polarization, the longer it is before the economy will stabilize.

Uncertainty about transition's winners and losers is explained in Fernandez and Rodrik (1991) as 'individual-specific uncertainty'. The public will initially be opposed to reform because those who start out as 'losers' cannot know with certainty whether the reform will make them winners or whether they will still turn out losers, or even lose more. So the median voter will prefer the *status quo* over reform so long as there is uncertainty about the welfare impact of the programme. Political support is therefore lowered by the incompleteness of information, and the uncertainty over the identities of winners and losers can prevent the adoption of efficiency-enhancing reforms, even if a majority were to gain over the longer run, at the outset of reforms it is not known with any certainty who will move from the group of 'losers' to 'winners' as a result of the changes. If the public is biased against reforms, it may be difficult to enact the needed policies (under a democratic system) until a sufficient quorum of winners can push the burden of adjustment on to the losers, or until the majority calculates that the lack of reform has become much more costly than continued delay. Alternatively, a reform programme could be imposed, either by an autocrat or by a government, both of which would rely on their ability to weather public protest against the transitional costs of reform.

But ultimately, once the reformed economy starts to provide net benefits, interest groups will come to support the measure which they previously opposed. Voters can switch their support, with those originally opposed to the reform approving of it if they are revealed to be winners. Furthermore, different socioeconomic groups can reach different estimates of their probability of winning or losing. For example, workers could weigh the probability of becoming winners by the likely demand for their skills in the new environment. Individual uncertainty can exist even where aggregate uncertainty is absent, and individual uncertainty can accumulate and thus distort aggregate preferences.

In the Polish case, however, the first and second possibilities were not political impediments to reform in 1989. As shown in Chapter 2, there was a large political consensus in favour of reform. In the face of economic collapse, the aggregate preference was for radical stabilization and liberalization. Yet there was a great deal of uncertainty about the risks of the process and whether all would share in progress. After the 1989 semi-free election, the Solidarity-led government carried an enormous level of political capital, what Balcerowicz (1994) called the period of 'extraordinary politics'. The policy makers were granted a very high level of discretion to form and conduct policy, with the added benediction (and domestically useful constraint) of the international financial institutions.

Given the nature of transition in Poland, it might be useful to consider what can be termed an 'anti-*status quo* bias model'. In this perspective, the majority of the population is in favour of reforms prior to their implementation and for a short time after reform begins. But as the costs of transition make themselves felt, those who have sustained losses may turn against the continuation of reform. If the public knew beforehand with certainty that this would be the distribution of gains and losses, a majority would not support the reform. In this sense, some individuals who fall into the 'loser' category after the event may have been wrong in overestimating the future benefits of reform.

The public opinion data presented in Chapter 2 show that there was a dip in public evaluations of the state of the economy, its prospects, or its advantages relative to the socialist-era economy which roughly aligned with the drop in GDP and rise in unemployment during Poland's 'transformational recession'. Again, in the 1998–1999 downturn, there has been some weakening in the support for rapid reforms, but the Polish public remains generally more positive and more optimistic than publics in other Central European countries. However, nearly half the public still perceive themselves to be in the 'loser' category, although there has been a rise in the proportion of 'winners' over the past decade. But this raises questions about what it means to be a loser – does it mean that one is quantifiably worse off than before the reform, for reasons directly connected with the reform itself and not for personal or exogenous reasons, or can one be a loser by failing to gain as much as initially expected, or even if one has gained less than one's neighbour? Costs (or lack of benefit) that are too great, last too long, or are distributed too unevenly may function as a loss which induces voters to back retarded reforms. The sense from preceding chapters is that most who consider themselves losers really have sustained deteriorations in their living standards. But it is also likely that perceptions of loss can be greater than the actual loss in income or consumption. For instance, a consumer could complain about the price of oranges when a few years ago there were no oranges to be had in retail shops.

The distributive question in this framework aligns with the previous chapters' association of uncertainty with socioeconomic status.

Through their voting preferences, workers, farmers, professionals and the unemployed (among others) display concentrations of policy preferences which appear to be oriented towards advancing their own welfare, even if the burden of transition then becomes shifted more on to someone else.

There are economic grounds for dissatisfaction with reform after the event, rooted in erroneous assumptions about what liberalization and stabilization would actually do. Under late socialism, private sector activity (frequently grey or black) was often extraordinarily profitable because private traders and other private economic actors exploited the distortions caused by administrative controls and subsidies. If the public's idea of reform was mainly that of liberalization, there may have been an expectation that this highly profitable private sector would be simply opened up to all takers. However, once liberalization took effect, these distortions largely disappeared. Another source of disillusion – one which has again raised its head under the present AWS government – is that a Solidarity-led government would formalize state sector workers' 'entitlements' to their firms' property into actual ownership of either shares or control rights. This assumption may be rooted in the *de facto* exercise of property rights by workers' councils. If the reforms turned out to be neither as enfranchising nor as lucrative as hoped, disillusionment may have unavoidably followed.

Farmers may have been especially misled by the behaviour of relative prices in late 1989. From the mid-1970s, the closed economy and persistent disequilibrium in the food market strengthened farmers' income earnings. In August 1989, food prices were liberalized but industrial prices, including those for chemical inputs, were still administrated. Farmers' incomes rose 16% more than those in workers' households. The food market was liberalized first, in August 1989, and brought farmers unprecedented profits. Many farmers held back supplies from the market, as the inflationary instinct told them to hold out for even higher prices. It seemed as though farmers would soon attain untold prosperity. However, the 'big bang' of January 1990 caused a strong terms-of-trade shock for farmers as industrial price rises outpaced food prices. The overall jump in consumer prices, which may have overshot the level needed to absorb excess demand, caused real incomes to fall, reducing the aggregate demand for food. But perhaps most importantly, farmers on small farms with low levels of mechanization found it increasingly difficult to compete with imports from European Union countries, reducing the demand for Polish goods further at the same time as the costs of inputs and consumer goods were rising. It soon became apparent to farmers that they were the losers in the new environment (Górecki and Wiśniewski 1995). Peasant parties, especially the PSL, quickly mobilized to advocate a peasant-oriented development model incorporating import tariffs and debt relief and cheap credits for farmers.

The key dynamic may be the trade-off between the pace of reforms and security. This trade-off may help explain the rise in support for the post-communist parties in 1993. In the wake of more than three painful years of transition, rising unemployment and stagnant wages, the electorate shifted towards those parties which promised to alleviate the costs of reform. Although the SLD–PSL government adopted a slower pace of reform and delivered impressive growth rates, they were not rewarded in the 1997 election. The SLD–PSL coalition fulfilled many of its promises, but did not gain electoral support. In fact, after four years of economic expansion and growing consumer confidence, the SLD increased its total number of votes from 2.8 million in 1993 to 3.5 million in 1997. Despite this, the party received fewer seats in the Sejm (down from 171 to 164) because the AWS gained more popular votes in 1997 (4.4 million) and was thus able to benefit from the electoral law provision which rewards larger parties. In part, the AWS was able to attract most of the votes which the splintered centre-right gained in previous elections. But it is probable that the positive economic situation in 1997 made people more willing to support the AWS, which promised further progress in reforms.

That said, people wanted not just faster but also efficient reforms. Just more than a year after taking office, the AWS–UW coalition implemented an ambitious package of reforms to the pension, health care, education and local government systems. However, a series of external shocks, including the emerging markets crisis of 1997–1998 and the EU slowdown, had a negative impact on Polish economic performance. Unemployment surged upwards and GDP growth rates slackened. Moreover, the public was confused over the rapidly implemented reforms, which were blighted by the funding crisis in the state-run benefit agency ZUS and problems in allocating funds to the new health care funds (*kasy chorych*). By the end of 1999, the SLD led the AWS by about two to one in the opinion polls. Early elections held at the end of 1999 would undoubtedly have resulted in a swing back to the left. What happens if the parliament proceeds to full term may depend not only on economic performance, but also on internal issues including 'lustration' and external factors such as the progress of EU accession talks.

However, this should not detract from Poland's impressive political achievement. Within less than ten years, Poland has held three completely free and fair parliamentary elections, and had numerous peaceful transfers of power. Two relatively large and stable political blocs have formed. The post-communist bloc has strengthened its already cohesive structure, while the centre-right is chastened into cooperation through its disastrous showings in 1993 and 1995. The polarization of the party structure may lead to some policy blocking, yet it also seems to have precluded the electoral success of upstart populist parties.

6.3   CONCLUSIONS

After Poland's 1993 parliamentary election, there was an increase in public discussion of the impact of the 'social costs' of transition on voting behaviour. A common interpretation of the victories of post-communist parties and politicians was that they had resulted from a general public dissatisfaction with the course of reform. However, there was initially scarce empirical work done either on weighing the gains and losses of transition for households' well-being or on whether there are discernible relationships between economic variables and party support. While the overarching crisis of the socialist system was a factor behind political transition, the political situation during the subsequent decade of transition appears to have been driven by socio-economic interests on the one hand, and ideology on the other. In several ways, Poland's new political economy developed a resemblance to those in advanced market economies, especially with regard to unemployment and poverty. As in European Union countries, agriculture and sunset industries have posed considerable challenges to the forces of economic restructuring. Generally speaking, most political opposition to the reform process has centred upon extracting protection or subsidization in the face of the need for painful restructuring and increased efficiency.

The case of Poland was considered for several specific reasons.

Poland was the first of the Central and East European countries to introduce political competition in the 1989 semi-free elections. After Lithuania, Poland experienced one of the first peaceful transfers of governmental power from the former opposition to the reconstituted former-communist, social democratic opposition. Another advantage, in addition to relatively good availability of statistical data, is the ethnic and religious homogeneity of the population which should make it easier to isolate economic factors in political choice. During the 1990s, elements of a substantive democratic system such as free media reinforced the peaceful transfer of power in a number of relatively transparent elections. Yet at the time this research project was started, in late 1993, Poland also provided several analytical challenges, including a divided party system, perceived political instability, and just the beginning steps toward recovery from a deep and painful recession.

However, it appears in retrospect that some of the costs of transition unfolded quickly, such as the rapid and deep fall in real income, but other effects (notably unemployment) took longer to emerge and have evidently become sensitive to fluctuations in macroeconomic perform-ance and expectations. But the positive aspects are also there, from the fact that real income did not keep falling, and that there was not only no sustained deterioration in the consumption of food and basic goods but also, for many, a real accumulation of long-scarce durable goods.

The main social (rather than individual) cost of reform is the gap between the winners and losers of transition, between those more and those less able to take advantage of the opportunities of the new economic, political and social environment. The losers are primarily those who have lost from the withdrawal of subsidies, shifts in the terms of trade, or both (farmers, and workers in uncompetitive indus-tries). But a larger section of the population than is often assumed appears to fall into a middle category, in which material conditions have not deteriorated as sharply as was originally thought. In addition, by some measures the majority of the population experienced an improvement in material conditions, even during the recession years of 1990–1991. In the latter half of the decade, rising real wages and falling unemployment indicated that the benefits of reform were finally becoming more widely distributed, with more gains accruing to a wider share of the public. However, the downturn in 1997–1999 shows that, like all market economies, Poland is not insulated from shocks to the international economy.

Living standards – and in particular the adverse impact of transition on unemployment and poverty in Poland – were shown not only to be of great concern for the Polish public, but also politically consequential. In the initial stages of transition, most Poles shared a common interest in arresting high and escalating inflation and restructuring the economy to ensure sustainable growth. But by the time of Poland's first freely contested election in November 1990, inflation was still high but stable, yet registered unemployment was rising towards 10%. As the reform process evolved from stabilization to transformation, the public's economic interests became more diverse. Privatization and social security both emerged as important and interrelated policy issues. Farmers and the unemployed were hit particularly hard during transition, whereas entrepreneurs and more skilled private-sector employees fared relatively well. Education, skill, age and gender took on added significance for individuals' vulnerability to unemployment and poverty.

That said, the unemployed by themselves were never a group large enough to swing the results of national elections. However, Chapter 3 showed how the incidence of unemployment can have an impact beyond individuals upon their community and region. At the regional level, unemployment emerged as an important factor not just for personal well-being and the performance of the local economy, but also for the level of support for political parties. Experience appears closely linked to attitudes towards market reform, but there also appears to be an internal consistency in people's attitudes to reform, whether positive or negative. Furthermore, the socioeconomic distinctions of different parties' constituencies reflect the placement of these parties along an economic spectrum ranging from interventionist to free market.

From these findings, it was proposed that voting patterns would also reflect differentiation according to economic performance. On the basis of the findings of Kramer (1971) and Lewis-Beck (1988), evidence of economic voting could be found through relating candidates' share of the vote to regional variations in unemployment, per capita income, and selected variables reflecting structural factors such as the level of urbanization, private sector activity and local dependence on farming. Considering the complex nature of Polish politics, it was surprising how much of the variation in voting patterns could be explained by these few variables. Furthermore, the consistency of these results across time is also impressive.

The regional data and survey data provided evidence that *voting patterns do display differentiation by socioeconomic group and regional economic performance.* Regions and groups with higher personal incomes and lower jobless rates were more likely to vote for pro-reform parties. Areas where lower-paid, industrial labour dominates are larger supporters of the 'centre-right', socially conservative and pro-labour parties. There is a substantial level of support for agrarian parties in rural areas. This study also concluded that *the most important factor behind the rise in support for the SLD has been the rise in unemployment.* While the SLD is the largest pro-reform grouping in the Sejm, it is perceived to be more inclined towards redistributive policies than the UW is, and has arguably marketed itself as the more socially responsive and pragmatic choice. This argument takes into account the risk factor, whereby a riskier economic environment – witness the rising levels of unemployment during 1990–1993 – has affected voters' electoral choices.

Through these chapters, the theme of unemployment emerged repeatedly with strong implications for political behaviour. The role of unemployment in economic voting, and its influence behind the rise of the SLD, may be the most important finding. But the most inspiring aspect is that the enormous and wrenching changes of Poland's transition have not proved lethal to the nascent democratic system. Instead, there is continued, widespread acceptance of democracy, and little support for a reversion to a socialist or an authoritarian system. A considerable amount of voting behavior can be explained in terms of rational choice, where the Polish electorate made informed calculations about their economic interests and voting accordingly. But the re-emergence of ideology – a concept admittedly not fully pursued here – indicates that the identity of winners and losers is not a purely economic idea. Although Poland has moved rapidly away from the socialist system in the past ten years, to the point where it can safely be described as a democracy and a market economy, the past continues to exercise a role in Poland's political economy.

NOTES

1. Significance = 0.000 unless otherwise noted.
2. In the 1999 data set, this covers 62% of the total sample.

Appendices

QUESTION WORDINGS FOR OFFICE OF RESEARCH SURVEY DATA

1999: People have different ideas about how much the government should be involved in the economy. I am going to ask you a series of short questions about the role of government in the economy. Bearing in mind that benefits paid for by the state are really paid for from taxes on individuals and businesses, please give me your opinion on each of the following:

A. Should the state provide health care for all citizens, only the poorest citizens, or no citizens of [survey country]?

B. Should the elderly in our country primarily rely on the government for their standard of living or primarily rely on their personal savings and their family?

C. Should child care for pre-school children be provided and paid for by the state, or should *parents* pay for child care?

1990–1999: If the parliamentary election were held tomorrow, which party would you vote for? [IF SAYS 'DON'T KNOW':] Which party are you leaning toward voting for? [SHOW CARD]

1991: In general do you feel things in Poland are going in the right or in the wrong direction?

1990–1991: In your opinion, is the pace of economic reform in Poland too slow, too fast, or just right?

1999: Looking back over the past ten years, if economic reform could have been handled differently, which option would you choose for our country's economic reform? A more radical (faster) economic reform, a more gradual (slower) economic reform, no economic reform

1990–1999: What would you say is the most urgent issue facing our country at the present time? [OPEN-ENDED]

1993, 1999: Thinking about what life in general was like in Poland under communism compared to what it is today, would you say that things today tend to be better or worse than they were under communism?

1992–1999: Thinking about our country's political system under communism compared with our political system today – would you say that our political system today tends to be better or worse than under communism?

1991–1992, 1999: Have the changes that have taken place over the past ten years had a good or a bad effect on: Standard of living?

1992–1999: Thinking about our country's economic situation under communism compared with our economic situation today – would you say that our country's economic situation today tends to be better or worse than it was under communism?

1990–1999: And how would you describe your household's financial situation at the present time. Would you say it is very good, fairly good, fairly bad, or very bad?

1990–1999: How would you describe the current economic situation in Poland? Would you say the economic situation is very good, fairly good, fairly bad, or very bad?

1993: Do you favour or oppose Poland's attempts to become a full member of the European Community (EC)? Is that strongly or somewhat?

1994–1999: If Poland had the opportunity to become a full member of the EU, would you strongly favour, somewhat favour, somewhat oppose, or strongly oppose our country doing so?

1993–1997: If Poland had the opportunity to become a full member of NATO, would you strongly favour, somewhat favour, somewhat oppose or strongly oppose our country doing so?

1998: As you may know, our coutry was invited to join NATO. What is your view of our country's joining NATO – do you strongly favour, somewhat favour, somewhat oppose or strongly oppose our country's membership of NATO?

1999: As you may know, our coutry has joined NATO. What is your view of our country's joining NATO – do you strongly favour, somewhat favour, somewhat oppose or strongly oppose our country's membership of NATO?

1990–1996: Some people feel that the majority of businesses should be privately owned. Others think that only some businesses should be privately owned and that the government should continue to run the majority of businesses in our country. Which of the two alternatives is closer to your own view?

1993–1999: Do you personally feel that the creation of a free market economy, that is one largely free from state control, is right or wrong for Poland's future?

1997–1999: Some people feel that the majority of large businesses should be privately owned. Others think that only some large businesses should be privately owned and that the government should continue to run the majority of large businesses in our country. Which of the two alternatives is closest to your own views?

1990–1999: There are different opinions about foreign investment. Some people think that foreign investment is necessary and will have a positive influence on the development of our economy. Others say that foreign investment is dangerous because it allows outsiders too much control over our affairs. Which view is closer to your own?

1991–1995: Some people feel that there should be no unemployment in Poland, even if it means that the Polish economy will not improve and modernize in the near future. Others feel some unemployment in Poland is acceptable, if that's what it takes to improve and modernize the economy. Generally, which position comes closer to your point of view?

1990–1997: Here is a set of statements that describe how people often feel. Please tell me whether you strongly agree, somewhat agree, somewhat disagree, or strongly disagree with each of these statements. 'The Church is too involved in politics and is losing sight of its main spiritual role.'

1993: How satisfied are you with the progress we have made towards becoming a democracy? Are you very satisfied, somewhat satisfied, not very satisfied, or not satisfied at all with the progress we have made towards becoming a democracy?

1990–1999: Here is a set of statements that describe how people often feel. Please tell me whether you strongly agree, somewhat agree, somewhat disagree, or strongly disagree with each of these statements. 'Poland is only for the Poles'

1990–1999: Do you attend religious services more than once a week, once a week, once a month or so, a few times a year, once a year or less, or never?

1993: How satisfied are you with the progress of economic reform in our country – very satisfied, somewhat satisfied, not very satisfied, or not satisfied at all?

APPENDICES FOR CHAPTER 2

Table 2A.1 Forecast direction of change (%)

	11/87	3/88	6/88	9/88	11/88	3/89	5/89	6/89
Economic situation								
Improve	23.0	20.0	20.1	18.5	32.7	33.0	28.5	35.0
No change	19.0	24.4	25.4	29.3	28.0	27.3	30.5	32.3
Worsen	45.4	41.5	39.1	31.9	18.4	24.3	31.3	17.7
DK/NA	11.9	14.0	14.7	20.3	20.9	15.5	9.0	15.0
Political situation								
Improve	22.0	17.7	23.1	25.6	28.4	39.3	46.0	45.3
No change	43.1	51.6	49.8	37.8	44.3	35.1	28.2	24.2
Worsen	19.9	16.9	12.6	14.2	9.1	9.5	11.7	9.8
DK/NA	14.2	13.7	14.4	22.4	18.0	16.7	14.0	20.6
Material situation		5/88				1/89		
Improve		11.6			24.4	18.2	17.9	26.4
No change		32.2			30.6	24.7	25.0	29.2
Worsen		39.4			19.8	37.1	47.3	28.7
DK/NA		16.8			25.2	19.7	9.7	15.7

Source: Selected data from CBOS 1989, 'Nastroje społeczne po pierwsze turze wyborów do Sejmu i Senatu', Report No. 475/89, Warsaw, June.

Table 2A.2 Factor analysis for Poland 1999

Factor	1	2	3	4	5	6
Issues						
Life better now	**0.7366**	0.0456	–0.0056	0.0320	0.0240	0.0545
Living standards better	**0.6600**	0.0499	–0.0540	0.0737	–0.0332	0.0097
Economy vs socialism	**0.6708**	–0.0552	0.1102	0.0103	0.0369	0.0127
Political system better now	**0.5315**	0.1058	0.2023	–0.0834	0.1051	0.3341
Poland's economy	**0.5216**	–0.0636	0.1773	0.0148	–0.1755	–0.1913
Household situation	**0.3773**	–0.0765	–0.1108	0.1762	–0.1853	–0.0253
Religion practice	0.0276	**0.4385**	–0.0688	–0.0177	–0.0234	0.0249
Role for religious values	0.0004	**0.7129**	0.0660	0.0585	–0.0355	–0.0348
Join EU	0.0163	–0.0253	**0.6298**	0.0806	–0.0375	–0.0815
Join NATO	0.0240	-0.0317	**0.6553**	–0.0095	–0.0132	0.0380
Free price/limited supply	0.0392	–0.0492	–0.0007	**0.5292**	0.0445	0.2174
Market set prices	–0.0356	0.0138	–0.0052	**0.5262**	0.0082	–0.0357
Large firms privatized	0.1465	0.0127	0.0040	**0.3967**	0.0666	–0.0155
Utilities private	0.0724	–0.0392	0.1101	**0.3972**	0.0055	–0.0754
Foreign investment	–0.0518	–0.0164	0.2484	0.2979	–0.1205	0.0982
Wage controls	0.0109	–0.0368	0.0267	0.2957	0.0089	0.1480
Market economy	0.1308	–0.0403	0.0980	0.2795	–0.0530	0.0959
Trust government to do right	0.0667	0.1431	0.1767	0.0504	**–0.4968**	0.1318
Politicians good intent	–0.0407	0.0090	–0.0237	–0.0473	**–0.5539**	–0.0308
Expect much future	0.0928	0.0196	0.0926	0.1306	**–0.3985**	0.0098
Democracy best system	0.1906	–0.0422	0.1391	–0.0493	**–0.2956**	0.2286
Small firms private	0.0416	–0.0846	–0.0185	0.1807	–0.0348	**0.4391**
Return to security	0.2489	–0.1294	0.0873	0.0133	–0.1988	**0.3105**
Loss-makers closed	0.0536	–0.1616	–0.0015	0.1762	–0.1597	0.2564
Eigenvalue	6.36	1.69	1.26	1.172	1.105	1.015
(% var)	(26.5%)	(7.1%)	(5.3%)	(4.9%)	(4.6%)	(4.2%)

Notes: Chi Square: 242.100. DF 1470. Sig: 0.00000.
Standardized scores. Pattern matrix.
Oblimin rotation, maximum likelihood, missing values replaced by mean.
Source: Office of Research (1999).

APPENDICES FOR CHAPTER 3

Table 3A.1 Cumulative price indices (1984 = 1.00)

	1985	1986	1987	1988	1989	1990	1991	1992	1993	1994	1995	1996	1997
CPI	1.143	1.345	1.684	2.698	9.474	64.97	110.6	158.2	214.1	282.8	361.4	431.5	495.4
Food	1.157	1.326	1.614	2.411	10.13	68.33	99.83	136.7	182.6	242.7	308.2	369.3	415.8
Non-food	1.168	1.403	1.760	2.910	9.507	65.71	111.5	157.7	215.7	283.4	360.8	435.4	496.4
Services	1.226	1.464	1.916	3.133	8.487	74.75	173.0	290.0	400.5	530.7	686.2	823.4	982.4

Sources: Bell and Rostowski (1995); author's calculations from GUS data.

Table 3A.2 Real monthly per capita expenditure (1987 prices)

	Workers	Mixed	Farmers	Pensioners
1988	1.33	1.29	1.42	1.38
1989	1.25	1.29	1.42	1.19
1990	1.00	1.00	1.00	1.00
1991	1.05	0.96	0.88	1.11
1992	1.03	0.93	0.86	1.06
1993	1.09	1.00	0.97	1.14
1994	1.09	1.02	0.97	1.13
1995	1.09	1.08	1.06	1.15
1996	1.20	1.11	1.06	1.22
1997	1.20	1.11	1.03	1.26

Source: Author's calculations from GUS data.

Table 3A.3 Regression results for Wałęsa in second round, 1990

Variable	Coefficient	Standard Error	t value	Significance of t value
Constant	1.031	0.172	6.006	0.000
Income	-0.134	0.160	-0.839	0.406
Unemployment	-2.641	0.540	-4.893	0.000

Notes: N = 49. R square: 0.345. Adjusted R square: 0.317. SEE: 0.076. F-ratio (sig): 12.117 (0.000). All numbers rounded off to third decimal place.
Sources: Parysek *et al., 1991*; author's calculations from GUS data.

Table 3A.4 Regression results for Kwaśniewski in second round, 1995

Variable	Coefficient	Standard Error	t value	Significance of t value
Constant	0.208	0.175	1.190	0.240
Income	0.158	0.220	0.717	0.477
Unemployment	1.408	0.321	4.392	0.000

Notes: R square: 0.309. Adjusted R square: 0.279. SEE: 0.101. F-ratio: 10.295 (0.000)
All numbers rounded off to third decimal place.
Sources: Państwowa Komisja Wyborcza (1996); author's calculations from GUS data.

APPENDICES FOR CHAPTER 4

Table 4A.1 Regressions for centre-right candidates and parties

	1990 Round 1 Wałęsa	1990 Round 2 Wałęsa	1991 POC	1991 NSZZ S	1993 BBWR	1993 Ojczyzna	1993 PC	1995 Wałęsa	1997 AWS
R^2	0.3297	0.3350	0.0972	0.1528	0.0910	0.3724	0.0729	0.2138	0.7950
Adj. R^2	0.3005	0.3209	0.0776	0.1321	0.0716	0.2568	0.0523	0.1970	0.7814
Independent variables (significance)									
Constant	0.7153	0.8902	0.1159	0.0741	0.0666	0.0822	0.0303	0.4555	-0.0473
	(0.0000)	(0.0000)	(0.0000)	(0.0000)	(0.0000)	(0.0002)	(0.0000)	(0.0000)	(0.4446)
Unemployment (%)	-1.5227	-0.2514	-0.2460	*	-0.1011	*	*	-0.8577	*
	(0.0042)	(0.0000)	(0.0310)	*	(0.0352)	*	*	(0.0008)	*
Trade (% total employment)	-0.0252	*	*	*	*	*	*	*	-1.5309
	(0.0002)	*	*	*	*	*	*	*	(0.0001)
Farming (% total employment)	*	*	*	-0.0608	*	*	*	*	*
	*	*	*	(0.0096)	*	*	*	*	*
Pensioners (% population)	*	*	*	*	*	0.1495	*	*	*
	*	*	*	*	*	(0.0099)	*	*	*

Benefit recipients	*	*	*	*	*	*	*	*	*	*		*
(% population)	*	*	*	*	*	*	*	*	-0.1428	*		*
									(0.0176)			
Urban residents	*	*	*	*	*	*	*	*	-0.0702	0.0207	*	*
(% population)	*	*	*	*	*	*	*	*	(0.0081)	(0.0664)	*	*
Industry	*	*	*	*	*	*	*	*	*	*	*	-0.5413
(% employment)	*	*	*	*	*	*	*	*	*	*	*	(0.0000)
Turnout	*	*	*	*	*	*	*	*	*	*	*	1.5182
(% eligible)	*	*	*	*	*	*	*	*	*	*	*	(0.0000)

Source: Author's calculation from GUS and PKW data.

Table 4A.2 Regressions for SLD

	1990 Cimoszewicz	1991 SLD	1993 SLD	1995 Round 1 Kwaśniewski	1995 Round 2 Kwaśniewski	1997 SLD
R^2	0.1335	0.1838	0.4144	0.2077	0.3015	0.7438
Adj. R^2	0.1150	0.1476	0.3877	0.1733	0.2866	0.7205
Independent variables (significance)						
Constant	0.0533	-0.0428	0.0389	0.5324	0.3276	0.2491
	(0.0022)	(0.4900)	(0.2022)	(0.0000)	(0.0000)	(0.0051)
Unemployment (%)	0.6043	0.3959	0.1582	*	1.3157	*
	(0.0098)	(0.0056)	(0.0003)	*	(0.0000)	*
Per capita income	*	*	*	-0.5378	*	*
	*	*	*	(0.0175)	*	*
Trade	*	*	*	*	*	1.3599
(% total employment)	*	*	*	*	*	(0.0009)
Farming	*	*	*	*	*	*
(% total employment)	*	*	*	*	*	*

Pensioners (% population)	0.5762 (0.0380)	* *	* *	* *	* *
Benefit recipients (% population)	* *	* *	* *	* *	* *
Urban residents (% population)	* *	0.4639 (0.0002)	0.3538 (0.0000)	* *	* *
Industry (% employment)	* *	* *	* *	* *	0.6853 (0.0000)
Turnout (% electorate)	* *	* *	* *	* *	-0.8342 (0.0000)

Source: Author's calculation from GUS and PKW data.

Table 4A.3 Regressions for UD, KLD and UW

	1990 Mazowiecki	1991 KLD	1991 UD	1993 KLD	1993 UD	1995 Kuroń	1997 UW
R²	0.8134	0.5413	0.6852	0.3806	0.6206	0.8046	0.7551
Adj. R²	0.8053	0.5314	0.6784	0.3668	0.6033	0.7961	0.7439
Independent variables (significance)							
Constant	-0.0805	0.1092	0.1961	-0.0082	0.1924	0.1192	0.2085
	(0.0066)	(0.0000)	(0.0000)	(0.3150)	(0.0000)	(0.0000)	(0.0000)
Unemployment (%)	-0.7318	*	*	*	-0.2493	0.0659	-0.2182
	(0.0011)	*	*	*	(0.0013)	(0.0462)	(0.0034)
Trade (% total employment)	0.0338	*	*	0.3252	*	*	*
	(0.0000)	*	*	(0.0000)	*	*	*
Farming (% total employment)	*	0.1484	-0.2457	*	-0.2024	-0.1382	-0.2067
	*	(0.0000)	(0.0000)	*	(0.0000)	(0.0000)	(0.0000)
Pensioners (% population)	*	*	*	*	*	*	*

Benefit recipients (% population)	* *	* *	* *	* *	* *	* *	* *
Urban residents (% population)	* *	* *	* *	* *	* *	* *	* *

Source: Author's calculation from GUS and PKW data.

201

Table 4A.4 Regressions for PSL

	1990 Bartoszcze	1991 PSL	1991 PL	1993 PSL	1995 Pawlak	1997 PSL
R^2	0.6877	0.4220	0.5948	0.5501	0.7055	0.7252
Adj. R^2	0.6811	0.4088	0.5834	0.5401	0.6993	0.7124
Independent variables (significance)						
Constant	-0.0089 (0.4007)	0.0328 (0.0482)	-0.0325 (0.0474)	0.0395 (0.0797)	-0.0205 (0.0156)	0.1102 (0.0115)
Unemployment (%)	*	*	*	*	*	*
Trade (% total employment)	*	*	*	*	*	*
Farming (% total employment)	0.2820 (0.0000)	0.2371 (0.0000)	0.3262 (0.0000)	0.4622 (0.0000)	0.2383 (0.0000)	0.2788 (0.0000)
Pensioners (% population)	*	*	*	*	*	*

Benefit recipients (% population)	*	*	*	*	*
Urban residents (% population)	*	*	*	*	*
Turnout (% elgible)	*	*	*	*	−0.2296
	*	*	*	*	(0.0098)

Source: Author's calculation from GUS and PKW data.

Table 4A.5   Regressions for other parties

	1990 Tymiński	1995 Olszewski	1997 ROP	1990 Moczulski	1993 KPN	1993 UP	1997 UP
R^2	0.2610	0.5019	0.3229	0.1241	0.1008	0.1314	0.2463
Adj. R^2	0.2453	0.4802	0.3069	0.1055	0.0808	0.1121	0.2104
Independent variables (significance)							
Constant	0.1317 (0.0000)	0.0647 (0.0000)	0.0992 (0.0000)	0.0276 (0.0000)	0.7477 (0.0000)	0.0743 (0.0000)	0.1073 (0.0001)
Unemployment (%)	1.5540 (0.0002)	-0.1839 (0.0021)	* *	* *	-0.1282 (0.0297)	-0.1373 (0.0123)	* *
Trade (% total employment)	*	*	*	*	*	*	*
Farming (% total employment)	* *	0.1079 (0.0000)	* *	-0.1134 (0.0130)	* *	* *	* *
Pensioners (% population)	*	*	*	*	*	*	*

Benefit recipients (% population)	*	*	*	*	*	*	*
Urban residents (% population)	*	*	*	*	*	*	*
Industry (% employment)	*	*	-0.1567* (0.0001)	*	*	*	*
Turnout (% electorate)	*	*	*	*	*	*	-0.1217 (0.0160)

Source: Author's calculation from GUS and PKW data.

APPENDICES FOR CHAPTER 5

Table 5A.1   Budget shares for socioeconomic groups (percentage of total expenditure)

	1987	1989	1990	1991	1993	1995	1997
Employees							
Total (PZN)	1.62	9.33	48.87	87.97	168.01	274.93	435.61
Food	40.9	45.8	48.0	42.0	39.1	37.4	33.4
Alcohol and tobacco	4.0	4.0	3.2	3.4	3.0	3.0	3.3
Clothing	13.8	16.9	11.2	10.4	7.5	7.5	7.5
Housing	10.3	10.6	9.6	16.0	19.1	20.6	21.9
Rent		1.3		3.2	3.8	4.2	4.8
Energy	2.6	1.7	3.5	5.9	9.2	10.4	9.5
Health and hygiene	3.0	2.6	3.2	4.2	6.3	6.2	6.4
Leisure	9.7	10.1	11.2	11.4	8.7	6.6	7.0
Transport, communications	5.5	6.2	7.1	8.7	10.1	9.5	10.5
Worker-farmers							
Total	1.45	8.65	45.46	73.42	138.84	222.94	352.59
Food	43.6	46.7	50.8	46.9	47.9	46.3	40.3
Alcohol and tobacco	4.5	4.3	3.3	3.4	2.8	3.0	3.1
Clothing	14.6	17.9	10.8	10.2	7.6	9.0	8.0
Housing	12.3	14.1	11.4	10.6	16.6	15.3	19.3
Rent				0.3	0.3	0.4	0.8
Energy	3.0	2.3	4.0	6.7	8.8	7.5	8.4
Health and hygiene	2.1	1.8	2.3	2.9	5.0	5.4	5.7
Leisure	4.5	5.4	6.1	6.3	4.1	3.5	3.7
Transport, communications	5.8	5.6	8.0	8.8	10.1	9.1	10.7

Farmers							
Total	1.70	10.46	50.93	75.82	151.52	234.71	348.68
Food	43.4	45.3	51.8	50.3	48.8	47.2	44.5
Alcohol and tobacco	4.5	3.5	3.3	3.6	3.1	3.6	3.6
Clothing	12.1	14.7	9.0	8.8	7.0	8.0	6.9
Housing	12.6	16.5	11.2	15.3	16.7	16.0	18.0
Rent				0.2	0.2	0.3	0.4
Energy	3.5	2.6	4.6	7.3	9.4	8.5	8.8
Health and hygiene	2.0	1.6	2.2	3.0	4.9	2.8	5.5
Leisure	3.7	5.5	5.0	5.5	3.5	5.0	2.4
Transport, communications	6.0	7.7	8.2	7.8	8.7	9.6	10.3
Pensioners							
Total	1.63	8.29	48.60	92.39	189.80	310.78	469.28
Food	49.2	45.3	57.8	48.2	43.1	41.3	38.1
Alcohol and tobacco	3.2	2.5	2.4	2.7	2.3	2.5	2.7
Clothing	11.0	14.7	7.9	8.1	5.2	5.1	5.3
Housing	10.7	16.5	8.4	24.8	23.4	23.9	25.1
Rent				4.1	3.5	4.1	4.5
Energy	5.4	2.6	6.9	10.0	13.7	13.9	13.6
Health and hygiene	9.3	1.6	3.7	4.7	8.2	8.3	9.0
Leisure	5.7	5.5	5.8	6.5	4.6	4.0	4.1
Transport, communications	3.8	7.7	3.8	5.4	6.3	6.1	6.6

Note: Rent is part of 'housing' expenditures. From 1987 to 1994, heating is calculated as a separate category. From that point, it is included under utilities as part of housing expenditures. Figures for 1987 to 1994 should be added to approximate 1995 and 1997 spending patterns.
Source: Author's calculations from GUS data.

Table 5A.2 Budget shares as a percentage of nominal consumption expenditure

	Self-employed		Unemployed	
	1993	1995	1993	1995
Total (PZN)	216.44	341.48	107.03	158.54
Food	34.4	32.3	48.8	48.8
Alcohol and tobacco	2.8	2.4	3.7	4.1
Clothing	8.2	7.7	6.7	6.2
Housing	17.4	20.1	18.7	19.0
Rent	2.5	2.7	4.4	4.9
Energy	8.1	8.6	10.2	10.4
Health and hygiene	6.2	6.0	6.0	5.0
Leisure	9.5	7.7	6.8	4.5
Transport, communications	13.9	13.4	6.1	5.3

Source: Author's calculation from GUS data.

Table 5A.3   *Average consumption of food items, averages for 1986–1989 and 1990–1995*

	Employees			Worker-farmers		
	Average 1986–1989	Average 1990–1995	% change	Average 1986–1989	Average 1990–1995	% change
Wheat flour	1.15	1.03	-10.2	2.05	2.05	0.0
Bread	7.03	7.13	1.5	8.61	8.20	-4.8
Pasta	0.14	0.20	45.2	0.10	0.11	7.3
Grains	0.39	0.35	-11.1	0.48	0.48	.2
Potatoes	7.96	7.75	-2.6	9.69	9.46	-2.3
Vegetables	5.34	5.19	-2.9	5.93	6.11	3.0
Fruit	2.90	3.48	20.3	2.66	3.00	12.7
Meat	4.80	4.84	0.8	5.18	5.26	1.5
Fish	0.47	0.43	-9.1	0.30	0.29	-2.0
Edible fats	1.60	1.46	-8.4	1.73	1.61	-7.1
Cheese	0.93	0.72	-22.4	0.93	0.89	-3.8
Sugar	2.12	1.88	-11.6	2.71	2.54	-6.4

Continued overleaf

Table 5A.3 continued

	Average 1986–1989	Farmers Average 1990–1995	% change	Average 1986–1989	Pensioners Average 1990–1995	% change
Flour	2.51	2.35	-6.4	1.98	1.86	-6.3
Bread	9.19	8.87	-3.5	8.66	8.49	-1.9
Pasta	0.13	0.13	-2.6	0.23	0.30	28.3
Grains	0.72	0.54	-24.7	0.90	0.80	-11.2
Potatoes	10.37	10.18	-1.8	12.24	12.39	1.2
Vegetables	6.77	6.87	1.5	7.66	7.47	-2.4
Fruit	3.08	3.35	8.9	3.86	4.35	12.8
Meat	6.40	6.33	-1.1	5.44	6.04	11.0
Fish	0.36	0.37	3.8	0.62	0.57	-9.2
Edible fats	1.98	1.83	-7.4	2.18	2.06	-5.5
Cheese	1.04	0.86	-17.8	1.37	1.03	-25.1
Sugar	3.25	2.89	-11.2	3.03	2.66	-12.4

Note: In kilograms.
Source: Rocznik Statystyczny, various issues.

210

Table 5A.4 *Employee households' average per capita monthly food consumption*

	1986	1987	1988	1989	1990	1991	1992	1993	1994	1995	1996	1997
Flour (kg)	1.11	1.15	1.18	1.14	1.12	1.06	1.07	1.04	0.95	0.93	0.93	0.82
Bread	7.15	7.05	6.99	6.92	7.10	7.17	7.25	7.43	6.92	6.92	6.93	6.61
Pasta	0.14	0.14	0.14	0.14	0.14	0.18	0.20	0.23	0.23	0.24	n/a	n/a
Potatoes	8.10	7.69	8.03	8.01	8.29	7.91	8.02	8.14	6.84	7.32	7.01	6.51
Vegetables	5.43	5.32	5.56	5.06	5.20	5.35	5.14	5.35	5.00	5.07	5.02	4.74
Grains*	0.3	0.4	0.4	0.3	0.3	0.3	0.3	0.3	0.3	0.3	n/a	n/a
Fruit	3.27	2.36	2.95	3.00	3.04	3.39	3.50	4.05	3.39	3.53	3.63	3.82
Meat	4.69	4.68	4.83	5.01	4.96	5.14	4.90	4.91	4.51	4.62	4.73	4.68
Fish	0.47	0.47	0.47	0.46	0.39	0.43	0.44	0.45	0.42	0.42	0.43	0.43
Oils and fats	1.58	1.59	1.63	1.58	1.52	1.49	1.43	1.52	1.41	1.40	1.42	1.39
Cheese	0.90	0.93	0.96	0.92	0.76	0.71	0.69	0.74	0.72	0.70	0.75	0.79
Sugar	2.02	2.12	2.28	2.06	1.92	1.96	1.89	2.26	1.66	1.56	1.59	1.47
Milk (litres)		7.71	7.58		6.78	8.42	6.04	5.70	5.53	5.16	5.14	4.88
Eggs (units)		15.63	16.18		14.45	16.91	13.80	13.39	12.74	13.19	12.98	12.64

Note: * In Tables 5A.4–5A.7, from 1996 grains are included in the 'vegetable' category.

Table 5A.5 Worker-farmer households' average per capita monthly food consumption

	1986	1987	1988	1989	1990	1991	1992	1993	1994	1995	1996	1997
Flour (kg)	1.99	2.04	2.08	2.09	2.14	2.05	2.14	2.05	2.01	1.91	1.76	1.57
Bread	8.86	8.75	8.51	8.33	8.35	8.27	8.17	8.27	8.19	7.97	8.17	7.95
Pasta	0.11	0.10	0.10	0.10	0.07	0.09	0.1	0.09	0.15	0.16	n/a	n/a
Potatoes	9.77	9.70	9.57	9.70	9.82	9.64	9.02	9.64	9.72	8.94	9.08	8.92
Vegetables	5.91	5.95	6.09	5.78	5.95	6.13	6.01	6.13	6.30	6.15	5.96	6.10
Grains*	0.60	0.66	0.06	0.61	0.45	0.49	0.46	0.49	0.52	0.49	n/a	n/a
Fruit	3.06	2.04	2.82	2.72	2.70	2.85	3.17	2.85	3.15	3.26	3.14	3.52
Meat	4.99	5.06	5.21	5.45	5.38	5.31	5.05	5.31	5.22	5.27	5.30	5.25
Fish	0.28	0.31	0.30	0.30	0.24	0.26	0.3	0.26	0.35	0.34	0.34	0.39
Oils and fats	1.72	1.75	1.76	1.69	1.66	1.63	1.54	1.63	1.62	1.56	1.58	1.59
Cheese	0.97	0.95	0.80	0.98	0.95	0.92	0.87	0.92	0.88	0.80	0.78	0.73
Sugar	2.53	2.79	2.96	2.57	2.54	2.64	2.58	2.64	2.48	2.36	2.29	2.20
Milk (litres)		11.11	10.70		10.63	10.20	9.52	9.97	9.82	9.42	8.91	7.70
Eggs (units)		18.97	19.63		18.93	16.60	15.93	16.26	16.49	16.32	15.92	15.77

Note: * In Tables 5A.4–5A.7, from 1996 grains are included in the 'vegetable' category.

Table 5A.6 Farmer households' average per capita monthly food consumption

	1986	1987	1988	1989	1990	1991	1992	1993	1994	1995	1996	1997
Flour (kg)	2.48	2.51	2.56	2.48	2.51	2.41	2.25	2.46	2.34	2.11	2.02	1.96
Bread	9.40	9.39	9.11	8.87	8.81	8.94	8.98	9.30	8.72	8.48	8.52	8.44
Pasta	0.13	0.13	0.13	0.13	0.08	0.10	0.10	0.16	0.15	0.17	n/a	n/a
Potatoes	10.42	10.47	10.19	10.40	10.64	10.21	9.81	10.37	10.12	9.92	9.88	10.58
Vegetables	6.67	6.69	6.99	6.73	6.86	6.85	6.74	7.02	6.92	6.84	6.45	6.65
Grains*	0.72	0.76	0.72	0.66	0.49	0.54	0.51	0.61	0.54	0.54	n/a	n/a
Fruit	3.64	2.28	3.23	3.16	3.05	3.01	3.42	3.87	3.38	3.38	3.37	3.46
Meat	6.16	6.26	6.5	6.66	6.63	6.48	6.12	6.38	6.13	6.21	6.30	6.55
Fish	0.35	0.35	0.36	0.36	0.29	0.33	0.37	0.41	0.41	0.40	0.40	0.44
Oils and fats	1.99	2.02	1.99	1.90	1.88	1.83	1.80	1.93	1.80	1.73	1.73	1.74
Cheese	1.07	1.03	1.04	1.02	0.95	0.94	0.90	0.82	0.80	0.72	0.72	0.72
Sugar	2.86	3.42	3.6	3.12	2.98	2.93	2.73	3.36	2.79	2.52	2.47	2.38
Milk (litres)		13.09	12.74		12.74	11.94	11.11	11.53	10.83	10.17	9.72	9.52
Eggs (units)		22.86	23.10		21.88	19.20	18.95	18.67	18.54	18.65	18.18	18.82

Note: * In Tables 5A.4–5A.7, from 1996 grains are included in the 'vegetable' category.

213

Table 5A.7 *Pensioner households' average per capita monthly food consumption*

	1986	1987	1988	1989	1990	1991	1992	1993	1994	1995	1996	1997
Flour (kg)	1.85	1.95	2.07	2.06	1.91	1.84	1.8	1.93	1.86	1.8	1.75	1.68
Bread	8.72	8.70	8.72	8.49	8.42	8.51	8.4	8.99	8.28	8.36	8.34	8.13
Pasta	0.23	0.23	0.23	0.23	0.20	0.26	0.28	0.34	0.33	0.36	n/a	n/a
Grains*	0.84	0.93	0.92	0.90	0.69	0.77	0.75	0.91	0.84	0.82	n/a	n/a
Potatoes	12.37	12.01	12.07	12.51	12.96	12.28	12.78	12.91	11.73	11.68	11.14	10.96
Vegetables	7.59	7.66	8.14	7.23	7.41	7.55	7.48	7.72	7.31	7.34	7.18	7.09
Fruit	4.34	3.14	4.15	3.81	3.75	4.17	4.51	5.17	4.15	4.37	4.42	4.53
Meat	5.21	5.33	5.52	5.70	5.95	6.33	5.98	6.27	5.78	5.91	6.03	6.06
Fish	0.64	0.64	0.62	0.59	0.49	0.58	0.57	0.60	0.58	0.57	0.58	0.60
Oils and fats	2.09	2.19	2.26	2.19	2.11	2.04	1.96	2.21	2.05	2.01	2.03	2.01
Cheese	1.31	1.39	1.44	1.35	1.29	1.01	0.93	1.02	0.98	0.94	0.96	1.00
Sugar	2.80	3.05	3.35	2.93	2.05	2.78	2.65	3.28	2.64	2.54	2.48	2.48
Milk (litres)		12.10	11.98			9.74	9.41	9.69	9.25	8.89	8.66	8.52
Eggs (units)		21.11	22.05			18.12	17.89	18.03	17.41	17.95	17.45	17.49

Note: * In Tables 5A.4–5A.7, from 1996 grains are included in the 'vegetable' category.

Table 5A.8 *Non-wage and self-employed households' average per capita monthly food consumption*

	Non-wage income					Self-employed				
	1993	1994	1995	1996	1997	1993	1994	1995	1996	1997
Flour (kg)	1.08	0.97	0.99	1.00	0.95	0.93	0.84	0.89	0.83	0.76
Bread	7.68	7.05	7.23	7.21	7.06	6.62	6.19	6.16	6.13	5.91
Potatoes	8.79	7.98	7.93	8.52	7.48	6.96	6.29	6.34	6.36	5.52
Vegetables	4.82	4.41	4.71	4.70	4.26	5.39	4.95	5.03	5.12	4.89
Fruit	2.93	2.27	2.35	2.26	2.26	4.62	3.93	4.31	4.56	4.77
Meat	4.09	3.71	3.73	3.85	3.90	5.14	4.72	4.85	4.93	4.85
Fish	0.35	0.30	0.31	0.30	0.30	0.48	0.46	0.44	0.45	0.48
Oils and fats	1.47	1.36	1.37	1.36	1.41	1.42	1.31	1.30	1.31	1.30
Cheese	0.53	0.49	0.45	0.48	0.54	0.85	0.81	0.83	0.84	0.87
Sugar	1.64	1.52	1.49	1.53	1.52	1.57	1.52	1.55	1.42	1.35
Milk (litres)	6.07	5.93	5.64	5.28	5.29	6.08	5.70	5.60	5.38	5.31
Eggs (units)	11.65	10.78	11.60	11.60	11.52	13.81	12.45	13.25	13.03	12.71

Table 5A.9 Number of selected consumer durables per 100 households: employee households

	1985	1989	1990	1991	1993	1997
Radios	82.0	93.4	93.6	91.1	82.9	61.4
Colour televisions	23.1	50.7	67.1	82.9	95.1	108.4
Black and white televisions	90.5	78.1	66.1	50.3	24.5	8.5
Satellite and cable TV	n/a	n/a	n/a	n/a	31.4	51.2
Compact disc players	n/a	n/a	n/a	n/a	n/a	12.5
Audio cassette players	67.0	70.3	77.1	81.5	32.8	n/a
Radio-cassette players	n/a	n/a	37.0	46.0	77.2	n/a
Stereo music systems	n/a	n/a	n/a	n/a	n/a	35.5
Videocassette recorders	n/a	4.7	20.1	41.0	63.2	71.6
Video cameras	n/a	n/a	n/a	n/a	2.1	3.1
Personal computers	n/a	n/a	n/a	n/a	11.0	13.6
Washing machines and spin driers	118.6	137.2	136.3	68.0	59.7	45.4
Automatic washing machines	38.7	59.1	63.5	67.2	70.9	79.0
Refrigerators and freezers	103.7	101.0	99.8	99.9	98.4	98.6
Freezers	n/a	20.3	23.8	27.4	32.3	33.3
Electric vacuum cleaners	94.8	97.7	97.6	97.6	96.2	97.1
Microwave ovens	n/a	n/a	n/a	n/a	3.5	11.5
Dishwashers	n/a	n/a	n/a	n/a	0.7	0.9
Sewing machines	53.6	60.2	60.5	59.6	56.7	45.4
Electric sewing machines	32.9	43.8	45.6	47.0	n/a	n/a
Bicycles	80.9	94.3	93.0	93.3	69.7	75.1
Motorcycles	10.5	10.8	10.6	9.5	7.1	3.6
Automobiles	27.2	30.7	33.2	38.3	44.7	49.2

Table 5A.10   Number of selected consumer durables per 100 households: worker-farmer households

	1985	1989	1990	1991	1993	1997
Radios	82.4	88.6	87.2	87.9	81.5	70.1
Colour televisions	6.6	20.8	37.6	52.6	74.2	101.8
Black and white televisions	99.3	99.1	90.6	80.0	49.3	15.9
Satellite and cable TV	n/a	n/a	n/a	n/a	5.3	16.4
Compact disc players	n/a	n/a	n/a	n/a	n/a	6.1
Audio cassette players	46.9	59.1	66.8	74.4	25.9	n/a
Radio–cassette players	n/a	11.7	20.1	29.8	65.3	n/a
Stereo music systems	n/a	n/a	n/a	n/a	n/a	19.5
Videocassette recorders	n/a	0.9	6.9	19.1	37.0	55.9
Video cameras	n/a	n/a	n/a	n/a	0.3	0.9
Personal computers	n/a	n/a	n/a	n/a	2.3	5.6
Washing machines and spin driers	116.4	134.9	137.2	101.1	98.2	88.6
Automatic washing machines	12.9	29.4	33.2	34.2	32.7	54.8
Refrigerators and freezers	105.9	101.0	99.2	99.8	98.7	100.2
Freezers	n/a	33.3	44.1	52.7	59.9	68.8
Electric vacuum cleaners	70.2	81.5	84.2	87.8	86.4	92.7
Microwave ovens	n/a	n/a	n/a	n/a	1.2	7.3
Dishwashers	n/a	n/a	n/a	n/a	0.4	0.7
Sewing machines	70.8	79.4	74.9	75.3	72.8	58.6
Electric sewing machines	25.3	39.1	38.2	39.8	n/a	n/a
Bicycles	137.0	149.6	141.8	139.2	119.9	132.2
Motorcycles	32.6	31.4	29.0	26.1	20.5	12.6
Automobiles	21.6	28.1	35.1	43.4	53.5	67.5

Table 5A.11   Number of selected consumer durables per 100 households: farmer households

	1985	1989	1990	1991	1993	1997
Radios	80.2	86.0	86.2	82.7	82.3	72.7
Colour televisions	7.2	19.8	28.4	38.1	57.1	92.7
Black and white televisions	92.0	94.0	88.6	80.6	60.0	23.3
Satellite and cable TV	n/a	n/a	n/a	n/a	4.6	10.7
Compact disc players	n/a	n/a	n/a	n/a	n/a	4.2
Audio cassette players	31.6	41.0	49.7	55.7	20.1	n/a
Radio-cassette players	n/a	8.0	14.9	21.8	55.1	n/a
Stereo music systems	n/a	n/a	n/a	n/a	n/a	13.2
Videocassette recorders	n/a	0.9	4.7	10.8	25.3	42.0
Video cameras	n/a	n/a	n/a	n/a	0.5	0.8
Personal computers	n/a	n/a	n/a	n/a	2.1	3.4
Washing machines and spin driers	108.8	124.2	125.0	99.6	97.8	93.2
Automatic washing machines	11.3	23.2	24.8	25.6	28.6	40.5
Refrigerators and freezers	97.4	96.2	95.6	96.1	95.4	99.1
Freezers	n/a	33.7	42.9	50.5	57.3	73.3
Electric vacuum cleaners	53.8	68.9	70.4	72.9	74.6	84.9
Microwave ovens	n/a	n/a	n/a	n/a	1.4	5.3
Dishwashers	n/a	n/a	n/a	n/a	0.5	0.9
Sewing machines	63.9	70.6	65.8	66.0	65.4	54.8
Electric sewing machines	17.9	26.8	26.6	27.2	n/a	n/a
Bicycles	121.5	140.0	136.5	129.3	117.0	131.7
Motorcycles	23.4	24.4	23.7	20.6	17.8	13.9
Automobiles	23.7	30.4	36.4	40.9	49.8	66.9

Table 5A.12   Number of selected consumer durables per 100 households: pensioner households

	1985	1989	1990	1991	1993	1997
Radios	76.8	82.3	81.6	80.7	87.3	78.1
Colour televisions	8.4	21.0	28.3	43.4	64.6	90.3
Black and white televisions	87.1	83.7	78.3	67.6	43.8	17.2
Satellite and cable TV	n/a	n/a	n/a	n/a	12.6	27.8
Compact disc players	n/a	n/a	n/a	n/a	n/a	2.6
Audio cassette players	17.3	18.5	21.9	27.6	13.5	n/a
Radio–cassette players	n/a	4.3	7.0	11.2	33.6	n/a
Stereo music systems	n/a	n/a	n/a	n/a	n/a	8.9
Videocassette recorders	n/a	0.7	2.8	8.4	19.7	31.2
Video cameras	n/a	n/a	n/a	n/a	0.4	0.7
Personal computers	n/a	n/a	n/a	n/a	1.5	2.4
Washing machines and spin driers	98.0	114.0	114.1	81.6	74.4	64.8
Automatic washing machines	14.4	27.3	30.4	35.5	42.0	53.5
Refrigerators and freezers	90.7	94.3	95.0	95.5	95.9	97.0
Freezers	n/a	9.1	11.4	14.3	21.7	26.4
Electric vacuum cleaners	71.0	n/a	79.1	81.9	83.8	87.9
Microwave ovens	n/a	n/a	n/a	55.4	1.2	3.7
Dishwashers	n/a		n/a	n/a	0.3	0.3
Sewing machines	52.2		53.5	55.4	54.4	46.0
Electric sewing machines	15.6		21.9	26.0	n/a	n/a
Bicycles	38.8		42.4	44.2	45.8	51.6
Motorcycles	4.8		4.9	4.7	4.3	3.2
Automobiles	7.3		9.5	13.9	18.8	23.8

Table 5A.13 Number of selected consumer durables per 100 households: non-wage income and self-employed households

	Non-wage income		Self-employed	
	1993	1997	1993	1997
Radios	74.0	56.1	87.1	64.4
Black and white televisions	31.9	19.3	3.3	7.4
Colour televisions	63.6	84.0	105.6	116.6
Satellite and cable TV	14.6	25.2	41.9	56.2
Compact disc players	n/a	4.5	n/a	21.6
Tape recorders	20.9	n/a	39.1	n/a
Audio cassette players	58.0	n/a	86.6	n/a
Stereo music systems	n/a	15.6	n/a	52.6
Videocassette recorders	32.8	38.4	76.2	83.8
Video cameras	0.7	0.6	6.7	10.4
Personal computers	2.9	3.2	20.0	24.4
Washing machines and spin driers	70.0	65.1	52.1	39.3
Automatic washing machines	36.3	43.4	87.7	90.3
Refrigerators	91.4	94.7	99.6	99.7
Freezers	14.6	18.2	54.5	52.0
Electric vacuum cleaners	79.5	82.5	99.1	98.9
Microwave ovens	2.2	5.5	9.8	26.6
Dishwashers	0.6	0.4	2.8	4.3
Sewing machines	36.0	27.3	61.9	51.5
Bicycles	48.6	60.6	77.2	89.8
Motorcycles	6.0	3.1	7.0	3.9
Automobiles	17.2	16.4	88.7	90.1

APPENDIX FOR CHAPTER 6

Table 6A.1 Regression results using 1999 factor scores

	SLD–AWS			Left–Right		
OLS regression	B	Beta	sig	B	Beta	sig
Factor 1	0.131	0.242	0.0004	0.151	0.279	0.0000
Factor 2	0.193	0.300	0.0000	0.125	0.189	0.0000
Factor 3	0.067	0.108	0.0917	0.079	0.134	0.0141
Factor 4	-0.027	-0.043	0.5413	0.047	0.081	0.1694
Factor 5	0.077	-0.125	0.0555	-0.057	-0.094	0.0798
Factor 6	0.018	0.027	0.6553	0.011	0.017	0.7274
Constant	0.391		0.0000	0.424		0.0000

$N = 372, 553$. R square: 0.2329, 0.2580

	SLD–AWS			Left–Right		
Logit regression	B	sig	R	B	sig	R
Factor 1	0.659	0.000	0.135	0.724	0.0000	0.149
Factor 2	1.016	0.0000	0.225	0.676	0.0000	0.144
Factor 3	0.418	0.0567	0.057	0.518	0.0046	0.089
Factor 4	-0.143	0.5347	0.000	0.204	0.2663	0.000
Factor 5	-0.372	0.0899	-0.042	-0.285	0.1059	-0.028
Factor 6	0.117	0.5892	0.000	0.095	0.5812	0.000
Constant	-0.585	0.0000		-0.438	0.0000	

Continued overleaf

Table 6A.1 continued

	Per cent correct			Per cent correct
0 (SLD)	31.90		0 (Left)	75.58
1 (AWS)	62.25		1 (Right)	70.40
Overall	73.92		Overall	73.24

N = 372, 553. Chi-square = SLD–AWS: 96.901 (0.0000); Left–Right: 165.107 (0.0000)

Bibliography

Adam, J., 1993, 'Letter to the Editor', *Economics of Planning*, Vol. 26, pp. 183-184.

Akcja Wyborcza Solidarność, 1997, Electoral Programme, Warsaw: District Electoral Staff.

Alesina, A., 1988, 'Credibility and Policy Convergence in a Two-Party System with Rational Voters', *American Economic Review*, Vol. 78, pp. 796-805.

——, 1994, 'Political Models of Macroeconomic Policy and Reform', in S. Haggard and S.B. Webb, eds, *Voting for Reform: Democracy, Political Liberalization, and Economic Adjustment*, Oxford: Oxford University Press for the World Bank, pp. 37-60.

—— and Drazen, A., 1991, 'Why are Stabilizations Delayed?', *American Economic Review*, Vol. 81, pp. 1170-1188.

—— and Tabellini, G., 1987, 'A Positive Theory of Fiscal Deficits and Government Debt in a Democracy', NBER Working Paper No. 2308, National Bureau for Economic Research.

Alt, J.E. and Chrystal, K.A., 1980, *Political Economics*, Berkeley: University of California Press.

Atkinson, A.B. and Micklewright, J., 1991, 'Economic Transformation in Eastern Europe and the Distribution of Income', in A.B. Atkinson and R. Brunetta, eds, *Economics for the New Europe*, Basingstoke: Macmillan.

——, 1992, *Economic Transformation in Eastern Europe and the Distribution of Income*, Cambridge: Cambridge University Press.

Balcerowicz, L., 1994, 'Fallacies and Other Lessons', *Economic Policy*, supplement, December 1994; also published as Working Paper No. 11, European Bank for Reconstruction and Development, London.

——, 1995, *Socialism, Capitalism, Transformation*, Budapest, London and New York: Central European University Press.

Bell, J., 1997a, 'Unemployment Matters: Voting and Economic Reform in Poland 1990-1995', *Europe–Asia Studies*, Vol. 49, No. 7, pp. 1263-1291.

——, 1997b, *The Effects of Economic Transition on Voting Patterns in Poland: 1990-1997*, PhD thesis, School of Slavonic and East European Studies, University of London.

——, 1999, 'Winners, Losers, and How They Vote: Poland 1990-1999', in J. Miklaszewska, ed., *Democracy in Central Europe, 1989-99: Comparative and Historical Perspectives*, Cracow: Meritum, pp. 41-85.

—— and Mickiewicz, T., 1997, 'Unemployment and State Sector Insiders during the Economic Transition in Poland', *MOCT-MOST Economic Policy in Transitional Economies*, Vol. 7, pp. 131–157.

——, and Rostowski, J., 1995, 'A Note on the Confirmation of Podkaminer's Hypothesis in Post-liberalisation Poland', *Europe–Asia Studies*, Vol. 47, No. 3, pp. 527–530.

Berg, A., 1993, 'Measurement and Mismeasurement of Economic Activity during Transition to the Market', in M.I. Blejer *et al.*, eds, *Eastern Europe in Transition*, Discussion Paper 196, Washington, DC: World Bank, pp. 39–63.

——, 1994, 'Does Macroeconomic Reform Cause Structural Adjustment? Lessons from Poland', *Journal of Comparative Economics*, Vol. 18, No. 3, pp. 376–409.

—— and Sachs, J., 1992, 'Structural Adjustment and International Trade in Eastern Europe: The Case of Poland', *Economic Policy*, No. 14.

Beskid, L., Milic-Czerniak, R. and Sufin, Z., 1995, *Polacy a Nowa Rzeczywistość Economiczna: Procesy przystosowywania w mikroscali*, Warsaw: Wydawnictwo IFiS PAN.

Bivand, R., 1994, '"Return of the New": The Regional Imprint of the 1993 Parliamentary Elections in Poland', *European Urban and Regional Studies*, Vol. 1, No. 1, pp. 63–83.

Blazyca, G. and Rapacki, R., 1996, 'Continuity and Change in Polish Economic Policy: The Impact of the 1993 Election', *Europe–Asia Studies*, Vol. 48, No. 1, pp. 85–100.

Boeri, T., 1994, '"Transitional" Unemployment', *Economics of Transition*, Vol. 2, No. 1, pp. 1–25.

Bossak, J., ed., 1995, *Poland: International Economic Report 1994/95*, Warsaw: World Economy Research Unit, Warsaw School of Economics.

Bresser Pereia, L.C., Maravall, J.M. and Przeworski, A., 1993, *Economic Reforms in New Democracies: A Social-Democratic Approach*, Cambridge: Cambridge University Press.

Calvo, C. and Coricelli, F., 1993, 'Output Collapse in Eastern Europe', *IMF Staff Papers*, Vol. 40, No. 1, March, pp. 32–52.

CBOS (Centrum Badanii Opinii Społecznej), various reports.

Chan, K.K.-L., 1995, 'Poland at the Crossroad: The 1993 General Election', *Europe–Asia Studies*, Vol. 47, No. 1, pp. 123–145.

Chelkowski, S., 1989, 'Co z tym bezrobociem?', *Życie Gospodarcze*, 12 November, p. 2.

Chilosi, A., 1993, 'Economic Transition and the Unemployment Issue', *Economic Systems*, Vol. 17, No. 1, pp. 63–78.

Chmaj, M., 1996, *Sejm 'Kontraktowy' w Transformacji Systemu Politycznego Rzeczpospolitej Polskiej*, Lublin: Wydawnictwo Uniwersytetu Marii Curie-Skłodowskiej.

Cichomski, B. and Sawinski, Z., 1993, *Polish General Social Surveys 1992–93, Machine readable data file*, Warsaw: Institute for Social Studies, University of Warsaw, October.

Coricelli, F. and Revenga, A., 1992, 'Wages and Unemployment in Poland: Recent Developments and Policy Issues', in F. Coricelli and A. Revenga, eds, *Wage Policy during the Transition to a Market Economy. Poland*

1990–91, Discussion Paper No. 158, Washington, DC: World Bank.

Coricelli, F., Hagemejer, K. and Rybinski, K., 1995, 'Poland', in S. Commander and F. Corricelli, eds, *Unemployment, Restructuring, and the Labor Market in Eastern Europe and Russia*, EDI Development Series, Washington, DC: World Bank, pp. 39–90.

Crow, G. and Rees, T., 1999, '"Winners" and "Losers" in Social Transformations, *Sociological Research Online*, Vol. 4, No. 1, <<http://www.socresonline. org.uk/socresonline/4/1/crow_rees.html>>.

Czarny, E. and Czarny, B., 1992, *From the Plan to the Market: The Polish Experience 1990–1991*, Warsaw: Friedrich Ebert Foundation.

Czekaj, J., Hausner, J., Indraszkiewicz, J. and Owsiak, S., 1991, *Polityka i Gospodarka: Polska w Latach 80'*, Warsaw: Państwowe Wydawnictwo Ekonomiczne.

Davies, N., 1984, *Heart of Europe: A Short History of Poland*, Oxford: Oxford University Press.

Deaton, A. and Muellbauer, J., 1980, *Economics and Consumer Behaviour*, Cambridge: Cambridge University Press.

Dohalnik, J., 1993, 'Profile swiatpodlagowe elektoratów poszczególnych partii i osób nieuczestniczacych w wyborach', in S. Gebethner, ed., *Polska Scena Polityczna a Wybory*, Warsaw: Wydawnictwo Fundacji Inicjatyw Społecznych 'Polska w Europie', pp. 155–165.

Donosy, e-mail newsletter, various issues.

Dornbusch, R. and Simonsen, M.H., 1998, 'Inflation Stabilization: The Role of Incomes Policy and Monetization', in R. Dornbusch (ed.), *Exchange Rates and Inflation*, Cambridge, MA and London: MIT Press, pp. 439–465.

—— and Edwards, S., 1991, *The Macroeconomics of Populism in Latin America*, Chicago: University of Chicago Press.

Downs, A., 1957, *An Economic Theory of Democracy*, New York: Harper.

Drazen, A., 1994, 'The Political Economy of Delayed Reform', Paper prepared for the conference *Economic Reform: Latin America and the Transition Economies*, Washington, DC: Georgetown University, 12–13 May; also in *The Journal of Policy Reform*, Vol. 1, No. 1 (1996), pp. 25–46.

Drewnowski, J., 1982, 'The Anatomy of Economic Failure in Soviet-Type Systems', in J. Drewnowski, ed., *Crisis in the East European Economy*, Beckenham: Croom Helm, pp. 72–86.

Easterlin, R.A., 1974, 'Does Economic Growth Improve the Human Lot? Some Empirical Evidence', in P.A. David and M.W. Reder, eds, *Nations and Households in Economic Growth: Essays in Honor of Moses Abramovitz*, New York and London: Academic Press.

Ekiert, G. and Kubik, J., 1998, 'Collective Protest in Post-Communist Poland 1989–1993: A Research Report', *Communist and Post-Communist Studies*, Vol. 31, No. 2, p. 102.

Elster, J., Offe, C. and Preuss, U., 1998, *Institutional Design in Post-Communist Societies*, Cambridge: Cambridge University Press.

Evans, G. and Whitefield, S., 1994, 'The Politics and Economics of Democratic Commitment: Support for Democracy in Transition Societies', mimeo, Oxford University.

Fair, R.C., 1996, 'Econometrics and Presidential Elections', *Journal of Economic Perspectives*, No. 3.

Fernandez, R. and Rodrik, D., 1991, 'Resistance to Reform: Status Quo Bias in the Presence of Individual-Specific Uncertainty', *American Economic Review*, Vol. 81, pp. 1146–1155.

Fidrmuc, J., 1997, 'Political Support for Reforms: The Role of Unemployment and the Private Sector', mimeo, Tilburg, The Netherlands: Center for Economic Research, Tilburg University.

Financial Times, various issues.

Freeman, R., 1993, 'What Direction for Labour Market Institutions in Eastern and Central Europe?', Discussion Paper No. 157, London: Centre for Economic Performance, London School of Economics, July.

Frentzel-Zagorska, J. and Zagorski, K., 1993, 'Polish Public Opinion on Privatization and State Interventionism', *Europe–Asia Studies*, Vol. 45, No. 4, pp. 705–728.

Fretwell, D. and Jackman, R., 1994, 'Labour Markets: Unemployment', in N. Barr, ed., *Labour Markets and Social Policy in Central and Eastern Europe: The Transition and Beyond*, Oxford: Oxford University Press for the World Bank and London School of Economics, pp. 160–191.

Frey, B.S., 1984, 'Modelling Politico-Economic Relationships', in D.K. Whynes, ed., *What is Political Economy? Eight Perspectives*, Oxford and New York: Basil Blackwell, pp. 141–161.

Gebethner, S., 1997, 'Partie i ich kolacje przed wyborami parlimentarnymi 1997 r.', in S. Gebethner, ed., *Wybory '97: Partie i Programy Wyborcze*, Warsaw: Dom Wydawniczy Elipsa.

Gibson, J. and Cielecka, A., 1995, 'Economic Influences on the Political Support for Market Reform in Post-communist Transitions: Some Evidence from the 1993 Polish Parliamentary Elections', *Europe–Asia Studies*, Vol. 47, No. 5, pp. 765–785.

Główny Urząd Statystyczny (Central Statistical Office, Poland)
    Aktywność Ekonomiczna Ludności Polski w 1998 roku
    Biuletyn Statystyczny, various issues.
    Budżety Gospodarstw Domowych, various issues.
    Information on Social and Economic Situation in Poland 1993
    Mały Rocznik Statystyczny, various issues.
    Poland: Quarterly Statistics, June 1996.
    Registered Unemployment in Poland, III Quarter 1998, Information and Statistical Papers
    Rocznik Statystyzny, various issues.

Golata, K., 'Polska Prywatna', *Wprost*, 1993, pp. 64–65.

Golinowska, S., 1996, 'State Social Policy and Social Expenditure in Central and Eastern Europel', *Studies and Analysis*, No. 81, Warsaw: Centre for Social and Economic Research (CASE).

Gomułka, J., 1995, 'Changes in consumption in Poland during the first two years of transition', mimeo, London School of Economics, 6 May 1995.

Gomułka, S., 1993, 'The Financial Situation of Polish Enterprises 1992–3 and its Impact on Monetary and Fiscal Policies', mimeo, London School of

Economics.

——, 1994, 'Economic and Political Constraints During Transition', *Europe-Asia Studies*, Vol. 46, No. 1, pp. 89–106.

Góra, M., 1995, 'Rynek pracy w Polsce w latach 1990–1993', in M. Dąbrowski, ed., *Polityka gospodarcza okresu transformacji*, Warsaw: CASE and Wydawnictwo Naukowe PWN, pp. 140–161.

——, 1996a, 'Institutional Sources of the Increase in Unemployment in Poland', mimeo, Warsaw School of Economics.

——, 1996b, 'W worku "bezrobocie" sa wszystkie polskie problemy społeczne', *Rzeczpospolita*, 29 August.

Górecki, B., 1994, 'Evidence of a New Shape of Income Distribution in Poland', *Eastern European Economics*, May–June, pp. 32–49.

—— and Wiśniewski, M., 1995, 'Economic Conditions of Polish Households 1987–1993 (New Patterns of Income Mobility, Saving and Spending)', mimeo, University of Warsaw.

Grabowska, M., 1991, 'System partyjny – w budowie', *Krytyka*, Vol. 37, pp. 24–33.

Grabowski, M., 1995, 'Informal Sector in Poland – Assessment and Policy Implications', in M. Grabowski and P. Jedrzejowicz, eds, *Informal Economy in the Polish Transformation*, Economic Transformation Series No. 52, Gdańsk Institute for Market Economics.

Gucwa-Lesny, E., 1995, 'Zmiany poziomy życia i ich ocena', mimeo, Institute of Social Studies, University of Warsaw.

——, 1996, 'Four Years after Velvet Revolution: Who is Better off? Who feels Better? in New Socio-Economic Conditions', Economic Discussion Paper No. 30, Warsaw: Faculty of Economic Sciences, University of Warsaw, September.

Gujarati, Damodar N., 1995, *Basic Econometrics*, 3rd edn, New York: McGraw-Hill.

GUS, 1995, *Mały Rocznik Statystyczny*, Warsaw.

Haggard, S. and Kaufman, R.R., 1989, 'Economic Adjustment in New Democracies', in J.M. Nelson, *et al.*, eds, *Fragile Coalitions: The Politics of Economic Adjustment*, New Brunswick, NJ: Transaction Books.

——, 1992, 'The Political Economy of Inflation and Stabilization in Middle-Income Countries', in S. Haggard and R.R. Kaufman, eds, *The Politics of Economic Adjustment: Institutional Constraints, Distributive Conflicts, and the State*, Princeton, NJ: Princeton University Press, pp. 270–315.

Haggard, S. and Webb, S.B., 1993, 'What Do We Know about the Political Economy of Economic Policy Reform?', *The World Bank Research Observer*, Vol. 8, No. 2, pp. 143–168.

Hibbs, D.A., Jr, 1977, 'Political Parties and Macroeconomic Policy', *American Political Science Review*, Vol. 71, pp. 1467–1487.

——, 1987, *The Political Economy of Industrial Democracies*, Cambridge, MA: Harvard University Press.

Illarionov, L., Layard, R. and Orszag, P., 1994, 'The Conditions of Life', in A. Åslund, ed., *Economic Transformation in Russia*, London and New York: Pinter Publishers, pp. 127–156.

Indraszkiewicz, J., 1994, *Demokracja i Gospodarka: Swiadomosc zmian ustrojowych w Polsce*. Cracow: Towarzystwo Autorów i Wydawców Prac Naukowych 'Universitas'.
Inglot, T., 1995, 'The Politics of Social Reform in Post-Communist Poland', *Communist and Post-Communist Studies*, Vol. 28, No. 3, pp. 361–373.
Iwanek, M. and Ordover, J.A., 1993, 'Transition to a Market Economy: Some Industrial Organizational Issues', in H. Kierzkowski, M. Okolski and S. Wellisz, eds, *Stabilization and Structural Adjustment in Poland*, pp. 153–170.
Jackman, R. and Rutkowski, M., 1994, 'Labour Markets: Wages and Employment', in N. Barr, ed., *Labour Markets and Social Policy in Central and Eastern Europe: The Transition and Beyond*, Oxford: Oxford University Press for the World Bank and London School of Economics, pp. 121–159.
Jasiewicz, K., 1992, 'Polish elections 1989–1991: Beyond the "Pospolite Ruszenie"', in P.M.E. Volten, ed., *Bound to Change: Consolidating Democracy in East Central Europe*, New York and Prague: Institute for EastWest Studies, pp. 191–211.
——, 1993, 'Polish Politics on the Eve of the 1993 Elections: Towards Fragmentation or Pluralism?', *Communism and Post-Communist Studies*, Vol. 26, No. 4, pp. 387–411.
——, 1996, 'Wybory prezydenckie 1995 roku a kształtowanie się polskiego systemu partyjnego', *Studia Polityczne*, No. 51, pp. 7–16.
——, 1998, 'Polish Politics After the 1997 Parliamentary Election: Back to a Polarized Polity?', Washington, DC: National Council for Eurasian and East European Research.
——, 2000, 'Dead Ends and New Beginnings: The Quest for a Procedural Republic in Poland', *Communist and Post-Communist Studies*, Vol. 33, pp. 101–22.
—— and Zukowski, T., 1992, 'The Elections of 1984–1989 as a Factor in the Transformation of the Social Order in Poland', in G. Sanford, ed., *Democratization in Poland, 1988–90: Polish Voices*, New York: St Martin's Press.
Johnson, S. and Kowalska, M., 1994, 'Poland: The Political Economy of Shock Therapy', in S. Haggard and S.B. Webb, eds, *Voting for Reform: Democracy, Political Liberalization, and Economic Adjustment*, New York: Oxford University Press for the World Bank, pp. 185–240.
Kabaj, M. and Kowalik, T., 1995, 'Who is Responsible for Postcommunist Successes in Eastern Europe?', *Transition* (World Bank), Vol. 6, No. 7–8, July–August, pp. 7–8.
Kaminski, B., 1991, *The Collapse of State Socialism: The Case of Poland*, Princeton, NJ: Princeton University Press.
Kaminski, M., 1998, 'Fragmentation and Stability: The Political Consequences of Pre-Electoral Coalitions in the 1993 and 1997 Parliamentary Elections in Poland', paper presented to the APSA convention, Boston, 3–6 September.
Katsenelinboigen, A., 1977, 'Coloured Markets in the Soviet Union', *Soviet Studies*, Vol. 29, No. 1, pp. 62–85.
Kaufman, R.R. and Stallings, B., 1992, 'The Political Economy of Latin Ameri-

can Populism', in R. Dornbusch and S. Edwards, eds, *The Macroeconomics of Populism*, Chicago and London: The University of Chicago Press.

Keech, W.R., 1995, *Economic Politics: The Costs of Democracy*, Cambridge: Cambridge University Press.

Kierzkowski, H., Okolski, M. and Wellisz, S., eds, 1993, *Stabilization and Structural Adjustment in Poland*, London: Routledge.

Kinder, D.R. and Kiewiet, D.R., 1979, 'Economic Discontent and Political Behavior: The Role of Personal Grievanaces and Collective Economic Judgments in Congressional Voting', *American Journal of Political Science*, No. 23, pp. 495–517.

Kitschelt, H., 1992, 'The Formation of Party Systems in East–Central Europe', *Politics and Society*, Vol. 20, No. 1, pp. 7–50.

Koen, V., 1992, 'Price Liberalization in Russia: Behavior of Prices, Household Incomes, and Consumption During the First Year', Occasional Paper 104, Washington, DC: International Monetary Fund.

Kolarska-Bobińska, L., 1989, 'Poland Under Crisis: Unreformable Society or Establishment?' in R. Clarke, ed., *Poland: The Economy in the 1980s*, London: Longman, pp. 126–138.

——, 1990, 'The Myth of the Market and the Reality of Reform', in S. Gomułka and A. Polonsky, eds, *Polish Paradoxes*, London: Routledge, pp. 160–179.

——, 1991, 'Changing the Polish Economy: Social Attitudes and Interests 1980–1990', *Economic Systems*, Vol. 15, No. 1.

——, 1994, 'Social Interests and Their Political Representation', unpublished mimeo.

Kolodko, G.W., 1989, *Reform, Stabilization Policies, and Economic Adjustment in Poland*, WIDER Working Paper 51, January.

Korbonski, A., 1989, 'The Politics of Economic Reforms in Eastern Europe: The Last Thirty Years', *Soviet Studies* Vol. 41, No. 1, pp. 1–19.

Kornai, J., 1980, *Economics of Shortage*, Amsterdam: North-Holland.

——, 1986, 'The Soft Budget Constraint', *Kyklos*, Vol. 39, No. 1, pp. 3–30.

——, 1992, *The Socialist System: The Political Economy of Communism*, Oxford: Clarendon Press.

Kramer, G.H., 1971, 'Short-Run Fluctuations in U.S. Voting Behavior, 1896–1964', *American Political Science Review*, No. 65, pp. 131–143.

Krueger, A.O., 1979, 'The Political Economy of the Rent-Seeking Society', *American Economic Review*, Vol. 64, pp. 291–303.

Kudrycka, I., 1993, 'Distribution and Differentiation of Incomes in the Years 1989–1991', in L. Zienkowski, ed., *The Polish Economy in 1990–1992: Experience and Conclusions*, Warsaw: RECESS (GUS and SGH), pp. 149–157.

Kwiecinski, A. and Leopold, A., 1993, 'Situation in Agriculture', in L. Zienkowski, ed., *Polish Economy in 1990–1992: Experience and Conclusions*, Warsaw: RECESS.

—— and Quaisser, W., 1993, 'Agricultural Prices and Subsidies in the Transformation Process of the Polish Economy', *Economic Systems*, Vol. 17, No. 2, pp. 125–154.

Layard, R. and Richter, A., 1995, 'How Much Unemployment is Needed for

Restructuring?: The Russian Experience', Discussion Paper No. 238, Centre for Economic Performance, London School of Economics.

Layard, R., Nickell, S. and Jackman, R., 1991, *Unemployment: Macroeconomic Performance and the Labour Market*, Oxford: Oxford University Press.

Lewis, P.G., 1994, 'Political Institutionalisation and Party Development in Post-communist Poland', *Europe–Asia Studies*, Vol. 46, No. 5, pp. 779–799.

Lewis-Beck, M.S., 1988, *Economics and Elections: The Major Western Democracies*, Ann Arbor: University of Michigan Press.

—— and Rice, T.W., 1992, *Forecasting Elections*, Washington, DC: Congressional Quarterly Press.

Lipset, S.M., and Rokkan, S., 1967, 'Cleavage Structures, Party Systems, and Voter Alignments: An Introduction', in Lipset and Rokkan, eds, *Party Systems and Voter Alignments: Cross-National Perspectives*, New York: The Free Press, pp. 1–63.

Lopez Murphy, R. and Sturzenegger, F., 1994, 'The Feasibility of Money Control: Theory with an Application to the Argentine Case', Paper prepared for the conference *Economic Reform: Latin America and the Transition Economies*, Washington, DC, Georgetown University, 12–13 May; also in *The Journal of Policy Reform*, Vol. 1, No. 1, (1996), pp. 47–73.

McAuley, A., 1994, 'Social Welfare in Transition: What Happened in Russia?', Research Paper No. 6, Transition Economies Division, World Bank, January.

Małkiewicz, A., 1994, *Wybory Czerwcowe 1989*, Warsaw: Institute of Political Studies, Polish Academy of Sciences (IFiS PAN).

Maret, X. and Schwartz, G., 1993, 'Poland: The Social Safety Net During the Transition', Working Paper 93/42, International Monetary Fund, Washington, DC, May.

Markowski, R., 1997, 'Political Parties and Ideological Space in East Central Europe', *Communist and Post-Communist Studies*, Vol. 30, No. 3, pp. 221–254.

Marody, M., 1995a, 'Three Stages of Party System Emergence in Poland', *Communist and Post-Communist Studies*, Vol. 28, No. 2, pp. 263–270.

——, 1995b, 'Social and Psychological Consequences of Transformation', paper presented to the Fulbright Commission conference on Education for Transition to Market Economy in Countries of Central and Eastern Europe, Warsaw, 29–30 June.

Mateju, P. and Vlachova, A., 1998, 'Values and Electoral Decisions in the Czech Republic', *Communist and Post-Communist Studies*, Vol. 31, No. 3, pp. 249–269.

Mickiewicz, T., 1993, 'Dobra publiczne, gra tchórza', *Życie Gospodarcze*, 31 October.

—— and Bell, J., 2000, *Transitional Unemployment: Labour Markets in Central and Eastern Europe*, Reading: Harwood Academic Publishers.

Milanovic, B., 1992, 'Poverty in Poland, 1978–1988', *Review of Income and Wealth*, September, pp. 329–340.

——, 1993, 'Social Costs of the Transition to Capitalism: Poland 1990–1991', Working Paper No. 1165, Washington, DC: World Bank, August.

——, 1996, 'Income, Inequality and Poverty during the Transition: A Survey of the Evidence', *MOCT-MOST*, Vol. 6, pp. 131–147.

——, 1997, 'Increased Ownership of Consumer Durables Does Not Necessarily Indicate Higher Real Incomes', *Transition*, February, p. 15

——, 1998, *Income, Inequality and Poverty During the Transition from Planned to Market Economy*, Washington, DC: World Bank.

Millard, F., 1995, 'The Polish Parliamentary Election of September, 1993', *Communist and Post-Communist Studies*, Vol. 27, No. 3.

Muellbauer, J., 1987, 'Professor Sen on the Standard of Living', in G. Hawthorn, ed., *The Standard of Living*, Cambridge: Cambridge University Press, pp. 39–58.

Mueller, D.C., 1989, *Public Choice II*, Cambridge and New York: Cambridge University Press.

—— and Murrell, P., 1987, 'The Voting Paradox', in C.K. Rowley, ed., *Democracy and Public Choice*, Oxford: Basil Blackwell, pp. 77–99.

Nordhaus, W.D., 1975, 'The Political Business Cycle', *Review of Economic Studies*, No. 42, pp. 1969–1990.

Offe, C., 1991, 'Capitalism by Democratic Design: Democratic Theory Facing the Triple Transition in East Central Europe', *Social Research*, Vol. 58, No. 4, pp. 865–892.

Office of Research, 1990, Data from a face-to-face survey of 997 adults age 18 years and over in November. The Center for Public Opinion and Market Research at Jagiellonian University in Cracow conducted the surveys for the Office of Research.

——, 1991a, Data from a face-to-face survey with 1,047 adults 18 years and over in May. The research firm Demoskop in Warsaw conducted the surveys for the Office of Research.

——, 1991b, Data from a face-to-face survey with 1,002 adults 18 years and over in September. The research firm Demoskop in Warsaw conducted the surveys for the Office of Research.

——, 1995a, Data from a face-to-face survey of 992 adults age 18 and over, conducted 11–28 March 1995. The research firm Demoskop in Warsaw conducted the surveys for the Office of Research.

——, 1995b, Data from a face-to-face survey of 898 adults age 18 and over, conducted 24 November–12 December 1993. The research firm Demoskop, based in Warsaw, conducted the surveys for the Office of Research.

——, 1999, Data from a face-to-face survey of 904 adults age 18 and over conducted 21 May–7 June 1999. The research firm Demoskop, based in Warsaw, conducted the surveys for the Office of Research.

Office of the Government Plenipotentiary for Social Security Reform, 1997, *Security Through Diversity: Reform of the Pension System in Poland*, Warsaw: Ministry of Labour and Social Policy.

Okolski, M., 1996, 'Czynniki zmian mobilności siły roboczej', in M. Okolski and U. Sztanderska, eds, *Studia nad reformowana gospodarka*, Warsaw:

PWN, pp. 137–170.

Olszewski, D., Pruban, G., Pawlica, M., Nojszewski, P. and Sibilska, M., 1993, 'Chronology of Economic and Political Events 1989–1991', in H. Kierzkowski, M. Okolski and S. Wellisz, eds, *Stabilization and Structural Adjustment in Poland*, pp. 255–291.

OMRI Daily Digest, various issues.

Opallo, M., 1995, 'Przestrzenne aspekty transformacji', *Wiadomości Statystyczne*, No. 8, pp. 22–31.

Organization for Economic Cooperation and Development (OECD), *Short Term Statistical Indicators*, various issues.

Orlowski, W., 1993, 'Prices, Wages and Money Supply', in L. Zienkowski, ed., *The Polish Economy 1990–1992: Experience and Conclusions*, Warsaw: RECESS.

Osband, K., 1992, 'Index Number Biases During Price Liberalization', *IMF Staff Papers*, Vol. 39, No. 2, June.

Osiatynski, J., 1992, 'Opposition Against Market-type Reforms in Centrally-planned Economies', in J.M. Kovács and M. Tardos, eds, *Reform and Transformation in Eastern Europe*, London: Routledge.

Osrodek Badanii Opinii Publicznej (OBOP), various reports.

Pacek, A., 1994, 'Macroeconomic Conditions and Electoral Patterns in East Central Europe', *American Journal of Political Science*, Vol. 38, No. 3, pp. 723–744.

Panek, T., 1997, 'Obszary ubóstwa', *Rzeczpospolita*, 7 January 1997, p. 22.

—— and Rytelewska, G., 1996, 'Budowa dobrobytu gospodarstw domowych w Polsce', *Bank i Kredyt*, September, pp. 4–17.

Państwowa Komisja Wyborcza, 1990, *Wyniki Wyborów Prezydenta Rzeczpopolitej Polskiej 25.11.1990 – 9.12.1990*, Warsaw.

——, 1991, *Wyniki Wyborów do Sejmu Rzeczpospolitej Polskiej: 27 pazdziernika 1991 r., Część II: Wyniki Głosowania i Wyniki Wyborów*, Warsaw.

——, 1993, *Wyniki Wyborów do Sejmu Rzeczpospolitej Polskiej: 19 wrzesnia 1993 r., Część II: Wyniki Głosowania i Wyniki Wyborów*, Warsaw.

——, 1996, *Wyniki Wyborów Prezydenta Rzeczpospolitej Polskiej 5 listopada i 19 listopada 1995*. Warsaw.

Parysek, J.J., Adamczak, Z. and Grobelny, R., 1991, 'Regional Differences in the Results of the 1990 Presidential Election in Poland as the First Approximation to a Political Map of the Country', *Environment and Planning A*, Vol. 23, pp. 1315–1329.

Persson, T. and Tabeilini, G., 1994, 'Introduction', in T. Persson and G. Tabellini, ed., *Monetary and Fiscal Policy – Volume 2: Politics*, Cambridge, MA and London: Cambridge University Press, pp. 1–28.

Pinto, B. and van Wijnbergen, S., 1994, 'Ownership and Corporate Control in Poland: Why State Firms Defied the Odds', Working Paper No. 1308, World Bank.

Podkaminer, L., 1982, 'Estimates of the Disequilibrium in Poland's Consumer Markets', *Review of Economics and Statistics*, Vol. 64, No. 3, pp. 423–431.

——, 1987, 'On Polish Disequilibrium Once Again', *Soviet Studies*, Vol. 39, No.

3, pp. 509–512.

Polish Press Agency, *Dzennik Internetowy*, various issues.

Polityka, various issues.

Przeworski, A., 1991, *Democracy and the Market: Political and Economic Reforms in Eastern Europe and Latin America*, Cambridge: Cambridge University Press.

——, 1996, 'Public Support for Economic Reforms in Poland', *Comparative Political Studies*, Vol. 29, No. 5, pp. 520–543.

Quaisser, W., 1986, 'Agricultural Price Policy and Peasant Agriculture in Poland', *Soviet Studies*, Vol. 38, No. 4, pp. 562–585.

Redor, D., 1992, *Wage Inequalities in East and West*, Cambridge: Cambridge University Press.

Roberts, B., 1993, 'The J-Curve is a Gamma Curve: Initial Welfare Consequences of Price Liberalization in Eastern Europe', Working Paper Series, UNU–WIDER, January.

Rodrik, D., 1993, 'The Positive Economics of Policy Reform', *American Economic Association Papers and Proceedings, American Economic Review*, Vol. 83, No. 2, pp. 356–361.

——, 1995, 'The Dynamics of Political Support for Reform in Economies in Transition', Discussion Paper No. 1115, London: Centre for Economic Policy Research, January.

Rogoff, K., 1990, 'Equilibrium Political Business Cycles', *American Economic Review*, Vol. 80, pp. 21–36.

Rose, A., 1999, 'Extraordinary Politics in the Polish Transition', *Communist and Post-Communist Studies*, Vol. 32, pp. 195–210.

Rose, R. and Haerpfer, C., 1996, 'Fears and Hopes: New Democracies Barometer Surveys', *Transition* (World Bank), Vol. 7, No. 5–6, May–June, pp. 13–14.

Rostowski, J., 1989, 'Market Socialism is Not Enough: Inflation vs. Unemployment in Reforming Communist Economies', *Communist Economies*, Vol. 1, No. 3, pp. 269–285.

——, 1993a, 'Problems of Creating Stable Monetary Systems', *Europe–Asia Studies*, Vol. 45, No. 3, pp. 445–461.

——, 1993b, 'The Implications of Rapid Private Sector Growth in Poland', Discussion Paper No. 159, London: Centre for Economic Performance, London School of Economics, July.

Rothert, A., 1997, 'Unia Wolności – między prawica a lewica', in S. Gebethner, ed., *Wybory '97: Partie i Programy Wyborcze*, Warsaw: Dom Wydawniczy Elipsa, pp. 215–232.

Rutkowski, M., 1995, 'Workers in Transition', Policy Research Working Paper No. 1556, Washington, DC: Office of the Vice President, World Bank.

——, 1996, 'High Skills Pay Off: The Changing Wage Structure During Economic Transition in Poland', *Economics of Transition*, Vol. 4, No. 1, pp. 89–112.

Rychard, A., 1992, 'Politics and Society after the Breakthrough: the Sources and Threats to Political Legitimacy in Post-Communist Poland', in G. Sanford,

234   *The Political Economy of Reform in Poland*

——, 1996, 'Beyond Gains and Losses: In Search of "Winning Losers"', *Social Research*, Vol. 63, No. 2, pp. 465–485.

Rzeczpospolita, print and internet editions, various issues.

Sachs, J., 1992, 'The Economic Transformation of Eastern Europe: The Case of Poland', *Economics of Planning*, Vol. 25, pp. 5–20.

——, 1993a, 'Reply to Jan Adam', *Economics of Planning*, Vol. 26, pp. 185–189.

——, 1993b, *Poland's Jump to the Market Economy*, Cambridge, MA and London: MIT Press.

——, 1995, 'Postcommunist Parties and the Politics of Entitlements', *Transition* (World Bank), Vol. 6, No. 3, March, pp. 1–4.

Sah, R.K., 1987, 'Queues, Rations, and Market: Comparisons of Outcomes for the Poor and the Rich', *American Economic Review*, Vol. 77, No. 1, pp. 69–77.

Sahay, R. and Végh, C.A., 1995, 'Inflation and Stabilization in Transition Economies: An Analytical Interpretation of the Evidence', *The Journal of Policy Reform*, Vol. 1, No. 1. pp. 75–108.

Schaffer, M., 1991, 'A Note on the Polish State-Owned Enterprise Sector in 1990', Discussion Paper No. 36, London: Centre for Economic Performance, London School of Economics, March.

——, 1992, 'The Economy of Poland', Working Paper No. 167, Centre for Economic Performance, London School of Economics, March.

Schneider, F. and Frey, B.S., 1988, 'Politico-Economic Models of Macro-economic Policy', in T.D. Willett, ed., *Political Business Cycle*, Durham, NC: Duke University Press.

Sen, A., 1976, 'Poverty: An Ordinal Approach to Measurement', *Econometrica*, Vol. 44.

——, 1987, 'The Standard of Living: Lecture I, Concepts and Critiques' and 'The Standard of Living: Lecture II, Lives and Capabilities', in A. Sen *et al.* with G. Hawthorn, eds, *The Standard of Living*, Cambridge University Press, pp. 1–19 and 20–38.

Shapiro, J. and Granville, B., 1995, 'Russian Inflation: A Statistical Pandora's Box', Discussion Paper 53, London: Royal Institute of International Affairs.

——, 1996, 'Less Inflation, Less Poverty: First Results for Russia', Discussion Paper 68, London: Royal Institute of International Affairs.

Slay, B., 1994, *The Polish Economy*, Princeton, NJ: Princeton University Press.

Smith, J.W., 1975, 'A Clear Test of Rational Voting', *Public Choice*, Vol. 23, pp. 55–67.

Socha, M. and Sztanderska, U., 1993, 'The Labour Market', in H. Kierzkowski, M. Okolski and S. Wellisz, eds, *Stabilization and Structural Adjustment in Poland*, pp. 131–152.

Sojusz Lewicy Demokratycznej, 1997, *Dobrze Dziś – Lepsze Jutro. Program Wyborczy Sojuszu Lewicy Demokratycznej*, Warsaw: Oficyjna Wydawnictwa 'Patria'.

Stahl, D.O. II and Alexeev, M., 1985, 'The Influence of Black Markets in a Queue-Rationed Centrally Planned Economy', *Journal of Economic*

Theory, Vol. 35, pp. 234–250.

Staniszkis, J., 1991, *The Dynamics of the Breakthrough in Eastern Europe: The Polish Experience*, Berkeley CA: University of California Press.

Subotic, M., 1997, 'Twardzi i miękcy w kampanii,' *Rzeczpospolita*, 7 August, p. 4.

Swianiewicz, P., 1996, 'The Policy Preferences and Ideologies of Candidates in the 1994 Polish Local Elections', *International Journal of Urban and Regional Research*, Vol. 20, No. 4, pp. 733–743.

Szamuely, L., 1996, 'The Social Costs of Transformation in Central and Eastern Europe', Discussion Paper No. 44, Budapest: KOPINT-DATORG.

Szulc, A., 1993, 'Consumer Expenditure Patterns during the Transition Period in Poland', *Statistics in Transition* Vol. 1, No. 2, pp. 187–199.

——, 1996, 'Ubóstwo materialne w Polsce w latach 1990–1994', in *Ubóstwo w Siwetle Badan Budzetów Gospodarstw Domowych*, in the series 'Studia i Analyzy Statystyczne', Warsaw: Główny Urząd Statystyczny, pp. 20–41.

Tufte, E.R., 1978, *Political Control of the Economy*, Princeton, NJ: Princeton University Press.

Tyszka, T. and Sokolowska, J., 1992, 'Perception and Judgements of the Economic System', *Journal of Economic Psychology*, Vol. 13, pp. 421–448.

Unia Pracy, 1997, 'Zaslugujesz na wiecej: deklaracja wyborcza', Warsaw: National Electoral Staff, 15 June.

UNICEF, 1994, *Crisis in Mortality, Health and Nutrition*, Regional Monitoring Report No. 2, Economics in Transition Studies, August.

Vinton, L., 1993, 'Polish Politics on the Eve of the 1993 Elections', *Communist and Post-Communist Studies*.

Wade, L.L., Lavelle, P. and Groth, A.J., 1995, 'Searching for Voting Patterns in Post-communist Poland's Sejm Elections', *Communist and Post-Communist Studies*, Vol. 28, No. 4, pp. 411–425.

Waldron-Moore, P., 1999, 'Eastern Europe at the Crossroads of Democratic Transition: Evaluating Support for Democratic Institutions, Satisfaction with Democratic Government, and Consolidation of Democratic Regimes', *Comparative Political Studies*, Vol. 32, No. 1, pp. 32–62.

Wanless, P.T., 1985, 'Inflation in the Consumer Goods Market in Poland, 1971–82', *Soviet Studies*, Vol. 37, No. 3, July, pp. 403–416.

Weclawowicz, G., 1996, *Contemporary Poland: Space and Society*, Changing Eastern Europe Series 4, London: UCL Press.

Wedel, J.R., 1992, *The Unplanned Society: Poland During and After Communism*, New York: Columbia University Press.

Weitzman, M.L., 1991, 'Price Distortion and Shortage Deformation or What Happened to the Soap?', *American Economic Review*, Vol. 81, No. 3, pp. 401–414.

Wellisz, S., Kierkowski, H. and Okolski, M., 1993, 'The Polish Economy 1989–1991', in H. Kierzkowski, M. Okolski and S. Wellisz, eds, *Stabilization and Structural Adjustment in Poland*.

Whitefield, S. and Evans, G., 1994, 'The Social Context of the December Elections in Russia: Public Attitudes and the Transition Experience', mimeo, Oxford University.

236 The Political Economy of Reform in Poland

Wiatr, J., 1993, Wybory Parliamentarne 19 września 1993: Przyczyny i następstwa, Warsaw: Agencja Scholar.

Winiecki, J., 1991, 'The Inevitability of a Fall in Output in the Early Stages of Transition to the Market: Theoretical Underpinnings', Soviet Studies, Vol. 43, No. 4, pp. 669–676.

——, 1994, 'East-Central Europe in 1993', Europe–Asia Studies, pp. 711–733.

Wiśniewski, M., 1996, 'Zmiany Rozkladu Dochodów w Latach 1987–1992', in M. Dąbrowski, ed., Polityka gospodarcza okresu transformacji, Warsaw: CASE and Wydawnictwo Naukowe PWN, pp. 232–268.

Wnuk-Lipiński, E., 1991, 'Deprywacje społeczne a konflikty interesów i wartości', in Polacy '90: Konflikty i zmiana, Warsaw: Institute of Political Studies, Polish Academy of Sciences (IFiS PAN).

——, ed., 1995, After Communism: A Multidisciplinary Approach to Radical Social Change, Warsaw: Institute of Political Studies, Polish Academy of Sciences (IFiS PAN).

Wojtaszczyk, K.A., 1992. 'Programy głownych ugrupowan politycznych', in S. Gebethner and J. Raciborski, eds, Wybory 1991 a Polska Scena Politycznych, Warsaw: Wydawnicwo Inicjatyw Społecznych Polska w Europie, pp. 27–40.

World Bank, 1995, Understanding Poverty in Poland, World Bank Country Study, Washington, DC: World Bank.

Wprost, various issues.

Zagorski, K., 1994, 'Hope Factor, Inequality, and Legitimacy of Systemic Transformations', Communist and Post-Communist Studies, Vol. 27, No. 4, pp. 357–376.

Zubek, V., 1994, 'The Reassertion of the Left in Poland', Europe–Asia Studies, Vol. 46, No. 5, pp. 801–838.

——, 1995, 'The Phoenix Out of the Ashes: The Rise to Power of Poland's Post-Communist SdRP', Communist and Post-Communist Studies, Vol. 28, No. 3, pp. 275–306.

Zubek, Z., 1997, 'The Eclipse of Walesa's Political Career', Europe–Asia Studies, Vol. 49, No. 1, pp. 107–124.

Żukowski, T., 1997, 'Mapa wielu Polsk', Gazeta Wyborcza, 25 September 1997, p. 10.

Życie Gospodarcze, various issues.

Życie Warszawy, various issues.

Index

240   *The Political Economy of Reform in Poland*

multi-party system 43
  see also parties, party system
Murrell, P. 87

nationalism 103, 120, 162, 163, 168,
    169, 170
NATO 159, 161, 165, 167, 175
Non-Party Reform Bloc 34
Nowy Sącz 122
NSZZ 'S' *see* Solidarity

occupational groups 124–71
  see also directors; entrepreneurs;
    farmers; workers
Ojczyzna 34, 57n, 96, 97, 110, 111,
    196
Olbrzych 80
Olechowski, Andrzej 37
Oleksy, Józef 36
Olszewski, Jan 38, 42, 98, 99, 102,
    120, 121
opposition 36, 40, 116, 183
  to communism 9, 20, 21, 22, 24,
    26, 52
  to reform 2, 7, 8, 29, 32, 53, 54,
    55, 64, 104, 182
OPZZ trade union 5, 22
output 10, 28, 60
  see also production
owners (of businesses) 2, 12
  see also entrepreneurs; self-
    employed
ownership 157, 159, 161, 162, 153,
    165, 167, 168, 169

parties, party system 3, 5, 8, 9, 16,
    17, 31–3, 34, 35, 36, 39, 40, 86,
    87, 88, 89, 93, 95, 99, 101, 103,
    156–70, 172–85
  post-communist 5, 17, 20, 32, 35,
    37, 40, 92, 99, 101, 104, 111–
    18, 122, 163–70, 181, 182
  see also SLD; PSL
  post-Solidarity 5, 17, 20, 33, 36,
    40, 53–4, 93–4, 99, 101, 104,
    111, 157–63, 169, 182
  see also AWS; ROP

Party 'X' 27, 33, 34
Pawlak, Waldemar 35, 36, 38, 98,
    99, 102, 118, 119, 166
PC (Centre Aliance) 34, 57n, 96, 97,
    158, 196
  see also POC
pensions 6, 15, 16, 32, 37, 39, 40,
    57n, 64, 65, 69–72, 126, 127–9,
    132, 138, 153, 181
  pensioners 5, 29, 48, 51, 71,
    109–10, 111, 113, 115, 122n,
    125, 127, 128, 129–30, 132,
    133, 137, 138, 140, 141, 142–
    3, 144, 145, 146, 147, 150,
    151, 153, 154, 155, 156, 158,
    160, 164, 166, 168, 170n, 193,
    196, 199, 200, 202, 204, 207,
    209, 214, 219
perestroika 21
Piła 81
PL (Peasants' Union) 28, 31, 33, 93,
    94, 119, 123n
  see also Rural Solidarity
POC (Civic Centre Alliance) 31, 93,
    94, 162, 163, 196
  see also PC
Podkaminer, L. 63–4, 142, 171n
policy 3, 7, 8, 12, 36
Polish Peasant Party *see* PSL
Polish United Workers' Party *see*
    PZPR
popiwek (excess wage tax) 71, 127,
    128
poverty 3, 10, 43, 71, 79, 128, 129,
    133, 152–3, 170n, 182, 184
Poznań 103
PPPP (Polish Friends of Beer Party)
    31, 94
prices 16, 23, 25, 36, 37, 59, 60–62,
    62–6, 67, 87, 106n, 125, 135, 139,
    142, 143, 148, 154, 180
  see also inflation
private sector 10, 15, 48, 52, 59, 110,
    123n, 126, 131, 152, 154, 162,
    169, 170n, 180, 184
privatization 30, 32, 39, 43, 58n,
    123n, 124, 169, 184